# Amazing Infinite Love

by
Charles Duey Taylor

Order this book online at www.trafford.com
or email orders@trafford.com

Most Trafford titles are also available at major online book retailers.

Note for Librarians: A cataloguing record for this book is available from Library
and Archives Canada at www.collectionscanada.ca/amicus/index-e.html

Printed in Victoria, BC, Canada.

ISBN: 978-1-4269-1384-6

*Our mission is to efficiently provide the world's finest, most comprehensive
book publishing service, enabling every author to experience success.
To find out how to publish your book, your way, and have it available
worldwide, visit us online at www.trafford.com*

*Trafford rev.08/19/09*

 www.trafford.com

**North America & international**
toll-free: 1 888 232 4444 (USA & Canada)
phone: 250 383 6864 ✦ fax:  812 355 4082

# IN MEMORIUM

*To my beloved wife*
*Anne Shelley Taylor, of*
*of nearly sixty-three years, without*
*whose encouragement and inexhaustible*
*desire to support and use her own talents, my*
*life and everything I have done  would have been*
*seriously lessened.*
*Charles D. Taylor*

# Table of Contents

# Preface

This is not intended to be a scholarly book, although I hope there are some good scholarly things in it. It is an effort to make available to interested followers of Jesus a journey which I have made throughout during my seminary days and throughout my life and to apply the results of that journey to a study of the life and teachings of Jesus as based on the Gospel Parallels (The New Revised Standard Version of 1989). Much of the material comes from years of teaching a university course in "The Life and Teachings of Jesus." I can only offer to the reader the intellectual struggles I have gone through and the conclusions I have reached which answer my questions. My hope would be that my journey will be of some value to others.

There are some real tragedies which are the result of theological controversies that have arisen concerning the study and explanation of the Bible. Perhaps the most damaging effect lies in the dogmatic assertions which often come out of those conflicts. There are numerous examples of councils decreeing that all who do not agree with the conclusions of the council are heretical and must be suppressed. (In reality a "heretic" appears to be someone who understands something differently.) There are also some good things which result from our debates. Each of us is in some way forced to explain his/her positions a little more clearly, if only to ourselves. We should all be reminded that St. Paul wrote in what we call 1st Corinthians to the effect that we all now see in a mirror dimly and that all of our knowledge is only fragmentary and partial. (Incidentally, that does not only apply to Biblical thought but to all of what humans call "knowledge.")

The particular interests of any age may determine the concerns which create the debates. In our own country a few decades past one big issue was that of divorce and every reader has probably heard of all kinds of decrees indicating that divorced people who married again were living in adultery. While divorce is not the ideal, most of us do not share the previously stated position, but those who are Biblical literalists often impose that burden of guilt on any of those who have been caught up in divorce. In this day, multiple issues relating to morality have been pushed to the forefront by advances in understanding in other fields, as seen in the issues of evolution, abortion, homosexuality, stem cell research and many others, and we often find harsh attacks and dogmatic conclusions being applied. Those emphases will probably change in the future, but the battles and scars will remain for many people.

The underlying issue with which this study is involved has to do with the nature of Biblical Literature. Do we struggle with the issues as they come up or do we dogmatically ignore them and dismiss concepts which do not mesh with ours with a simple, "Well, the Bible says" statement? To this writer it has always been difficult to attack the problems about Biblical Literature and to point out inconsistencies because, if one stops in fear and does not battle through to solid conclusions, there may be either a statement of damnation of some heretical view or there might come about a lack of confidence in what we call Scripture which causes the individual to dismiss the Bible! On the other hand a lack of honesty in dealing with problems in this area allows us to live with no solutions - just dogmatic decrees and denunciations of those who raise questions.

I have chosen to express my journey through the issue of the nature of Biblical Literature because to me it is primary in any effort to understand Jesus. What is often called the Historical Critical Method is necessary to even come close to getting back to the life situation. One must go through twenty centuries of culture, change from a Jewish culture through a Graeco-Roman one and come to our own; one must deal with at least three, perhaps more, language barriers; while doing all of that one must deal with the hallowed atmosphere which surrounds the Bible or any religious text. This controversy has divided numerous denominations and I hope that my pre-occupation with it does not get me involved in something which you have already settled and which will render much of what is said here as unnecessary. I feel rather confident from my experiences with students that the issues are relevant for each of us.

My one other hope is that the reader will diligently pursue the work to its completion. The essence of my journey is climaxed in the last chapter and while it may be meaningful only to me, stopping short of the end will cause much of it to lose its meaning.

# CHAPTER I
## "My Journey"

The first parts of this work will be devoted to an explanation of my efforts to deal with the problems I discovered when I began a serious study of Biblical Literature. After that they will attempt to show how those perplexing problems aided me in the study of the life and ministry of Jesus.

When I completed the Seminary phase of my preparation, I decided that my stewardship would not be that of a scholarly writer, but rather that it would consist of trying to interpret and share with lay people what I had been introduced to regarding theological principles. Consequently, I have spent my entire career in attempting to provide for college students and for church congregations an opportunity to deal with what I consider to be a pursuit of truth. (I learned long ago from one of the brilliant old professors with whom I came in contact that everything I call my knowledge is simply the best understanding I have at that particular time, no matter what issue I am dealing with.) In the latter days of my graduate work, I had the privilege of hearing Dr. W. O. Carver deliver a series of lectures when the was 83! His body was almost gone, but his mind was a clear as ever. One morning he said, "Young Gentlemen, last evening as I was reviewing the material for this session, I discovered that for all of my life I had been wrong about this issue and I changed my mind." I don't even remember what the specific issue was, but I do remember praying that somehow God would help me to avoid dogmatism and keep me learning with an open mind as long as learning is possible. That did not and does not mean that there would be no convictions! It simply meant that all of my convictions, even the most prized ones, were open to scrutiny.

So I know the struggle about the nature of Biblical Literature first hand. My purpose here is not to persuade the reader to agree with my conclusions, but rather to get him/her to follow my journey. I want to be honest about my dilemmas and to present some of the conclusions at which I have arrived. In this introductory chapter I only want to share where I was and what I have come to believe, and how, for me, these answers came.

This journey began long ago in my pre-seminary days and continued through a larger part of that seminary training, and still continues. When I first heard the Gershwin lyrics, "It ain't necessarily so. The things that you're liable to read in the Bible, it ain't necessarily so," I was furious! My reaction was the same as some today - "Well, if you can't believe one part of the Bible you can't believe any of it!" So I mentally fought a battle of faith. (Maybe you have done the same.) I read, not long ago, that a man who claims to be an inerrantist said that there were no errors in the Bible if it was interpreted correctly. Well, interpreted by whom? Now, let me be certain that you know that throughout my journey and even now, I believe in God's message in the Bible and more specifically I believe that the complete message relating to the nature, character, and purposes of God is revealed to us in the life, the message and teachings, the death and resurrection of Jesus, the Christ. But that did nothing to stop my struggle with the nature of that record.

Most of us understand that all religions and particularly our Hebrew/Christian heritage, attempt to find some way to lead us from this materialistic, finite world to the ultimate spiritual world. Parenthetically, if you do not believe that the spiritual realm is the ultimate, you cannot make this journey with me, and in all probability you will have difficulty in understanding my struggles. If humanity is to open up to any understanding of the spiritual realm, it must do so through symbols. In fact, any communication must be done through symbols. Words are symbols and as you hear words they convey a personal meaning. Sacraments or rituals are symbols; smiles, hugs, and nods are symbols. We simply cannot communicate without them. The meaning of the term "symbol" as I am using it here is: something that points beyond itself to a greater reality and in some mysterious sense participates in that to which it points. I reject the idea that something is merely_ a symbol and therefore, insignificant. Symbols are vital, necessary elements in personal growth and communication and most especially in spiritual understanding.

Shortly after World War II I was sailing along in my dogmatic certainty when I bumped into my first major "pothole." I began a class under a brilliant New Testament scholar who challenged me and opened up some problems I had never seen. One day when I was in his office I asked what was probably a very naïve question. He did not answer me at all! Instead he laughed and it made me so mad that I determined to find my own answer, but he had cracked my shell. Not long after that I met on the pages of a book on Church History a Gnostic "heretic" named Marcion. Marcion believed that the whole creation was composed of a dualism. What we knew as the material realm was totally evil, in and of itself. Therefore, a good God could never have been a part of creating it. So the theory of Gnosticism suggested that the good God created a god who was a little inferior, less good that the original, and that lesser god created an even lesser god until finally there was one who created this evil mess. (I have wondered since the time when I first met that idea how that makes the good God any less responsible since He created the very first of those emanations) Because Marcion sensed many problems with the God of the Old Testament, he assumed that this ultimately evil and inferior God should be identified with the God of the Hebrews. Since some of the Old Testament stories seemed to present to Marcion an image of God that was not compatible with Jesus and His message, what was to be done in the face of that problem? To most of us Marcion's primary conclusion that the God of the Old Testament must be a different God from the one Jesus taught about is not the proper answer. However, Marcion had great influence in the Church at Rome and he tried to call the church back to what he thought was the gospel of Christ and that of Paul. He discarded the Old Testament and everything in the New which seemed to be too Jewish.

Is it any wonder that his efforts to persuade the church to follow him resulted in his excommunication.

Now, if the answer of Marcion was not acceptable, I was at that time so engrossed in the problem that some other answer had to be found, because Marcion had messed up my playhouse! (There are those who can confront major problems like this and not be bothered by the issues at all. I am not one of those!) My earlier position had been that everything in the Bible was literally exact and had been given in God's own words, no questions asked! But my world had been disturbed and I could no longer avoid the difficulties of an Old Testament God whose character appeared to be inconsistent with what Jesus taught about the Father. Either the new found difficulties had to be ignored in a fit of intellectual dishonesty or some other answer had to be found.

The first step in that journey was to try an education model. If God revealed bits and pieces of information to men of old, like the order Samuel, the prophet, gave to Saul to slaughter all the people of Amalek (woman, infants, animals and all) and then later we hear Jesus telling us to love our enemies, that must have been because the people simply were not ready yet for the words of Jesus. So God revealed something to Abraham and the a little more to Moses and so on until He could finally bring us to understand Jesus. That is much like teaching the beginning principles of elementary mathematics or science or any other subject, before moving to a higher level. We all know the necessity of pre-requisites in all fields. (One cannot begin to teach physics to a first grader) For a while I thought the problem was solved. I found that the theory of "Progressive Revelation" indicated that God had revealed bits and pieces of information, but had not revealed higher things because mankind was not ready. I even used the first chapter of Hebrews as a proof text, for it did say that "in bits and pieces" our fathers of old were spoken to by God through the prophets. That meant that Ezra's commands to break up families and send foreign wives home, the prohibitions against allowing any foreigners in the congregation of Israel, and many others were God's responsibility! (No wonder that 'racial' exclusiveness developed!) People were left with a confusing and inadequate picture of the nature and character of God, and if Jesus' portrayal of God was correct the earlier representation might be false! (In 1 Corinthians 7:12-16 St Paul offered a very different solution than that of Ezra.) To me, "Progressive Revelation" <u>was not a satisfactory answer any longer.</u> Once again, inside my being, my playhouse had collapsed and I wondered if I should ever find satisfaction.

Then I read a book by a great scholar of the Twentieth Century, John Baille (*The Idea of Revelation in Recent Thought*, [New York: Columbia University Press, 1956]) Baille suggested that revelation was not about information bits at all. Instead, just as all person to person revelation takes place, God revealed Himself - not information! (While in the Bible God may not be specifically called a person, He is thought of in personal terms throughout its pages, and so we may say He reveals Himself as a person.) That meant that men who were open to God interpreted God according to their own culture and understanding. The Bible then became a record of men's interpretation of who God is and in the great events of their lives and experience and under God's leadership (inspiration), little by little, man's understanding of God reached higher and higher. It was not and is not a steady upward incline, but it moved in jagged peaks and lower valleys. For instance, students of the Bible have recognized that there is development in the understanding of God's nature among the Hebrews. At one time they were probably polytheists. If you remember, when Jacob and Rachel left her Father's home, she stole the household gods. (Genesis 31:19) They must have believed in them! But in the story of the giving of the ten commandments the first three deal with how one is to reverence God, and the very first one suggests henotheism and says, "You shall have no other gods before me!" That simply means that there may be other gods, but there is only one for us. That command is a far cry from understanding that there is only one God. The prophets continued to battle against polytheism and henotheism and during the eighth century B. C. E. they appear to have reached toward an ethical monotheism.

This more appropriate answer may be called "Progressive Understanding." It means that even though God is the "same yesterday, today, and forever," as he reveals Himself, people interpret that revelation in the light of their own culture and time. God is not responsible for how one interprets Him, He simply reveals Himself. (This is true also in the matter of mankind having free choice. There could never be worship or meaningful commitment if God did not allow mankind to reject His revelation.) So, for example, Israel came to understand that human sacrifice is not consistent with the nature and character of God. It remained for St, Paul to explain that we must offer Him our lives as living sacrifices. That kind of understanding probably began with the Abraham/ Isaac story and from that time on there are only rare incidents of human sacrifice. That kind of progressive understanding continues. God's people have, even recently, come to know that every person deserves honor and dignity and that things like slavery or abuse are not consistent with who and what God is. We have also come to understand that what St. Paul wrote in Galatians - that "in Christ there is no Jew nor Greek, no bond slave or free man, no male or female" is consistent with the being of God. It has taken a long time and, for the human family, learning about God's nature is not finished, but liberating all humans into first class citizens in Christ is God-like.

From an understanding of a God who dictated bits of information based on what men could use to an understanding of a God who gives Himself and whom we come to understand progressively is a long journey. But it has been the solution to my struggle. Of course, the climax of all of that came when God mysteriously translated Himself into human terms. The basic theological position of nearly all Christian thought has been that whatever you wish to know about the nature and character of God can be seen in the one whom some have called the God-man, Jesus! Is that not some of the explanation of why there had to be an incarnation, so men could really come to know God?

Now to some fundamental issues, if we are to deal with the nature of Biblical Literature:

The current theological arguments about every word of the Bible being literally true hinge on the word "inerrant." Most of us are not willing to claim for the Bible what it does not claim for itself, and it is very doubtful that the Bible makes the inerrant claim. We know, in fact, that even one little variation would discredit that theory and any of us can point out not one variation, but many. Just two examples, one of which is from the Old Testament and one from the New, suffice for this work. In Exodus 6:2-3 the narrative says something which one might never catch in an English translation. It says, God spoke further to Moses and said to him, "I am the Lord and I appeared to Abraham, Isaac, and Jacob as God Almighty (El Shaddai), but by my name The Lord (<u>Yahweh</u>), I did not make myself known to them." Yet that name

(Yahweh) is used in Genesis as early as chapter two and Abraham used it in naming the mountain upon which the experience of the sacrifice of Isaac took place. He called that mountain "Yahweh Will Provide." In the account in Mark 2:26 that narrative says that Jesus said, "Have you never read what David did when he was in need and became hungry, he and his companions, how he entered the house of God in the time of Abiathar, the high priest, and ate the consecrated bread, which is not lawful for anyone to eat except the priests, and he gave it also to those who were with him?" Someone made a slip of memory, for in the account in I Samuel 21:1-6 the Old Testament record states that when this event occurred Ahimilech was the priest and not Abiathar. Because of his fears and suspicions Saul had the entire household of Ahimilech murdered. Abiathar was the only surviving member of Ahimilech's family and he later became the priest. Both Matthew and Luke have corrected this by leaving the reference to the high priest out entirely, but Mark can hardly be inerrant here (in all probability Mark, or whoever contributed the information, remembered it wrongly). All of the better manuscripts which scholars trust in dealing with matters of textual criticism follow the reading "when Abiathar was high priest."

One term which must be dealt with before the study of the message of Jesus can be attempted is "revelation." Revelation literally means an uncovering, the lifting of an obscure veil, so as to make known something which was formerly hidden. One may say in regard to something he comes to understand that "I discovered it,' and say of another thing. "it was disclosed to me." There is one sense in which all valid knowledge may be regarded as being revealed, for human knowledge is the result of coming to understand what is already there. That means that each mind must select and integrate whatever confronts it. It also means that the mind is both active and passive, for if nothing ever confronts a mind, it knows nothing. If that assumption is correct it follows that human interpretations of anything are conditioned by the circumstances surrounding it.

Yet there is a tremendous difference in dealing with coming to know a thing and coming to know a person. One may be able to catalog precisely what he/she has come to know about a thing, be it a virus or an asteroid, but when one tries to do the same thing in regard to a person, even a close friend, it can never be done exhaustively or maybe even accurately. If one tries to describe a friend to another, the efforts will take the form of telling the characteristics that have been observed or recounting some words the friend has said, but it can never be exhaustive or completely accurate. The hearer will then fill up his/her understanding from what is known of other personalities, and that will be the interpretation of said friend. The describer is using abstractions from the personality as he understands them and the hearer understands everything that is said in his own manner, he may derive both something right and something wrong. The same thing is true when one meets a person. That person reveals himself, and some reveal more than others, but the process of knowing a person is a continuing one and one of interpretation.

But the revelation of the being of God is not just a matter of qualities or information about God. That information may be what our understanding communicates, but to know God is to meet a person. Yet from very early times there was an emphasis on right opinion or orthodoxy. Everyone knows the divisive nature of the situations that came about during the Protestant Reformation. There were numerous efforts at conciliation, but none of them succeeded and by the time of the Council of Trent (1545-1563 A. D.) the whole of scripture was seen as given by the dictation of the Holy Spirit. Emil Brunner has said, "Among the teachers of the Reformation the difference in the view of the Scriptures was not so much one of confessional position as of generations. The Reformers of the first generation, Luther and Zwingli, are not favorable to the doctrine of verbal inspiration, whereas Melanchthon, Calvin, and Bullinger are. Calvin is very fond of talking about the *Oracula Dei* and of divine dictation." (*Revelation and Reason*, trans by Olive Wyon [London: Student Movement Press, Ltd. 1947] 127-128)

It would appear that Luther and Zwingli were not favorable to the doctrine of verbal inspiration, but others like Calvin seemed to be happy with that theory. In the revealing of God we have in all cases human attempts to repeat and produce this word of God in human thoughts and words with regard to particular human situations. That self disclosure is often spoken of as coming to us in two ways:

a) General Revelation: Even St. Paul indicates that there is something that comes to us through the natural order somewhat like the manifestation of God as the great architect. (Romans 1:19-23) Not many Christian theologians consider this type of revelation to be adequate for salvation.

b) Special Revelation: The other type comes through historical events and from the Christian perspective it is climaxed in the appearance in history of Jesus, the incarnate God. It almost goes without saying that since God is a person, that person can only reveal Himself through some kind of interaction with other persons. Since nature is in itself impersonal, that means that the personality is often hidden behind the systems of nature and the "hidden person" might never be revealed to us as anything more than what the 18th century Deists proposed. But in the New Testament faith is a trustful obedience and commitment of a person to that other person whom we meet in Jesus Christ, not in bits of dogma!

John Baillie wrote about a sophisticated legal representative of a certain university who said to him, "You speak of trusting God, of praying to Him and doing His will. But it is all so one-sided. We speak to God, we bow down before Him and lift up our hearts to Him. But he never speaks to us. He makes no sign, it is all so one sided." (*The Idea of Revelation in Recent Thought,* [New York: Columbia University Press, 1956] 137). Have we not all felt that way and shouldn't we face that enigma honestly? (Much of what follows is an attempt to digest Baillie's concluding thoughts, for this introductory chapter has become much too lengthy. (If the reader is interested in following the argument to its conclusion he/she is advised to consult the "Epilogue" in Baillie's *The Idea of Revelation in Recent Thought.*)

Perhaps we should answer two questions before trying to deal with how God speaks to us. First, what kind of communication or sign would we accept? Jesus knew that dilemma and refused to give signs, but in the parable of Dives and Lazarus He indicated that any sign which would be given, even if one returned from the dead to give it, would be useless. (Luke 16:19-31) Has God not already done (and is continuing to do) all He can to make His will known and obeyed by us - at least short of denying us our freedom of will? Maybe we only hear partially what God reveals because we do not diligently listen to His message.

Remember the rich young man who came running to Jesus eager, and I believe sincere, to find answers? He got an answer! "Go, sell what you own and give the money to the poor, and you will have treasure in heaven; then come, follow me. When he heard this he was shocked and went away grieving, for he had many possessions." (Luke 18:18-30) The truth of that event is simply Jesus speaking a principle about God - if anything, money, power, prestige, family, ambition or any other thing, is more important to a person than obedience, that becomes his god and he cannot hear God. Do we diligently listen to Him?

If we have really listened, the second question is, have we obeyed? It seems that the saints we have each known in our lives began their journey by obeying what they heard. Someone has asked, "What right have we to blame God for our lack when we are not using what we have?" It may very well be that the "little voice" seeking to make itself heard, comes because of some dissatisfaction with ones way of life, some particular thing in ones life, some positive task that is challenging, or even some new insight, and is God speaking. Obviously, we are not so naïve as to think that God speaks to us in a physical voice, even though perhaps He could if He chose to. His revelation comes to us in a challenge or a guidance about the stewardship of our lives, and it is always consistent with what He has said to us in Jesus. In any case, God's revelation is not facts, it is a person to person unveiling that is meaningless unless we respond.

Another term which we must identify is "inspiration." There is some sense in which the writers of the New Testament assumed that inspiration was at work in the Old Testament. The nearest thing to a formal statement about inspiration is in II Timothy 3:16. The Greek text has no verb to help us translate it and as a result it may either say, "All scripture is inspired by God and is profitable for teaching, etc." or it may say, "Every God-inspired writing is also profitable for teaching, etc." Both of these assume that God is at work but no matter which translation one uses, it is evident that the writer did not make any claim about the nature or manner of inspiration. It is also impossible to know what he meant by the term "scripture" or "writing." Certainly not the New Testament for it had not been completed or canonized when II Timothy was written and most readers will know that what we now call the canon of the Old Testament was not set until around 90 A.D.

(at the council of Jamnia) and there are several references in the New Testament to works which were not later included in the canon.

The old dictation theory, called Plenary Verbal, has already been referred to. But the Bible makes no such claim for itself, and if the concept espoused in this work (i.e. that God reveals Himself instead of information or decrees) is correct, some other concept of inspiration must be employed. The outcome of all of this is simply that God inspired (in breathed) men who surrendered themselves to Him. They subsequently wrote out of their own culture and understanding, using their own sources, vocabulary, and patterns of thinking. The literary methods of their times were not the same as ours and much of what they used had been preserved in oral tradition, both in the Old Testament and in the Gospels. In this sense, the initiative in Biblical Literature was always with God and not man and the authors of Biblical works represent God's use of human talents and abilities to express their response.

Does not God still inspire people (not that they will write new scripture, for that was done under different circumstances and restraints and perhaps with different goals in the Divine intention)? Does He still speak and lead His servants so that they express what they understand to be His challenges? It should be obvious, as we listen to various speakers and predictors of the future that not everything that is said to be God's will is an accurate representation of the said will. Yet the measure of accuracy of that message should always be its consistency with the total message, its strengthening of the committed fellowship, and most of all, its identity with the message and mind of Jesus as best we can understand it. Whenever we try to capture the mind of Christ we must couch it in His cultural situation, including the religious debates and pre-conditions under which He labored, and carefully try to represent the essence of His language. Another issue which any student must face is in the process of letting Jesus be human (and thus with certain limitations) and at the same time recognizing what He really is, the Incarnate God.

# CHAPTER II
## RELIGION AND CHRISTIANITY

In any effort to study one of the great religions of the world, it is necessary that we begin by defining the term "religion." A definition that will suffice for any of what we call religions, seems to be "that which is the Ultimate Concern of its followers." It has also been called by other scholars the "Pivotal Value." (Monk, Hofheinz, Lawrence, Stamey, Affleck, Yamamori, *Exploring Religious Meaning ,5th ed.* [Upper Saddle River, New Jersey: Prentice Hall, 1998] 3-14) But even though that definition will cover the Christian faith, it is necessary to add to the definition. Christianity is an effort by God to re-establish a right relationship with God, from whom humanity is estranged.

Christianity makes the claim that man exists with his/her basic problem and that problem is estrangement because of the refusal to allow God to be God. The story is best illustrated by the early chapters of Genesis in which it is assumed that at the beginning, there was perfect harmony between God and the creation He called good. God exists with His unique nature and purposes. Whatever may have been included in the initial desire of God one thing is clear - He wanted creatures with whom He could have voluntary fellowship on their behalf and that seems to be represented in the early narrative by the idea, that God came and walked and talked with Adam and Eve (mankind). But since worship and love can only be expressed by free beings, there is always the possibility that they will abuse their freedom So something happened and there is always the temptation that humanity yields to, which denies God His right of "Godness." That is told in terms of disobedience and refusal to exercise faith that God knows what is best. When this happened, the whole atmosphere changed and the next time God came to walk and fellowship with the human pair, they hid from God. Immediately after their disobedience; they want nothing to do with Him and so a barrier is thrown up between man and God, placed there by the disobedience of mankind.

The major question of the Bible from that point on seems to be how can that barrier be removed and who can break through it and create the possibility of restoration? Two things are essential. Man must be able to really know God and even though he has created the dilemma himself, man must have access to God.

There are multiple religions in the world and those many expressions indicate a diverse understanding of the nature of God. Incidentally, even though Christianity offers its explanation of the nature and character of God, there are misunderstandings even within the Christian fold about the nature of God. There are many different types of worship and all claim to point to the same kind of objective, but it would appear that the different concepts of the nature of God may explain why there is so much divergence in their applications and worship.

It has already been said that. if restoration is to occur, man must know God. That calls forth the discussion in the introductory chapter and indicates that there can be no valid religion without revelation. That involves a self-disclosure by God of His own character and nature and since God is a person He must make that disclosure. By the time of the first century it had become the hope that a complete revelation of God and His power would occur, and the message of the New Testament is that in Jesus the full impact of God's character is revealed. That means that we can know God's character; it is revealed in human terms in Jesus of Nazareth. So it is the purpose of God to bring humanity back into fellowship in a personal relationship. That requires what appears to be a central part of Jesus' message, the necessity of transforming of individuals into the character likeness of God. That may be basic to the content of life eternal!

The definition used for the Bible in this work is that it is the record of the revelation of God to man. In a real sense the Bible is a word about the WORD for the true WORD of God is Jesus of Nazareth.. Revelation comes to men and they record the results from their understanding of history, the culture, the science of the time and all other factors that influence their understanding. So the Synoptic Gospels become a part of that interpretation of God as revealed in Christ. To appreciate those great works we must attempt to find out each writer's intention, and it would appear that each had a different purpose So the record must be analyzed as to how it came about and what each intends to show about Jesus.

# CHAPTER III
## A BRIEF SURVEY OF JEWISH BACKGROUNDS

A very short outline of Jewish history may enable one to determine where these people came from and the conditions under which the Jewish Kingdom arose. All Judaism maintains that Abraham is the ancestor with whom it identifies itself. Abraham did not please God because of his great honesty or morality, he pleased God because of his faith. A shocking, but probably honest evaluation of Abraham makes him a liar, a cheat, and at least a bigamist, but it would be a mistake to expect to judge Abraham by the nobler standards of Jesus.

Our best efforts at placing Abraham in History seem to focus on the time around 1800 B.C.E. The story of his family is seen in the chart below:

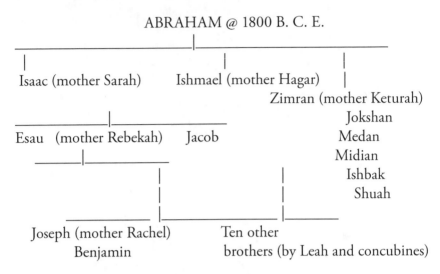

## ABRAHAM @ 1800 B. C. E.

Isaac (mother Sarah)    Ishmael (mother Hagar)

Zimran (mother Keturah)
Jokshan

Esau  (mother Rebekah)    Jacob

Medan
Midian
Ishbak
Shuah

Joseph (mother Rachel)    Ten other
Benjamin    brothers (by Leah and concubines)

Parental favoritism, deceit and many other factors

combined to force Jacob to flee to Haran, where some kindred lived. The beautiful story of his meeting with Rachel and exhibiting his physical prowess to her by rolling the stone from the well so that Rachel could water Laban's sheep and then serving Laban for seven years in order to have Rachel as wife is darkened somewhat by the "trickery" of Laban, who passed off the older sister, Leah, as Jacob's first wife. It may seem puzzling to us, but apparently, Jacob did not know until the next morning that he had married the wrong sister. When he confronted Laban, a deal was worked out that gave him both wives (one on the lay away plan and the other on the installment plan). The story followed the life of Joseph, one of Rachel's sons, who because of jealousy was sold into slavery in Egypt. Later, that became the salvation of Jacob's family and the family lived in Egypt until the Exodus. (That entire story may be found in Genesis. chapter 29 through the end of the book,)

Father Abraham was a Semite and is considered the ancestor of the Hebrew people, but as the people, later led by Moses and Joshua, entered and conquered Canaan many other Semites probably joined them, swelling their ranks. (Since there were no vowels in the Hebrew language, one must note the linguistic identity between the terms Hebrew [HBR] and a group who are later described as being in Palestine called the Habiru [HBR].) After the land had been partially conquered there was a period of very loose political connection between the tribes and the rule, if it can be called such, was done by judges. (@1200-1020 B. C.) The first King of Israel was Saul who reigned from 1020-1000 B. C. David reigned as the second King from 1000-961 B. C. At David's death Solomon ruled from 961-922 B. C. and when Solomon died the kingdom was split:

The Nothern Kingdom was called Israel. It lasted until 722 B.C.E. when it was captured by Assyria and the elite were taken to Babylon. The Southern Kingdom was called Judah. It lasted until 586 B.C.E. when it was captured by the Babylonians and the elite were taken to the area of Babylon also.

Leaders were allowed to return to Judea in 535 B. C. E. under Ezra and Nehemiah, and they began what we now know as Judaism and hence the term "Jew." The Temple, originally built in great splendor by King Solomon, was rebuilt around 520-515 B. C. E. The Jewish/Samaritan feud, so prominent in Judaism and in the first century, grew out of the confrontation with Sanballat when his offer to help was rejected. That led to a division and much prejudice which later produced a Temple on Mount Gerizim in Samaria in competition with the Temple in Jerusalem on Mount Zion.

Although the Jewish people were living in the land we know as Palestine and had very little control exercised over them, they were still subject to the Persians until the time of Alexander the Great, the Greek ruler, who then conquered Palestine as he campaigned to rule to entire world. But Alexander died in 323 B. C. E. and his kingdom was divided among four of his generals. The Palestinian area was initially under the control of the Ptolemies (who also ruled Egypt) from 323 until 198 B. C. E. At that time the Seleucids gained control. The much more rigid control of the Seleucids continued until the Maccabean revolt against Antiochus Epiphanes in 167-164 B. C. E.

## THE LAND OF PALESTINE

To understand the conditions under which Jesus ministered, it is necessary to know something of the cultural, geographical, and political circumstances in which he found himself. The territory known as Palestine has exerted influence far beyond what its size would suggest, largely because of its location. It served as the connecting link between Egypt and Syria and is often called the Fertile Crescent. The influence of the Greeks and what is known as "Hellenism" dominated the culture, the language and even affected the religion of the area. There were many foreigners living in Palestine and many Jews had left the area to become what is known as "Diaspora" Judaism. However, the area, especially Judaea, was predominantly Jewish and resistance to foreign influences and to foreigners was very strong. With the coming of Roman power in 63 B. C. E. all hope for independence seemed to vanish.

The land of Canaan had always been an agrarian territory, used mostly for herding sheep, goats, and cattle. Grains, olive oil, wines, fruits, nuts, dates, and fish from the Sea of Galilee were the main staples. It was a small area about 75-100 miles East to West and about 130 miles North to South. The Jordan River Valley divided it so that about 6,000 square miles lay on the eastern side and about 4,000 on the western. The climate of the Jordan Valley was semi-tropical, and while Old Testament peoples called the territory a land flowing with milk and honey, that description may be relative to the conditions out of which they came. The area was mountainous on either side of the Jordan Valley. There were rolling hills and valleys, particularly in Galilee, and the area was thickly populated with small farmers, peasants, and day laborers, and marketing of foods, various goods, and craftwork dominated the area. The trade routes served to bring caravans to the area so that contact with the outside world was common and as a result, in Galilee, both Greek and Aramaic were spoken. To the north the Lebanon Mountains, especially Mount Hermon, towered to about 9300 feet. To the South was the Negev desert; to the East lay the Arabian desert; to the West was the Mediterranean Sea with its rather rugged coastline.

Probably one of the most noted features was the Sea of Galilee. Although it was only about twenty miles from the Lebanon Mountains, its surface was already 686 feet below sea level, a drop of some 10,000 feet. Galilee was a small fresh water lake, about six to eight miles wide and some fourteen miles long, but it was a prosperous source of fish and produced a thriving economy. There is an intriguing discussion of first century fishing methods by Mendel Nun entitled, "Cast Your Net Upon the Waters". (*The Biblical Archeology Review Vol. 19 Number 6*, [The Biblical Archeology Review, 1993] 47-56)

About 65 miles to the south of the Sea of Galilee the course of the Jordan River led to the Dead Sea. That sea is in the deepest part of the depression of a geological fault and has no outlet.  It's surface is about 1300 feet below sea level and also appears at its deepest point to be about 1300 feet deep.  The sea is roughly fifty miles long and ten miles wide.  Because there is no outlet except by evaporation, the waters of the Dead Sea are unbelievably dense with various minerals, salts, tars, phosphorous, and the area around it is generally very arid.  A more thorough discussion of the Land  has been developed by C. Milo Connick, (*Jesus, the Man, the Mission, and the Message* [Englewood Cliffs: Prentice Hall, Inc. 1974] 18-36)

## POLITICAL DIVISIONS:

First century Palestine was divided into six major sections. In the time immediately prior to the first century, Herod the Great ruled the entire area.  He was king from 41- 4 B.C. and was a lover of Graeco-Roman culture and spent tremendous amounts of money building cities, an artificial harbor in Caesarea and other remarkable construction projects.  All of these were financed by heavy taxes and the confiscation of property.  He was never popular with the Jews, even though he attempted to pacify them by rebuilding the Temple with great extravagance. (That effort began in 20 B.C. and was not completed until just a short time before its destruction by the Romans in 70 A.D.) His loyalty to the Roman Emperors secured his control over the area, but he was always uncertain about efforts, real or imagined, to de-throne him.  He had many of his own family, of whom he became suspicious, put to death and even had his wife Mariamne, executed in a fit of jealous rage.  Josephus, the Jewish historian, labels him as a tyrant, yet anyone examining his tenure as king will find a political genius, but one who totally lacked morality.

When he died his will divided the territory  among his three remaining sons and the Emperor Augustus approved the terms of that will.

To Herod Archelaus he willed the areas of Judaea, Samaria, and Idumea, but after ten years, there were so many complaints against him that  Augustus deposed him and placed the three areas under a Roman procurator.  For the people the situation was even worse than under Herod because of the presence of a Roman garrison, the abuses of bartering for the office of high priesthood, which was at this time appointed by foreign rulers, and the hated graft of the publicans.

To Herod Antipas he left Galilee and Peraea (on the eastern side of the Jordan river) which he ruled from 4 B.C. E. to 39 C. E. His rule was somewhat satisfactory partially because of a much less conservative populace. The area seems to have been populated by many Gentiles as well as some Jews and that may also account partially for his lengthy and successful rule. He ruled over most of the territory in which the major part of the ministry of Jesus took place and is of particular interest to Biblical students because of his dealing with John the Baptist. He too favored Hellenism and there was close contact with some of the cities of the Decapolis, which were proud of their Hellenistic institutions, theaters, sporting arenas, and schools.

To Herod Philip he willed the control of Northeast Palestine which he ruled from 4 B.C. to 34 A.D. He is sometimes described as the best of the Herods, but much of this may also be because most of his subjects were Gentiles and their Greek sympathies made them easier to deal with.

## SOCIAL AND ECONOMIC OUTLOOK:

Slavery was rampant in the Roman Empire. Many of those who were slaves had been captured in battle and sold into slavery or sold because of indebtedness and even many Jews seem to have owned slaves. The status of women was very poor. Although the Jews were seldom guilty of the practice, others often exposed baby girls or they were sold for future prostitutes. Women had very few rights and were almost completely dependent on husbands or family for their livelihood, with practically no way to make their own living. Marriage required betrothal and dowry.

The group known as publicans and often in the gospels classed with "sinners" were people who were employed by the Romans to collect taxes. Since the taxes went to a foreign power, most Jews saw those who worked for the Romans as traitors to both God and the people. Generally the material conditions were terrible. Daily wages seem to have amounted to 19/20 cents, barely enough to buy grain for the day. There were some small landowners but many were tenants. In the first century there was some trading done with foreign caravans, but there were few luxuries and economic conditions were very poor. Since there was a good bit of travel, people came in contact with both their native Aramaic language and with Greek. Latin was, of course, the official language of the Empire, but the Hellenistic influence had made the use of Greek almost universal and Latin did not supplant Greek. All of these conditions led to tensions and economic uncertainty.

## RELIGIOUS CONDITIONS

The Jewish people were proud of their long religious history and most of their practices were colored by that history. However, after so long a time in captivity, and so many failed struggles to gain freedom, there was intense pessimism. Many Jews wondered whether God really cared about them and those tough political fortunes led to questions in terms of a sovereign God and these subject people. Prophets had often indicated that their misfortunes were caused by sin, but in the light the behavior of everyone else, could Israel really be that sinful?

All around them were those who believed in a dualistic creation. That had probably originated in Persia and had influenced the exiles. It taught that there were two gods, one good and one evil and they continually struggled for control. In Jesus' time, many thought that the entire order was under the control of Satan and his demons. Every kind of sickness or deformity was considered the result of demon possession. As a result there were many professional exorcists. Into that atmosphere Jesus came and faced immediately four kinds of Messianic hope:

1) Some believed that God would have to send a great prophet like Moses who would challenge the entire nation. A prophet was not one who predicted the future primarily, but one who brought forth the message and truth of God to the people.

2) Others who saw the corrupted priesthood as a major problem were hoping for a great priest who would recover the reputation and confidence of the priesthood. A priest filled the other side of communication with God and he was charged with representing and leading the people to God.

3) Still others had lost hope in the ordinary things and believed that in some sense God would have to send a supernatural being to restore things to their proper condition. Many of these would have followed the hope characterized by apocalyptic literature. Apocalyptic literature was characteristically Jewish and had grown up in times of despair and hopelessness. It was written in signs and symbols, often because the works needed to be disguised from the authorities. Apocalyptic literature can be seen in the Old Testament primarily in the books of Daniel and Ezekiel and a bit in Joel, which Simon Peter quoted in the sermon on the Day of Pentecost. (Acts 2) The primary examples of that literature in the New Testament are seen in Matthew 24, Mark 13, and the entire book of Revelation. It appealed to the ordinary man, both then and now, because it may be interpreted very spectacularly, if its apocalyptic nature is disregarded, and because it promised hope.

4) Still others looked for the return of a great king like David, who would liberate them from the power of the Romans and that was probably the overwhelming popular hope. That idea can often be seen as one Jesus had to struggle against during His ministry such as the time when they tried to take Him by force and make Him be king (John 6:15). It may have also played a prominent role in the thinking of the people at the time of the arrest and crucifixion, since they still may have hoped he would restore the theocracy and the power and glory of Israel.

## RELIGIOUS SECTS OF JUDAISM:

During Jesus' entire ministry we are confronted with various religious groups. These gradually developed during what is often called the Intertestament Period. Most notable in the gospels were the Pharisees. They probably originated during the Maccabean period and arose to protect the Law. As a result they were extreme legalists who most likely began with the aims of separatism. They seemed to have minimal political interest and their beliefs have been described in the following ideas:

1) They accepted the Pentateuch and the Prophets as scripture. (The Writings did not become officially Jewish Scripture until 90 A.D.)

2) They accepted the Rabbinic Oral Tradition as binding.

3) They were intensely legalistic, minutely observing not only the laws but the oral interpretations of the laws. This later resulted in what is known as the "Mishnah" which is composed of hundreds of pages of regulations and interpretations. (Danby, *The Mishnah* [London: Oxford University Press, 1954])

4) They believed strongly in Divine Providence in all things.

5) They believed in life after death, but for them it was a resuscitation of the physical body.

6) They believed literally in a world saturated with demons and angels.

The second and probably the most powerful group were the Sadducees. They were probably descendants of the priest Zadok. They were an aristocratic group who were politically motivated. They do not appear to have avidly resisted Hellenism.

Their beliefs can be summarized as follows:

1) They accepted ONLY the Penteteuch as scripture and they applied it rigidly.

2) They were conservative in their religious acceptance, new ideas were not adopted easily.

3) Since the Pharasaic concept of resurrection was physical resuscitation they rejected that concept and consequently were often characterized as not believing in life after death.

4) They rejected the idea of a spirit world.

5) They denied "Divine Providence" as taught by the Pharisees.

The Sadducees had great power in the Temple. Many high priests were Sadducees. They were usually wealthy partly because of the Temple Tax which was 1/2 shekel for each male above 12 years of age and that amounted to about 1 and ½ days wages.

The third group were the Essenes. There is some controversy about which communities were Essene but most scholars tend to identify them with communities like the Qumran community of the Dead Sea Scrolls. Usually they were ascetic and lived communal lives. They seem to have been eclectic in speculation. Most, but not all, of the Essene communities practiced celibacy. They performed ceremonial lustrations and often wore white robes and prayed facing the sun. They avoided the conflict between the Pharisees and the Sadducees regarding life after death by accepting the Greek idea of the immortality of the soul, not resurrection. Although it is remotely possible that there was some influence on John the Baptist, few take that claim seriously. There is no mention of them in the New Testament.

The fourth group were the Zealots. Many believe that these originated with Judas of Gamala who led an aborted revolt against Rome in 6 A.D. They were extreme nationalists, always agitating for freedom from Rome. It is fairly certain that Simon Zealotes, one of the twelve, was a Zealot and Judas Iscariot probably was. The Zealots formed part of the background for the disastrous national revolt in 66-70 A.D.

The last major group are the Herodians. They were highly political and probably should not be called a religious sect. Their major goal was to have a restoration of a Herod to rule over Palestine. The group noted as scribes were not a sect, and while the majority may have been Pharisees they were scholars drawn from many of the groups to copy by hand, study and interpret the Law (TORAH) The scribes may have originated under the influence of Ezra.

## RELIGIOUS INSTITUTIONS IN FIRST CENTURY JUDAISM.

As would be expected, the major institution of Judaism was the Temple. The first Temple had been constructed under the leadership of King Solomon around 960 B.C. and even though it had been destroyed in 586 B.C. it was still revered by the populace as the dwelling of God. The foundation had been re-laid in 520 B.C. and it remained in place until the Temple was Rebuilt. The first century Temple was built by Herod (20 B.C. until 64 A.D.) but was destroyed by the Romans during the revolt of 66-70 A.D. It was a marvelous structure made of marble overlaid with gold. It was built on the sacred site of Mount Moriah, on a rectangular area about 1000 by 750 feet. There was one outer court, called the Court of the Gentiles and anyone could enter that part. Just inside that was the Court of the Women, for Jewish women and children, and beyond that court no women or children (including boys under twelve) could go. The next level was designated as the Court of Israel and Jewish men (and boys above twelve) could enter that court, but they could not enter the Court of the Priests or get closer to the Holiest place in Judaism. That was the building proper and it contained the Holy Place and the Holy of Holies. There is reason to suspect that the common people believed that the Holy of Holies was where God dwelt, since it was separated from the Holy Place by a tremendous veil, said to have been about six inches thick. No one went into the Holy of Holies except the High Priest and he went only once a year on the Day of Atonement. There were twenty four courses of priests who served in the daily administration of the Temple and the sacrifices. The priests lived normal lives except for two periods of two weeks a year when they served in Jerusalem, rotating their time of service. By the first century the Levites seem to have become little more than glorified Temple janitors.

|Holy Place &
Holy of Holies|
|Court of Priests|
Court of Israel|
Court of Women|
|Court of the Gentiles|

The other major institution was that of the synagogue. It was required that there be at least ten adult Jewish males for there to be a synagogue in a town. Synagogues probably originated during the Babylonian Exile (586-520 B.C.) and served as a place for teaching the Law, a social center, a worship center (usually on the Sabbath, Monday and Thursday), and a school. They were most often run by local laity, but visiting scribes and rabbis often gave homilies.

The ruling body, in terms of religious affairs, was the Sanhedrin (*Gerousia*). It is clear that while both Pharisees and Sadducees composed the seventy member court, the Pharisees must have been predominant. (W. O. E. Oesterly, *A History of Israel,* Vol ii, [London: Oxford University Press, 1951] 296) There is no evidence to show that before the Greek period any ruling body existed which had supreme authority over the entire Jewish nation. It is true that Rabbinical works have attempted to identify the Sanhedrin with the seventy elders Moses chose, at the suggestion of his father-in-law, to assist him (Exodus 18:14-26), but making a historical link between the Sanhedrin and those elders is extremely doubtful. (Emil Schurer, *A History of the Jewish People in the Time of Jesus Christ,* second division, vol. I, [New York: Charles Scribner's Sons] 165)

## THE FEASTS OF JUDAISM AND HOLY DAYS:

There were five feasts which were celebrated by the Jews. Passover (Pesach) was the oldest and was celebrated in March or April. It commemorated the deliverance of the Jews from Egypt under the leadership of Moses as the story is told in Exodus. Pentecost (Shavuot) was usually celebrated fifty days later in late May or early June. It reminded the Jewish people of the giving of the law under Moses and it later became a grain harvest festival. The feast of Tabernacles (Sukkot), held in October, commemorated God's care of the Israelites during the wilderness wandering of about forty years. A feast that developed late was called Lots (Purim) and occurred about the first of March. It reminded the Jews of their deliverance during the Babylonian exile, and in all probability the book of Esther was read during the feast and may have been composed for this occasion. The latest of the feasts was Dedication (Hanukkah). It was celebrated around December 20th and dealt with Maccabean cleansing and rededication of the Temple which had earlier been defiled by Antiochus Epiphanes.

Two other Holy Days held a spot in the Jewish calendar. The Jewish New Year (Rosh Hashanah) occurred in late September or early October and The Day of Atonement (Yom Kippur) reached back to Mosaic times and was celebrated also in October.

# CHAPTER IV
## NON-BIBLICAL COURCES FOR THE EXISTENCE OF JESUS

There have been those who have suggested that Jesus never existed and that he is a creation of the church. The sources looked at here will not provide anything of value for the life and teaching of Jesus, but they will authenticate his actual existence.

> *The Roman historian, Tacitus, who wrote around 115 A.D. made reference to Jesus in his Annals in connection with the fire in Rome during the reign of Nero. It is certainly not a reference in support of Christianity, but incidentally, provides evidence for the existence of Jesus. "a race of men detested for their evil practices, and commonly called Chrestini. The name was derived from Chrestos, who, in the reign of Tiberius, suffered under Pontius Pilate, Procurator of Judea. By that event the sect of which he was founder received a blow which for a time checked the growth of a dangerous superstition; but it revived soon after, and spread with recruited vigor not only in Judea . . . but even in the city of Rome, the common sink into which everything infamous and abominable flows like a torrent from all quarters of the world. Nero proceeded with his usual artifice. He found a set of profligate and abandoned*

*wretches who were induced to confess themselves guilty; and on the evidence of such men a number of Christians were convicted, not indeed on clear evidence of having set the city on fire, but rather on account of their sullen hatred of the whole human race. They were put to death with exquisite cruelty, and to their sufferings Nero added mockery and derision. Some were covered with skins of wild beasts, and left to be devoured by dogs; others were nailed to crosses; numbers of them were burned alive; many, covered with inflammable matter, were set fire to serve as torches during the night . . . At length the brutality of these measures filled every breast with pity. Humanity relented in favor of the Christians. "* (Will Durant, *The Story of Civilization: Part iii, Caesar and Christ.* [New York: Simon and Schuster, 1944] 281)

A second Roman source comes from Suetonius (@120 A.D.), who published in the *Lives of the Caesars* a statement which deals with conditions in the Empire during the time of Claudius Caesar (41-54 A.D.) and says that the Emperor Claudius expelled the Jews from Rome "because of constant tumults under the leadership of Chrestus." (J. W. Shepard, *The Christ of the Gospels,* [Grand Rapids: Erdman's Publishing Company, 1954] 1) That story parallels the story in Acts 18:1-2. Apparently, Aquila and Priscilla had just been banished from Rome by this edict. (There is no difficulty with the differences in vowels in "Christus" and "Chrestos.")

Pliny was a wealthy nobleman who had been appointed governor of Bythinia, and he wrote to ask advice as to how to deal with Christians during their trials.

*"Renegade Christians who worshipped your statue and the images of the gods and cursed Christ were pardoned. Faithful Christians were executed unless they were Roman citizens and those could be given the death penalty only by the Emperor."*

He also said,

*"They were in the habit of meeting on a certain fixed day before it was light when they sang in alternate verses a hymn to Christ, as to a god, and they bound themselves by a solemn oath not to do any wicked deeds, never to commit any fraud,*

> *theft or adultery, never to falsify their word nor deny a trust when called upon to deliver it up, after which it was their custom to separate and then reassemble to partake of food - but food of any ordinary and innocent kind."* (D. M. Beck, *Through the Gospels to Jesus*, [New York: Harper & Brothers, 1954] 69-70)

The last of these references comes from the satirist, Lucian. @165 C.E.:

> *'There was a man, Christus, who was nailed to the stake in Palestine, but who was still worshipped in Lucian's time. This Christus taught life hereafter and the brotherhood of men.'* (Shepard, 1)

There are two quotations from the Jewish Historian, Josephus, a man of high repute. He wrote:

> *"Now there was about this time Jesus, a wise man, if it be lawful to call him a man; for he was a doer of wonderful works, a teacher of such men as receive the truth with pleasure. He drew over to him both many of the Jews and many of the Gentiles. He was [the] Christ. And when Pilate, at the suggestion of the principal men amongst us, had condemned him to the cross, those that loved him at the first did not forsake him; for he appeared to them alive again the third day as the divine prophets had foretold these and ten thousand other wonderful things concerning him."*
> *(Antiquities XVIII, Ch. III:3)*

It must be admitted that there are those who believe that some elements of this passage are not an original part of Josephus' work, but even when the additions are deleted, it still supports the fact of Jesus' existence.

He also wrote that while Albinus, the successor of Festus, was on the road to Jerusalem, Ananus, the high priest,

> *"assembled the Sanhedrim of Judges and brought before them the brother of Jesus, who was called the Christ, whose name was James, and some of his companions; and when he had formed an accusation against them as breakers of the law, he delivered them to be stoned."* (Antiquities Book XX Ch. IX:1)

There is also a reference from the Talmud: (The Talmud is a running commentary on the law and an interpretation of the Midrash and the Mishnah. There is a Jerusalem Talmud and a Babylonian Talmud. Joseph Klausner reported some of these early statements about Jesus and tried to distinguish the untrustworthy ones. The list included the charge that Jesus' mother was divorced from her husband and that she was a adulteress and that Jesus was born as the result of an affair with a man named Pandera who is sometimes identified as a Roman soldier. (*Jesus of Nazareth, His Life, Times and Teaching* [London: George Allen & Unwin, Ltd, 1947] 17-24)

Klausner also suggests that the Talmud accuses Jesus of sorcery, leading Israel astray, expounding scripture like a Pharisee. His conclusion is "It is unreasonable to question either the existence of Jesus (as certain scholars have done both in the eighteenth century and in our own time) or his general character as it is depicted in these Gospels." All of this would indicate that no one would state such negatives about a person who never existed.

## EARLY EXTRA-CONONICAL LEGENDS.

It is not unusual for many legends to grow up around famous characters and Jesus was certainly no exception. In fact, we have no idea about the number of works which were composed in the early days of the Christian movement, but many have been found which were not included in those we call the canonical ones. There were probably many more which were oral and have been lost, but some have been preserved. There is no advantage in quoting many of these legends, but several out of the Apocrypha will help us once again to see that a man Jesus really existed and many legends grew up about his childhood. (Apocryphal stories are to be distinguished from apocalyptic literature.)

1. "And this little child Jesus when he was five years old was playing at the ford of a brook: and he gathered together the waters that flowed there into pools, and made them straightway clean, and commanded them by word alone.

2. And having made soft clay he fashioned thereof twelve sparrows. And it was the Sabbath when he did these things. And there were many other children playing with him.

3. And a certain Jew when he saw what Jesus did, playing upon the Sabbath day, departed straightway and told his father Joseph: Lo, thy child is at the brook, and he hath taken clay and fashioned twelve little birds, and hath polluted the Sabbath day.

4. And Joseph came to the place and saw and cried out to him saying: Wherefore doest thou these things on the Sabbath which it is not lawful to do? But Jesus clapped his hands together and cried out to the sparrows and said to them: Go! And the sparrows took their flight and went away chirping.

5. And when the Jews saw it they were amazed, and departed and told their chief men that which they had seen Jesus do."

*"Now his father was a carpenter and made at that time plows and yokes. And there was required of him a bed by a certain rich man, that he should make it for him. And whereas one beam, that which is called the shifting one, was too short and Joseph knew not what to do, the young child Jesus said to his father Joseph: Lay down the two pieces of wood and make them even at the end next to thee. And Joseph did as the young child said unto him. And Jesus stood at the other end and took hold upon the shorter beam and stretched it and made it equal with the other. And his father Joseph saw it and marveled; and he embraced the young child and kissed him, saying, 'Happy am I for that God hath given me this young child.'"*

*"Now after certain days Jesus was playing in the upper story of a certain house, and one of the young children that played*

*with him fell down from the house and died.   And the other children, when they saw it fled, and Jesus remained alone. 2. And the parents of him that was dead came and accused him that he had cast him down. (And Jesus said: I did not cast him down) but they reviled him still. 3. Then Jesus leaped down from the roof and stood by the body of the child and cried with a loud voice and said: Zeno (for so was his name called), arise and tell me, did I cast thee down?   And straightway he arose and said: Nay, Lord, thou didst not cast me down, but didst raise me up.   And when they saw it they were amazed: and the parents of the child praised God for the sign which had come to pass, and worshipped Jesus."* (M. R. James, ed., *The New Testament Apocrypha* [Berkeley, CA, Apocryphile Press, 2004], 49, 52)

# CHAPTER V
## THE SYNOPTIC GOSPELS

There are four kinds of critical studies which must be considered as the Synoptic Gospels are studied. These are Source Criticism, Form Criticism, Redaction Criticism and Textual Criticism. A very brief explanation of the first three of these studies will be made in this chapter, but the introduction to Textual Criticism will be reserved until an appropriate place in the body of the work. No effort will be made to deal with the way these studies affect the Old Testament except to say that some of the difficulties expressed earlier (p.11) can easily be dealt with by the JEPD theory which arose from the Form Critical work with the Old Testament.

Scholars for a number of years have recognized that there are significant differences between the Synoptic Gospels and the Fourth Gospel. Those which are called Synoptic ( Matthew, Mark, and Luke) all seem to look at the life and ministry in the same general way and use much of the same material and assume a chronological order, even though materials are sometimes placed in different contexts. The Fourth Gospel simply sets out to prove that Jesus was the logos of God and no chronological order is attempted. One example is the story of the cleansing of the Temple. In John it is placed early in the work with the story of the first miracle in Cana of Galilee. Some have tried to suggest that Jesus cleansed the Temple twice, once at the beginning of his ministry and the other at the very end. It is highly unlikely that this event occurred twice since the story in the Synoptics indicates that the Temple cleansing was "the straw that broke the camel's back" and within a few days it precipitated the arrest, trials, and crucifixion of Jesus. Very early the Fourth Gospel was called the "Spiritual Gospel." Because of this obvious difference, in this work, the Synoptics will be the basic source of the study of the teachings of Jesus.

In dealing with the sources, the purposes, and dates of the Synoptic Gospels, the benefits that have come from the study called Source Criticism will be of great value. The term "criticism" may bring up negative images and since it is an analytical study, it could be called Source Analysis. Regardless of that, Source Criticism is the science of attempting to find what the sources were for the materials the writers used. Most people who read the Bible simply do so in a devotional way, but for this type of study it is necessary to attempt to find the sources behind the writings as we have them. Some of those, may have been lost forever, since many were oral and may never have been committed to writing. The reference to a saying of Jesus by St. Paul, "Happiness lies more in giving than in receiving" (Acts 20:35 NEB) is an example of things that were lost probably because they were oral. There also seem to be distinct purposes which each gospel writer had in mind and pursued. It is necessary that those be examined, because they may affect they choice, placement, and use of the materials. This work will rely heavily on a basic work on the Four Document Hypothesis for the sources of the Gospels. (B. H. Streeter, *The Four* Gospels [London: Macmillan and Co. Limited, 1951])

## MARK:

Mark's purpose was to preserve the gospel story, probably as preached by Simon Peter. The traditional view of the authorship of Mark is that John Mark, who was for a short time with Paul and Barnabas and later appears to have been with Simon Peter, was the author. There is a passage, quoted by the historian Eusebiuis and relating to an elder Papias.

*"This also the elder used to say, 'Mark indeed having*

> *been the interpreter of Peter, wrote accurately, howbeit not in order, all that he recalled of what was either said or done by the Lord. For he neither heard the Lord nor was he a follower of his, but, at a later date (as I said) of Peter; who used to adapt his instruction to the needs of the moment, but not with a view of putting together the Dominical (Lord's) oracles in orderly fashion so that Mark did no wrong in thus writing some things as he recalled them, for he kept a single aim in view; not to omit anything of what he heard, not to state anything falsely." (Eusebius, Ecclesiastical History III, 39)*

Mark seems to have used an almost hidden idea of the Messianic Secret (although there are those who do not ascribe to this). He used no proof texts and ordered the stories to accomplish his purpose of preserving Peter's message. The gospel, was probably the first to be written and most likely dates from after the death of Peter (@65 C.E.) and shortly after the destruction of Jerusalem. Mark's gospel served as some of the source material which both Matthew and Luke used.

## MATTHEW:

Matthew's purpose seems to have been to show that Jesus' teaching was the genuine consummation of Judaism. Many scholars have doubts that the apostle Matthew wrote the work, but believe that it got its name from the special source material that the author used. However, the writer tried to prove that Jesus was the Messiah of Old Testament expectations and wherever possible he tied the ministry of Jesus to those Old Testament expectations. (My own conviction, arrived at after years of teaching a course in the Life and Teaching of Jesus, is that the author of Matthew had come to understand that Jesus' message constituted the real Judaism and supplanted it.) He followed the Rabbinic method of using numerous proof-texts. (A proof text is taking a passage out of its context and using it to support a particular idea to which the author applies the text.)

1) Matthew used about eighty percent of the gospel of Mark. By taking the Greek manuscripts and placing them side by side, one can easily see this usage, many times 'ver-batim'.

(Modern ideas about plagerism have no bearing on first century writers.)

2) There is also a source which is peculiar to Matthew and scholars have labeled this as the "M" source. It may very well be the "logia" that Papias wrote about, "So then, Matthew compiled the oracles (*logia*) in the Hebrew language, but everyone interpreted them as he was able."Some date this source from around 65 C.E. and from Jerusalem.

3) Matthew also used a source called "Q". The "Q" material is that which is common to Matthew and Luke but which is not found elsewhere. There is no extant document "Q"; it is a hypothetical source. Calling it hypothetical does not in any way indicate that it is not a very early authentic source. It is obvious that Matthew and Luke are using common material, even though sometimes there are a few variations. The language is similar, if not identical, and it requires a simple source to explain it. It may very well have been a part of the Christian oral tradition and (perhaps) dates from before 50 C.E. There have been numerous scholars who have recently studied this material and have even tried to postulate a different community from that which is seen in the canonical gospels. It is difficult to doubt that this source played a heavy part in the early community. (Burton L. Mack, *The Lost Gospel, The Book of Q and Christian Origins* [San Francisco,1993] 44-49) "Q" has some unique characteristics: There is no account of the birth of Jesus, the Passion, or the Resurrection. It appears to consist of a collection of miscellaneous sayings arranged topically and is mostly positive religious and moral teaching. It may have been an early catechetical manual for instruction in the duties of the Christian life, taken from the teaching of Jesus. The material, whether it was a written document or not, was held in high regard by the community, between 30-50 C.E. Most probably the need for "Q" ceased when the written gospels began to appear.

4) Then there are some special infancy stories found only in Matthew.

Since there are evidences that Matthew used the gospel of Mark and since that book has been dated from around 70 C.E., the conclusion must be that Matthew was written a little later than Mark, There are other evidences that the work came after the destruction of Jerusalem. In the twenty-fourth chapter of Matthew, the chapter that used apocalyptic imagery, Jesus responded to questions from his disciples. The first question had to do with when the magnificent Temple would be destroyed; the second dealt with when the Messiah would come (return), and the third dealt with the end of the age. Jesus indicated that no one knew anything about the time of the end (Mt. 24:36) and he referred to a Daniel figure ("the abomination of desolation", which most scholars who date the book during the revolt against Antiochus Epiphanes in 167-165 B.C.E. take to be a reference to desecrating the Temple) in talking about the destruction of the Temple which occurred under the Romans. There is in that discussion a parenthetical remark, "let the reader understand," which seems to imply that anyone reading the book will know what he is talking about, and therefore, it would appear that the book must be dated after the destructive war in 66-70 C.E. The probability is that the best date for the composition of Matthew is around 75 C.E.

## LUKE:

The purpose of Luke appears to be to show the universality of the love of God with a special interest in the poor, and therefore, that Jesus was intended as the Savior of all men. If there should be any doubt that the gospel writers used sources, the introduction to the gospel of Luke should remove them. It plainly shows research!

"The author to Theophilus: Many writers have undertaken to draw up an account of the events that have happened among us, following the tradition handed down to us by the original eyewitnesses and servants of the gospel. And so, I in my turn, your excellency, as one who has gone over the whole course of these events in detail, have decided to write a connected narrative for you, so as to give you authentic knowledge about the matters of which you have been informed." (Luke 1:1-4, NEB)

Nearly all scholars accept the idea that the books of Luke and Acts were written by the same person and that they really form a two volume set. It is evident that the author of these works was a highly educated person for there is general agreement that the books of Luke, Acts, and Hebrews are set apart as providing the best Greek in the New Testament. Perhaps, if he were an educated physician it would indicate that Greek was probably his native tongue. There is some material in the New Testament which mentions the times when Luke was companion of Paul. That would fit with the fact that in Acts the writing is done with the third personal pronoun until the time when Paul had his experience in Troas of a man asking that he come over into Macedonia and help them. (Acts 16:6-10) Suddenly the narrative is given in the first person, saying, "We immediately tried to cross over to Macedonia." From that point on in Acts when Luke was present with the mission party the narrative used the first person and when he is not present it used the third person. The conclusion drawn here is that Luke was a Macedonian and may have been the subconscious source of Paul's vision and the author of these two works.

If Luke-Acts are read as a unity it becomes evident that he was attempting to show that Christianity was a universal religion. Luke selected and arranged the materials which supported the thesis of his work and he used approximately sixty per-cent of the gospel of Mark. Like Matthew he also used the "Q" source. There is also material in the work which is peculiar to Luke (designated "L") and it was probably put together as gleaned from certain eye-witnesses, most probably when he was with Paul in Palestine while Paul was in prison in Caesarea, around 56 C.E. It contains special teaching and parables which are not found elsewhere. Then Luke has his own series of infancy narratives, distinct from those in Matthew. There may have been a few sources that are not presently identifiable,

# CHART SHOWING THE POSSIBLE SYNOPTIC SOURCES

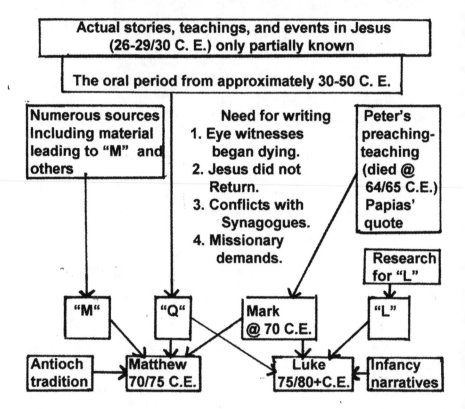

Actual stories, teachings, and events in Jesus (26-29/30 C. E.) only partially known

The oral period from approximately 30-50 C. E.

Numerous sources Including material leading to "M" and others

Need for writing
1. Eye witnesses began dying.
2. Jesus did not Return.
3. Conflicts with Synagogues.
4. Missionary demands.

Peter's preaching-teaching (died @ 64/65 C.E.) Papias' quote

Research for "L"

"M"

"Q"

Mark @ 70 C.E.

"L"

Antioch tradition

Matthew 70/75 C.E.

Luke 75/80+C.E.

Infancy narratives

# CHAPTER VI
## FORM AND REDACTION CRITICISM.

One of the studies which has had tremendous effect on recent New Testament study is that of Form Criticism (Analysis). This study deals with what happened during period before the materials were written. Using the methods of literary criticism it attempts to place the narratives in their original settings (Sitz-im-Leben) and to ascertain what impact and influence the early community had on the tradition. It is a valuable tool with limited powers but is probably the most subjective of the critical studies.

The movement began shortly after World War I and was led by two German scholars, Martin Dibelius and Rudolph Bultmann. It sought to answer the historical questions as to the nature and trustworthiness of our knowledge of Jesus and to dispel the doubts which had been raised about the existence of Jesus by Strauss and others. These two men worked independently and while their methods and procedures are similar their conclusions are often not. However, both concluded that we are in no sense at the mercy of those who doubt or deny that Jesus ever lived. Dibelius believed that the major formative influence was the early missionary preaching and the development of the *kerygma*. The *kerygma* is what scholars understand as the content of early Christian preaching and it answered questions about who Jesus was and what had he done. The sermons of Peter in the book of Acts may provide our best information about the content of early Christian preaching (Acts 2,3,4, and 10).

The *kerygma* apparently contained the following: (1) In Jesus the Messianic fulfillment came about. (2) Something was included about Jesus' descent from David, His ministry, His death and Resurrection. (3) The Holy Spirit is the promise of Christ for direction in the church. (4) An appeal for repentance and acceptance of God's grace. No two expressions of the *kerygma* were necessarily identical, but in general those early sermons and those by Paul and most likely some others contained some of these issues.

Bultmann, on the other hand, concluded that the forms the material took were closely related to the controversies of the early church, particularly between the church and the synagogue.

When looking at the oral period, a modern student must become aware of the vast difference between oral transmission during the period before the invention of the printing press and the current "untrustworthiness " of memory. The great majority of narratives were preserved in memory and that was a very trustworthy device. Any written material had to be done by hand and therefore was rather scarce. However, that does not mean that transmission of that material is as unacceptable as it would be in modern times. In dealing with the narrative of Abram rescuing Lot the band is described as consisting of 318 men. The following quote supports that and shows the reliability of the transmission of the narrative orally:

> " I believe the figure of 318 to be exactly correct, although aware of the fact that it had to be repeated from father to son for well over a thousand years before there was any possibility of committing it to paper. To this very day there are old men in the tents of Arabia who can recite the history of their ancestors for forty generations, and if  in their recital they stray but a jot from the facts, others within hearing will immediately correct them, or supply forgotten details" (Nelson Glueck, *The River Jordan* [Philadelphia: The Westminster Press, 1946] 74)

Anyone who has tried to read a book to a small child which has been read before may know that if one reads it incorrectly, the child, who cannot read, will promptly correct the reader. Or if you ask most any adult from any part of the United States to tell the story of "Little Red

Riding Hood" you will get essentially the same story, no matter what area one comes from or even what generation. That story was learned during the childhood years, before most could read and therefore it was preserved in the oral tradition manner. Some may think that the corruption of the use of memory is tragic, but the availability of printed material has done that to society and we sometimes, due to lack of effort, lose our abilities to remember accurately.

If scholars are correct in believing that the oral period covered from 30-50 C.E., perhaps some parts of the tradition (conflict stories, the Passion narrative and collections of specific sayings) began to be in written form around 50 C.E. There are many reasons to believe that new frontiers showed the need for a "full size" gospel and the teaching of new converts, who were ignorant of the Jewish background and the events of the life of Jesus, required some stabilizing of the material. There were other problems that faced the early community. Relatively few knew the gospel story, some of Jesus' sayings regarding the Kingdom of God seemed enigmatic and needed some interpretation, the manner of the death of Jesus in relation to the Suffering Servant concept had to be explained. When eye-witnesses began to die the dangers relative to losing the message became evident. So materials were needed for fellowship, for instruction, for missionary preaching and for worship.

Form Criticism saw all of these problems and looking at their assumptions, it is easy to understand their approach, even if one does not agree. The basic assumptions seem to be:

1. There must have been a twenty to thirty-five year oral period before the first gospel, Mark, was written.

2. During the oral period the narratives were passed down in isolated units.

3. The structure of the written gospels was created by the author and/or the community, therefore, there is little of biographical, chronological, or geographical emphasis in them.

4. The early community was, by and large, an unlettered community.

5. The early community expected the end of the world in their own generation.

6. Materials may be classified according to form and with that form it may be possible to find the original life situation.

This is not the place to try to give an exhaustive explanation of the Form Critical movement. That may be found a study of the effort by Basil Redlich. In his preface, Redlich says,

> *"Form Criticism has been termed a "discipline," and so it is. As a method of investigation it is about twenty years old, and the exponents of the From Critical school quite understandably overrate the value of their method, but there can be no doubt that Form Criticism has left its impress on the study of the gospels."* (*Form Criticism,* [London: Duckworth Press, 1948], 5)

While this school of thought has been valuable, it should be obvious that many will find shortcomings in the methodology. First of all, there is some disagreement about the classification of the gospel materials and it is extremely difficult to demonstrate many pure examples of a form. Also communities are much more likely to preserve and shape than they are to create. There appears to be a tendency to confuse the history of a form with the history of the subject matter. Multiple factors were involved in the growth and control of the tradition, not just the function of forms, and the identification of a form does not tell where and how the forms originated, nor how trustworthy they may be. There is probably little disagreement that the gospel tradition circulated in isolated units and with the possible exception of the Passion narrative, chronological relationship may be difficult to find. On the whole there is in the gospels no life of Jesus in the sense of a developing story or a chronological outline of the history of Jesus' ministry, but only isolated stories which have been provided contexts by the authors of the gospels. Some Form Critics are more radical than others in analyzing and deleting material from the record, but their contributions have been of great value.

## REDACTION CRITICISM:

A new type of study arose because of the way the gospel writers used the various materials. It is called "Redaction Criticism" and it attempts to determine the theological stances of the Synoptic writers. This assumes that the material has been brought together and redacted in various ways, so that the writers are seen as more than simple collector recorders. Redaction Critics tend to think of the evangelists as having a much more positive and creative role than the Form Critics allowed them. This study delves into the purposes of the writers and thus explains why the materials were used differently.

By the time Mark wrote his gospel (sometime soon after 65/70 C. E.) many of the first generation Christians had died, some by natural causes and some through martyrdom. As those who had known Jesus and witnessed the events died, it became important that the facts be preserved. Nearly all tradition holds that John Mark was the author of the gospel bearing his name. The following three quotations support the traditional view:

> *"Mark, having become the interpreter of Peter, wrote down accurately everything that he remembered, without however, recording in order what was said or done by Christ.".*
>
> *-Papias during the last half of the first century.*

> *"Mark, who was called stump fingered because his fingers were small by comparison with the rest of his body, was Peter's interpreter, and after Peter's decease wrote down this same gospel in the region of Italy."*
>
> *- from Anti-Marcionite Prologues to the Gospels*

> *"After their deaths (i.e. Peter's and Paul's) Mark, the disciple and interpreter of Peter, himself also gave us a written record of the things preached by Peter."*
>
> *-Irenaeus around 180 C. E.*

> *"Where the tradition is so unanimous we need not have the slightest hesitation in ascribing the Gospel to Mark, about whom, happily, we know quite a lot."* (A. M. Hunter, *The*

*Gospel According to Saint Mark,* [London: SCM Press LTD. 1955] 16)

As those who had known Jesus and witnessed the events died, preservation became vital. Mark, therefore, is one of those efforts to preserve the gospel story according to eyewitness accounts and he appears to construct the work around the idea of a "Messianic Secret" (by which he slowly unfolds the idea of Jesus as the Messiah and only allows that idea to be expounded when he feels it appropriate), and the horror of the rejection of Jesus which resulted in the Passion.

The account by Luke is designed to show that the message of Jesus was not limited to Jewish followers but that inherent in the teaching of Jesus was the universal application of the gospel with a particular emphasis on the poor. Whatever else they do, both Luke and Acts show the struggle that went on inside the early church to break out of the mold of Jewish isolationism and particularism. Luke appears to have ordered his gospel by choosing such powerful stories such as that of the "Good Samaritan" to show that people outside Judaism had acquired the spirit of Jesus' direction. It is not surprising that Luke often makes a hero out of a Gentile, or in the case of the parable mentioned, a Samaritan.

Matthew, whoever the author may have been, divided his work into five sections and in each instance the narrative is interrupted by a great discourse. The first of these in the Sermon on the Mount (5:1-7:28) and concludes with the statement, "When Jesus had finished these sayings." The second (11:1) concludes with some special instruction of the twelve and also concludes, "When Jesus had finished," in this case with the instruction. The third ends a series of great parables (13:53) and concludes, "When Jesus had finished these parables." The fourth division (19:1) concludes with the same general tone and the last (26:1) comes at the end of a long discourse and just before the beginning of the Passion narrative.

Whether the author meant to make his effort comparable to the five books of the Torah will remain speculation, but the work seems to teach that the Kingdom of God is inward and spiritual rather than national and political. And he opens the door to the same position that St. Paul took that Christ inaugurated the new and true Israel (Romans 9, 10, & 11). This would appear to lead to the conclusion that the long held idea of the favored position of the Jewish nation had been forfeited and, from the position of Redaction Criticism, it is easy to conclude that Matthew meant to show that Jesus taught that the rejection of His mission by the Jews, at the very least, meant that they are no longer a privileged people just because they are Jews.

# CHAPTER VII
## BEGINNING THE STORY

The remainder of the material in this work will follow *The Gospel Parallels* and the page numbers will be given so that the reader may follow the accounts and see the similarities and differences in the Synoptics. (The Synoptic material may be followed using ones New Testament, but that approach will forfeit some of the value of this work!)

### THE INFANCY NARRATIVES: pp. 1,2

Only Matthew and Luke give genealogies for Jesus. They differ somewhat in content, but the primary difference is in how they arranged and used that material. Keeping in mind that Matthew was interested in showing that Jesus was the promised Messiah of Old Testament hopes, it is not surprising that he begins the genealogy (Matt. 1:1-17) with Abraham, the father of the Jewish nation. He also divided the material into three sections of fourteen names each. Perhaps that was for mnemonic purposes, but in order to make that work it was necessary to use an event instead of a person for one of the listings. The first group of fourteen runs from Abraham to David and it omits two names that Luke places in his genealogy. He also adds one name that Luke did not include, but in general they agree.

The second group of fourteen finds the two authors differing considerably. While Matthew traces the genealogy through Solomon, who was born to Bathsheba, the wife of Uriah, Luke's account follows the descent through the line of Nathan. Matthew ends this series with the event of the deportation into captivity in Babylon. The genealogy listed in Matthew's third group of fourteen also differs from that in Luke. Only one of those differences needs to be dealt with here for most scholars simply believe that the two writers found and used two different traditions in regard to the genealogies. In any case the genealogies trace Jesus' lineage through Joseph and not through Mary. A serious difference can be seen in the account of who Joseph's father was. Matthew states that the father was Jacob and Luke names him as Heli. Obviously, both cannot be the father and it is highly unlikely that the two names refer to the same man. The most plausible explanation can be found in the Jewish rite of Levirate marriage (Deuteronomy 25:5ff). If this be the case Jacob was probably the brother who died and left no offspring, The belief that the dead brother's name and line would perish led to the responsibility of the next brother to marry the brother's widow and the first child born to that union would then be credited to the dead brother, thus preserving the line. That would mean that Heli would have been the natural father of Joseph while Jacob would have been the dead brother to whom Joseph was credited. If this is followed, Luke, being a Gentile and probably unfamiliar with the Hebrew Levirate marriage, might have named the real father while Matthew would have used the Levirate father. That tradition was also seen as functioning in the story of Ruth and Boaz and other Old Testament occurrences.

Efforts have been made to harmonize the two accounts. Some have suggested that Matthew is preserving a "regal" descent while Luke is giving Mary's genealogy. But there is no indication that either tried to trace the lineage through Mary, they both went through Joseph! There is probably no way that anyone can be certain as to how the two can be reconciled, if that is necessary at all. Jewish genealogical accounts offered legal descent and were not required to be literal accounts of each generation.

It is interesting that in Matthew's account there are five women mentioned; two are non-Jewish (Ruth and Rahab), three of them have sexual irregularities (Tamar, Bathsheba, and Rahab) and one is Mary.

It would appear that the main purpose of the genealogy in Matthew was to trace Jesus back through David to Abraham, while in Luke (keeping in mind his purpose) the genealogy traced him clear back to Adam and therefore included all humanity and showed the universal nature of Christ's purpose.

## THE ACCOUNT RELATING TO THE CHILD JOHN (Luke 1:4,5) pp. 4,5

The story of the annunciation of the birth of John to Zechariah indicates that it occurred while Herod was still ruling. Since Herod died in 4 B.C.E. (and there are some other things which also must have occurred before Herod died) a good estimate for the date of the announcement would be about 7 B.C.E. Zechariah was a priest and he and Elizabeth were advanced in years and were childless. Barrenness may have been considered as about the worst thing that could happen and it was especially hard for the wife. It meant that there would be no posterity for her husband. Probably taunts and even accusations of sin as the cause for her barrenness were made. In any case, Elizabeth probably felt that she was out of favor with God. Both Elizabeth and Zechariah were descended from priestly stock.

There were twenty four courses of priests and each course was responsible for one week twice a year. (Josephus, *Antiquities, VII. 14.7*) The incense was to be offered twice daily and a priest was chosen to enter the Holy Place to perform this function. Since the priests in each course were very numerous, the one who was to perform this task was chosen by lots and it may have happened only once in a lifetime. On this occasion the lot fell on Zechariah and as he attended to the function an angel, Gabriel, informed him that his prayer for a child had been heard and that the child was to be named John. In this religious "high" the vision came to Zechariah and even though he had prayed for a child, he could hardly believe this message. Due to his lack of belief in the vision he remained unable to speak until after the birth of the child. It must be remembered that posterity was particularly important to the Jews for it would appear that many believed that continuation of ones name, and perhaps ones continuous life, was bound up in having children. When, after some delay, Zechariah came out from the Holy

Place he was unable to speak and other priests realized that he had seen some kind of vision.

When the time of his service was ended, he went home and Elizabeth conceived and for five months kept herself in seclusion. She said, "This is what the Lord has done for me when he looked favorably on me and took away the disgrace I have endured among my people." (Luke 1:25) One would have to ask whether John was a Nazarite (compare Numbers 6:3) as implied in 1:15 and a forerunner of the type of Elijah.

## THE ANNUNCIATION TO MARY (Luke 1:26-38) pp. 5,6

Luke then proceeds to the annunciation to Mary regarding the birth of Jesus. It probably occurred about six months after that which Zechariah received since Mary's visit was described as in the "sixth month" (probably of Elizabeth's pregnancy) and it is also made by the angel, Gabriel. Mary is described as being "espoused" to Joseph. That was a procedure by which she was legally bound to Joseph, but there was as yet no marriage. Such espousal required a divorce proceeding to dissolve it. According to the narrative, Mary was puzzled about the type of greeting that the angel made and about the possibility of her having a child since she had never had sexual relations. In spite of her early questioning, Mary accepted what the angel said and the dangers which went with it. Obviously, this would have put a great strain on Joseph in regard to the espousal and Mary would have been open to the charge of adultery and perhaps even the punishment of being stoned.

## MARY VISITS ELIZABETH (Luke 1:39-56) pp. 6,7

The first issue that must be dealt with is that Mary and Elizabeth are kindred and Elizabeth was of the daughters of Aaron. There are those who pay no attention to this and simply affirm that Mary was of Davidic lineage, but it would appear that such a claim is open to question. Since each of the genealogies trace Jesus through the male side, (Joseph), one must assume that either Mary's lineage was of no significance or that the male legal lineage was all that was important. When Mary arrived at Elizabeth's home, the fetus jumped or kicked and that was taken as a sign of recognition. According to the narrative, Mary then sang or quoted the Magnificat, which is reminiscent of the song of Hannah (I Samuel 2:1-10). Many of those poetic passages refer to songs and praises from the Old Testament. Mary's visit lasted for three months which would take her to the time for the birth of John, but nothing is said about her being at that event.

## THE BIRTH OF JOHN (Luke 1:57-80) pp. 7,8

The main issue in the narrative about the birth of John lies in the naming of the child. At the annunciation Zechariah was told to name the child John, but there was no one in the family named John. Those present for the ceremony of circumcision and naming insisted that he should be named after his father, but Elizabeth stuck by the notion that his name should be John and when Zechariah wrote on a tablet that his name was John, immediately, he was released from his inability to speak and John was then identified as a prophet by his father. The message by Zechariah is again very reminiscent of the use of Old Testament references. The childhood of John is omitted, but he is said to have been "in the wilderness" from some unstated age until his public ministry began.

## THE BIRTH OF JESUS (Taken from Matthew's Antioch tradition 1:18-25) p. 2

The narrative about the birth of Jesus began with the dilemma that Joseph must have faced. When he discovered that Mary was pregnant, his options would have been to either dissolve the betrothal or later marry her. He appears to have been a man of great compassion and decided to put her away privately, hoping that that was the best thing to do. Then in a dream he was informed by an angel that the child was from the Holy Spirit and that he should be called "Jesus", which is the same name as Joshua and means, "Jehovah is helper" and indicates salvation. And Joseph decided to take Mary as his wife, but there was no sexual relationship until she had borne the child. Matthew then turned to one of his many proof texts. (Isaiah 7:14) A proof text takes a passage out of its original context and applies it to prove the issue under discussion, whether the original usage actually applied to the current issue or not. This particular passage may have been chosen because of the name "Immanuel" which meant "God with us" and that identified Jesus and implied the incarnation.

The original context was something else. The seventh chapter of Isaiah dealt with the Syro-Ephramitic War (735-732 B.C.E.). If one reads the passage without trying to super-impose Christian teaching on it the issue is perfectly clear. Ahaz, the King of Judah, is frightened. The narrative says, "The heart of Ahaz and of his people shook as trees of the forest shake before the wind," (7:2) because Rezin, the King of Syria, and Pekah, the King of the Northern kingdom, Israel, have made an alliance and are prepared to attack Jerusalem. So, Isaiah is told to go to Ahaz to challenge him. Isaiah had a peculiar trait in naming his children, in these cases boys, giving them names that meant something. He is told to take along his son, *Shear-yashub*, which means "a remnant shall return" apparently for encouragement, and to tell the king that the alliance will not succeed.

Then Ahaz is asked to request a sign, but for some reason he did not want to test God. Whether that was because of doubt or some sort of false humility one can never know. When he refused to ask for a sign, Isaiah offered him one anyway, "Therefore the Lord himself will give you a sign. Look, a young woman of marriageable age is with child and shall bear a son and will name him Immanuel." (from the Hebrew text - Isaiah 7:14) Matthew quoted this from the Septuagint, which described the young woman as a virgin. The Septuagint is a Greek translation of the Old Testament which was made during the latter part of the Intertestament Period when Greek was the predominant language. It is necessary to explore this problem, since the King James Version translated the Hebrew as "virgin". The Hebrew word used in this passage is *Almah* and it means a young woman of marriageable age who has not yet borne a child." That means she is minimally about twelve years of age. There is a Hebrew word which means virgin, *Bethulah,* and it covers a girl from her birth until she has her first intercourse. Assume that at twelve she becomes capable of bearing a child but does not marry and have a child until she is seventeen. During that period, from twelve to seventeen, she is both a *Bethulah* and an *Almah*. Of course, if no child was born until later, she remained an Almah as long as she was childless or until she became old enough to not be considered a young woman. When the Septuagint translators came to that term (*Almah*) there was no Greek term equivalent to it so they used the Greek *Parthenos,* the Greek word for virgin. What Isaiah told Ahaz was that the woman was already pregnant and would bear a child and before that child was old enough to distinguish between good and evil, the threat from the two kings would be over. (7:15) That encouragement must have been meant to apply to those immediate years, around 732 B.C.E. and it would have been of no encouragement value at all to say, "Hang in there, old boy, for in about seven hundred years relief will come." The question remains as to why Matthew used that text. It is not possible to get into his mind and state exactly what he thought, but it would appear that it was the promise of "God with us" that in those dark days offered hope to Ahaz and for Matthew it also paralleled the incarnation in the person of Jesus. Who the young woman was will remain a mystery, but since Isaiah named his previous children with names that meant something (*Shear-jashub*, meaning "a remnant shall return" and *Mahar-shal-ala hash-baz*, meaning "Hasten the spoil and speed the prey") there is a strong probability that she was his wife. Every time she would have called the child, the name would have said to everyone who heard, "God is with us." There is no record to support that idea, but polygamy was common and he may very well have had another wife who was pregnant but had not yet delivered her first child. One of the interesting things about the scriptural record is that it often has an immediate application, but also carries a principle which may apply much later.

> "While there was no real prediction, the New Testament occurrence reminded the Evangelist of the Old Testament passage or so resembled the Old Testament occurrence as to warrant the application to it of the same language. . . . Two things are to be observed, (1) The New Testament writers sometimes quote Old Testament expressions as applicable to gospel facts or truths, without saying that they are prophesies. . . . (2) It is often unnecessary, and sometimes impossible, to suppose that the prophet himself had in mind that which the New Testament writer calls a fulfillment of his prediction." (John A. Broadus, *An American Commentary on the New Testament, vol. 1* (Philadelphia: The American Baptist Publication Society, 1886] 11)

In the discussion in which Joseph is informed about the solution to the problem of Mary's pregnancy, the virginity of Mary is assumed and therefore, nothing is taken away from that concept even if the Isaiah passage (7:1-25) is allowed to be interpreted in its original sense. The principle is: Divine guidance in the scripture shows that there are great principles of truth which are true in one way in one generation and applicable in another way in another generation. In this passage Isaiah may not have seen beyond the problems facing Ahaz, but the principle of truth was and is that "God is with us." The same usage can be seen in the different ways as the Suffering Servant poems in Isaiah are interpreted. The discussion of Matthew's use of proof-texts really says nothing about the virgin birth. This story is clearly not something unique to Christianity, since there are virgin birth stories in the literature of other religions. It is also obvious that this narrative did not play an important role in early Christian dogma, at least from the information we have, since only the works of Matthew and Luke contain it and Paul, never referred to it at all. Of course, the normative Christian position accepts the story and recognizes that God can do anything He so chooses. The renowned British Scholar, William Barclay, indicated,

> *"The New Testament writers were not primarily concerned with the Virgin Birth as a literal and historic fact; they were concerned with it as a symbolic way of saying that from his very first entry into the world Jesus was in a special and unique relationship with God,"*

Barclay further stated,

> *"I do not think we are intended to take the Virgin Birth literally. . . . I think we are clearly intended to take the story of the Virgin Birth as a parabolic, symbolic, pictorial, metaphorical method of carrying the unique relationship with God back to the very birth of Jesus, quite irrespective of whether that birth was a virgin birth or a normal birth like the birth by which all men enter into the world."* (*The Mind of Jesus,* [New York: Harper and Brothers, 1961] 331-332)

The fact that many have come to be Christian even before they knew what a virgin was should show that it is not a requisite to believe the story literally - I myself, was one of those children too young to know what a virgin was. I am reminded about a story of a young first grader who had drawn a picture of the nativity scene. Everything was there that was supposed to be, but off to one side was a short, fat, round figure. When the teacher asked who that was the child replied, "That's Round John Virgin." However, for most Christians accepting the story literally presents no problem.

## THE BIRTH OF JESUS (Taken from Luke's Infancy Narratives - 2:1-20) p. 9

Probably one of the most beautiful narratives ever written is that which describes the birth of Jesus in Luke. It is couched in the time of Emperor Augustus Caesar, who ruled the empire from 27 B.C.E. to 14 C.E., and during the time of a census ordered taken by Quirinius, who is called the governor of Syria. A problem arises with the dating of that census during the time when "Quirinius was governor of Syria.." There is a record of a census taken in 6 C.E. when he was the governor and that census, which appears to have been the first, (Josephus, *Jewish Wars, II. 8.1)* caused a rebellion in Galilee which was suppressed only with great difficulty. However, the year 6 C.E. is much too late for the birth of Jesus, since both Matthew and Luke indicate that the birth took place when Herod was still King. Herod died in 4 B.C.E. and therefore, the birth had to occur at least ten years before that census of 6 C.E. Several attempts have been made to explain this difficulty, probably the most significant is the one by Sir William Ramsey in which he argues that Quirinius held a position of authority, perhaps a co-legate, when Saturninus Varus was called governor of Syria in 9-4 B.C.E. (*The Bearing of Recent Discoveries on the Trustworthiness of the New Testament,* [London, New York, Toronto: Hodder and Stoughton, 1915] 220-254) Whether those arguments are convincing or not will remain an unanswered question unless more inscriptions are discovered. At any rate, even if the Lucan Infancy Narratives are incorrect about Quirinius, the time frame is still set by the reign of Herod. It does appear that even though it may seem unnecessary to moderns, both the husband and wife were required to go to the city of the forefathers, and so Joseph and Mary traveled to Bethlehem. It is obvious that Luke uses the story to connect Joseph with the "house and lineage of David."

The birth of Jesus took place around 6-5 B.C.E. In the fifth or sixth century C.E. a monk named Dionysius Exiguus suggested that since, in his thought, Jesus was the dividing point of history, all time should be measured from the birth of Christ, (B.C meaning before Christ and A.D., *anno domini,* meaning in the year of our Lord.) All efforts to use the comparative reigns of sovereigns indicate that the present calendar is off by about 4-6 years. The birth occurred during the lifetime of Herod the Great and since Herod died in 4 B.C.E., Jesus could not have been born after that date. Dionysius erred in his calculation and hence the conclusion that the calendar is off by about four to six years. The following facts support the recognizing this error in date:

1. Jesus must have been between one and three when Herod the Great slaughtered the infants in Bethlehem, and Herod died in 4 B.C.E., therefore the birth would have occurred around 7/6 B.C.E..

2. The astronomer, Kepler, discovered the following in 1603-04.

> *"Each December at some planetariums the projector is run back to the year 7 B.C. and the demonstration for the public shows that there is a changed aspect of the sky from November 7 B.C. through May of 6 B.C. In February of 6 B.C. the three planets, Mars, Jupiter, and Saturn appear to be in triple conjunction low in the western sky, just after sunset. This verifies the calculation made by Kepler who observed Jupiter and Saturn in close connection on December 17, 1603 and in the autumn of 1604, when, while they were still near each other, Mars passed close to Saturn and Jupiter. Scientific curiosity led Kepler to calculate how often that phenomenon happened and he calculated an occurrence for 7/6 B.C. Such a planetary conjunction suggests an explanation of the "Star of the East" at the time of Jesus' birth. Another suggestion would be to identify the star of Bethlehem as a "Nova", i.e. a star that suddenly flares up, only to fade away after a few weeks or months, such as the Nova Herculis of 1834-35, which reached its maximum brilliance at Christmas time."* (Elmer

K. Mould. *Essentials of Bible History, 3rded.* [New York: The Ronald Press Company, 1966] 576-577)

We have no accurate date for the day for the celebration of the birth of Christ. The celebration of the "Epiphany" on December 25th began in the early Christian centuries and probably coincided with the pagan feast of Saturnalia, which was a Roman National Holiday, and no one would have been working. It should also be noted that the Eastern Orthodox Church celebrates January 6th as the birth date.

The praise of the angelic host and the homage of the shepherds would seem to fit late spring or early summer, possibly early fall (not after October when the rainy season set in). In a little village like Bethlehem there would have been limited accommodations and if our conjecture that people returned to their ancestral home is correct, space would have been at a premium. One needs to know that animals were kept very close to the human living quarters (that practice even prevailed in parts of Europe until after World War II) so when the story suggests that Joseph found space only in a stable, that should not be a surprise. The amazement of the shepherds and the message of the angels, "Glory to God in the highest heaven, and on earth peace among those with whom he is pleased," (Luke 2:14) lent an awesome atmosphere to the event. Mary, who should have understood more about it than anyone, is left pondering all these words. Both the story of the shepherds (attested by Luke) and that of the Magi (attested by Matthew) fit with the idea that Bethlehem was the place of the birth. There have been those who questioned this location and suggest that Nazareth was the birthplace, since travel would have been difficult for Mary. But returning to the place of ones lineage for a census appears to have been a Roman practice, and there is no evidence to support Nazareth as the birthplace..

## CIRCUMCISION. AND REDEMPTION. pp.9, 3-4, & 10

When Jesus was eight days old he was circumcised and named, as was the Jewish custom. The name given to him, Jesus, was that which both Mary and Joseph had been told of in the annunciations. Soon after that event, when Jesus was forty days old, he was taken to the Temple for a ceremony of redemption from the priesthood and for Mary it was a ceremony of purification. Early in the history of the Jews the first born son was to be the priest of the family. But when the Levitical priesthood developed, there was no need for more priests and so the first born was released from that obligation by a sacrificial ceremony. Also, when a woman had any kind of issue of blood, particularly after childbirth, she was considered unclean. Therefore, after forty days, when presumably the birth process was over, the sacrifice also served to announce her purification. (For some inexplicable reason, when the baby was a female the uncleanness lasted for eighty days.)

While they were in the Temple two figures came to tell the praises of the child and speak about his deliverance of the nation. The first of these was Simeon, who was looking for the coming of the Messiah and when he took the child he offered praise to God and, in keeping with Luke's universal approach, he indicated that the child would be a revelation to the Gentiles and to the glory of Israel. Also in the Temple at this time was an old woman, Anna, who had lived in marriage with her husband for seven years and after that as a widow for eighty-four years, It is difficult, although it probably doesn't make any difference in the story, to determine whether at the time of this event she was eighty-four years old or was a little more than one hundred and seven years. (This would assume that she was married at about thirteen to sixteen, lived the seven years in marriage and then lived for eighty-four years after her husband's death.) She also praised the child and spoke of the redemption of Jerusalem. Mary and Joseph seem to have been amazed at the things which had been said. According to Luke they returned to Nazareth where the child grew and became strong and was filled with wisdom. Nothing is said in Luke's account about the rampage of Herod, but trying to place the visit of the Magi in some chronological order, it probably came after this visit to the Temple and certainly before they went back to Nazareth.

The Magi were Babylonian astrologers who were probably aware of the Jewish hopes for Messiah. While they were in the East they saw a peculiar star and immediately set out on a journey to find the new king. They went first to the palace of Herod, where one would expect the next king would be born, but they were met with suspicion on the part of Herod. Matthew indicated that Herod, and all Jerusalem, was filled with fear. The priests and scribes quoted Micah 2:6 in regard to the Messiah being born in Bethlehem. Herod then, with false piety, sent the Magi on their way hoping that they would find the child and report the location to him. They went to Bethlehem and offered their gifts and worshipped the child.

Even though there has been a popular idea that there were three Magi, there is no indication of the number except that there were three gifts mentioned. When they arrived they worshipped the child and offered their gifts. We are not told whether they became suspicious of Herod because of his actions or what triggered the dream in which they were warned not to report to him, but they returned to their homeland, avoiding Jerusalem. Some time must have elapsed between the birth and this visit, for the Magi found them "in a house" and Herod chose to eliminate all male children up to two years of age.

Joseph was then also warned in a dream about Herod's madness and he took Mary and the child to Egypt to get away from the danger posed by Herod. That did not require a long trip to modern Egypt, just far enough to get outside Herod's control. They stayed there until Herod died. Matthew again used proof-texts in connection with these events.

The first of those is from Hosea 11:1,

> *"out of Egypt I have called my son."* *That text originally referred to Israel being brought out of Egyptian bondage under Moses.*

The second is from Jeremiah 31:15,

> *"A voice was heard in Ramah wailing and loud lamentation, Rachel weeping for her children; she refused to be consoled, because they were no more."*

It certainly must have been a fact that there was an atmosphere of sorrow in Bethlehem when the children were slaughtered. Even though the village was small and the number of male children two years and under would have been relatively small, still their deaths would have produced great sorrow. So Matthew found a similar situation in the Old Testament and quoted it. The passage in Jeremiah originally referred to the captives being taken away to Babylon and as some passed by the tomb of Rachel that sorrow was portrayed, figuratively, as Rachel weeping for her children and it showed some of their anguish. It was a sad day for the people. That Herod would have ordered such a deed should not be surprising. It is interesting that Augustus Caesar knew some of the cruelty of Herod and once said, in a play on words, that Herod was kinder to his pig (*huos* in Greek) than he was to his son (*hweos* in Greek). After the death of Herod, Joseph returned to Nazareth. Remember the will of Herod. Not only was Nazareth the home of Mary and Joseph, but Herod Antipas would have been much easier to live under in Galilee than Herod Archelaus would have been in Judea. Matthew used another proof-text to support this move.

He quoted from Isaiah 11:1 or from Judges 13:7,

*"He will be called a Nazorean."*

That text, if it comes from Isaiah refers to the term *nezer* which means a shoot or branch; if it is from Judges it refers to the Nazarite vow. In either case it did not designate a citizen of Nazareth, but Matthew found it applicable. There is no information about the childhood of Jesus from around 4 B.C.E. until 6/7 C.E. (Unless one places value on the Apocryphal tales).

## JESUS AT TWELVE. p. 10

The visit to Jerusalem in 6, 7, or 8 C.E. is of great importance in the study of the life of Jesus. Many have difficulty in allowing Jesus to be human and assume that he knew everything, including his mission, from the very beginning, but this narrative seems to indicate that some new religious awakening took place when he was able for the first time to be an accepted Jewish adult male (twelve years and up). Twelve is not an unusual age for children to feel special religious inclinations, especially Jewish children. In this story we are reminded that each year at the Passover Season families went to Jerusalem to observe the feast. We cannot know whether the whole family went each year, but this time was certainly one in which Mary, Joseph, and Jesus went and it had tremendous impact on Jesus. He was twelve and for the first time he was allowed to enter the Court of Israel! Keeping in mind that he would probably have also celebrated the Bar Mitzvah, the indication is that for the first time he began to express feelings about his mission in life. Perhaps the Temple surroundings awakened an awareness and he most definitely found a unique interest in what was going on. Some have been surprised that the parents could go a whole day's journey without knowing that Jesus was not with the group. That is not so difficult to explain. If he had gone with them in the caravans in earlier years, he would have been in the company of his mother and Joseph may have thought that was the case this time. The group traveled with the women separated until the end of the day, so Mary, who would have been acutely aware that her son was growing up, perhaps more than Joseph, would have probably thought he was with the men. It is only at the end of the day that they find him missing; not among their kindred; not among the boys playing; just not there! One can almost sense the panic, but they could not return to Jerusalem, up the dangerous road from Jericho to Jerusalem at night, and probably not without joining another caravan for protection. At any rate, it is not until later that they discovered him in the Temple, immersed in the discussions that were going on and asking questions. He was certainly an astute student and the teachers recognized that. When, in somewhat a spirit of anger the parents challenged him with the question, posed by Mary, with a bit of reprimand, "Why have you treated us this way?", his reply shows that he had a special feeling at that time and that he identified this event with "being in my Father's house" and that seems to have been beyond Mary and Joseph; they did not comprehend it all! But the narrative quickly moved on stating that the parents were puzzled and the fact that Jesus was obedient to them.

For what is sometimes called the "silent years" (more than likely eighteen of them) he grew, as Luke indicated, in all the ways that humans do, in physical size, in mental development, and in spiritual and social favor, indicating, once again, the mysterious human nature of Jesus. More than likely Jesus' synagogue schooling was finished. This narrative is the last which mentions Joseph and because of that many believe that soon after this time Joseph died and Jesus would have become responsible for the care of the family. He must have been subject to many influences among which were: 1)family love in the home; 2) Pharasaic emphasis on legal obedience; 3) nationalistic hope and zeal; 4) nature and everyday life; (note his illustrations and his concern for the poor) and 5) many of the prevailing ideas around him.

# CHAPTER VIII
## THE BEGINNING OF THE GOSPEL

### THE ATMOSPHERE

In the century immediately preceding the birth of Jesus, many things had gone wrong in the experience of the Jews. Even though there had been efforts to re-establish the nation, with the coming of the Romans in 63 B.C.E. all hope of independence was lost. Religious institutions had been compromised and while the Romans generally left conquered nations alone as far as religion was concerned, there had been the corruption of the high priesthood through efforts to buy and sell it. As a result the high priest was often appointed by the Romans and respect for the institution had dwindled. Annas was the high priest appointed by Quirinius, but he was so corrupt that after six years he was deposed and Caiaphas, who was Annas' son-in-law, held the office during Jesus' ministry. Annas still had huge amount of influence, even though officially he no longer served. Many of the prevailing philosophies which pervaded the area appealed to lust or pride. It is probably fair to say that many Jews had lost hope.

## THE MESSENGER AND HIS MESSAGE  (p.11 - 13)

Into that atmosphere came a rugged man reviving the office of prophet. John the Baptist was a very peculiar individual. He lived somewhat of a hermit life-style and his manner of dress indicated that he was not concerned with social acceptance. He was described as wearing a camel's hair garment with a leather thong tied about his waist. A modern person needs to be aware that the camel's hair of John's day was in no sense the luxurious camel's hair of the modern period. It probably was more like a burlap bag. He was also described as eating locusts and wild honey. (Matthew 3:4) That may turn the modern stomach; what is repulsive to one may be regular fare for another. During the occupation of Japan in 1945 at the close of World War II I had just finished a sumptuous Christmas feast and as I walked around the corner of a building I saw a Japanese workman pull out of his pickled lunch a grasshopper, wings and all, and eating it. Needless to say, I almost lost my lunch! John's message to the Jews was simple: "Repent, for the kingdom of heaven is right here on us." The word used in this passage is in the Perfect Tense and indicates that the Kingdom has already drawn near. John did not say how near, but his message indicated that it was immediate and he confirmed that message with a revival of the prophetic style. He used a common symbol of baptism, which was not new to the Jews for proselyte baptism had been used for Gentiles who converted to Judaism for some time. But John was calling for Jews themselves to be baptized! The Greek term *baptidzo* means to dip or plunge under and would indicate some kind of renewal.

John was born of a priestly family and the question of why he did not serve as a priest may disturb some. It should be remembered that since at the birth of John, Zechariah noted that he was a prophet perhaps the abdication of the priestly career did not disturb anyone, and apparently John considered himself as following a prophetic challenge.

The introduction of the concept of the Kingdom of God probably revived all of the nationalistic hopes of those who heard him for their hope was for an immediate restoration of the kingdom of Israel. While John in all probability held to the notion of a physical and national kingdom, he did indicate some new things. Physical descent alone was not sufficient to allow one to participate in this kingdom. His message was packed with moral connotations and those who received his baptism were characterized as having repented, changed their minds in regard to their sins. It was a rather harsh appeal to those who were a "brood of vipers." His estimate of himself reached back into Isaiah and all three Synoptics state that he saw himself as one who prepared the path for the Messiah, and his baptism is said by Mark to have been in reference (*eis aphesin hamartion*) to the forgiveness of sins While there appear to have been some who saw John as the Messiah, he did not see himself in that light, in fact, in the Fourth Gospel he expressly denies it and claims to be one preparing the way. His picture of the one who was to come was that of one bringing immanent judgment. The message of John indicates an apocalyptic expectation of separation. Many would have been familiar with the figure of an unfruitful tree being cut down and his reference that "even now the ax is lying at the root of the tree" indicates an expectation of immediate judgment. (That picture indicates that the swing of the ax has already occurred and the picture is stopped just as the ax bites into the tree root.) That characterization of John's message (calling for immediate judgment) is from the "Q" material and the similar phrase, "His fan is in his hand" would recall, for all of those people, the familiar sight of the threshing floor and the farmer throwing the wheat and chaff up into the air so that the wind would separate the chaff from the wheat. He expected the Messiah to bring in that judgment. Whereas previously God's wrath had been seen as directed against the Gentiles (and the Jews were safe) that was not what John preached. The Jews as a whole needed to get ready. The length of John's ministry is hard to estimate. Luke interrupted the account with the record of Herod Antipas' arrest of John and shutting him up in prison and set the stage for his death by indicating the issue of Herod's marrying Herodias and other evils that Herod had done were the basis for the imprisonment. Then he returned to the main narrative to tell of Jesus sharing in the baptism. With his preaching, John had excommunicated the entire Jewish nation. (Barclay, p.24)

## THE BAPTISM OF JESUS (p. 14)

Regarding the baptism of Jesus, only Matthew offers the introductory thought about John's hesitancy to baptize Jesus.

The account in the Fourth Gospel offers some question about what John knew about Jesus before the baptism. He does point people to the

"Lamb of God who takes away the sin of the world," but the narrative gives us little help in learning when and how much he understood of Jesus and the nature of his mission. Many have struggled with the question of why Jesus submitted to John's baptism. In the book of Hebrews, there is a statement which refers to Jesus as "without sin." (Hebrews 4:15) Apparently, early in Christian history there were those who wondered about the question, "Why the baptism?" In a non-canonical work an answer was offered:

> *"the mother of the Lord and his brothers said to him, 'John the Baptist baptizes for the forgiveness of sins; let us go and be baptized by him.' But he said to them, 'In what way have I sinned that I should go and be baptized by him? Unless, what I have just said is a sin of ignorance.'"* (Footnote quoted in *The Gospel Parallels, p. 14 from The Gospel According to the Hebrews*)

In an effort to answer the "why" question some have seen Jesus identifying himself with all human-kind and thus being baptized as a representative of all men. Perhaps a better thought is that just as his consciousness was aroused in the Temple when he was twelve, now his mission becomes clearer. So he made a decision to go public and for that some assurance was needed. In this moment of self dedication, the assurance came in the experience of the spirit coming on him as a dove. Matthew, who would be familiar with the figure of the dove representing the Spirit, indicated that when Jesus was baptized he, Jesus, saw the spirit coming on him rather swiftly as a dove comes down and he, Jesus, heard the voice. The message of that voice reflected Old Testament thought in identifying Jesus as the beloved Son in whom God was pleased. (Psalm 2:7 and Isaiah 42:1) There is an addition in some late texts of the rest of the verse "Today I have begotten you." (Psalm 2:7) That addition is supported by the late manuscript "D" and by some church fathers, Justin, Clement, Origen, and Augustine, and has given rise to some discussion of a Christology of adoption since at this point the Spirit came upon him, but the addition is not strongly enough attested in manuscript evidence as to be accepted. All of this raises the question whether the experience, at least the meaning of it, was probably internal and was vital to the ministry of Jesus and one which Jesus must have discussed with his disciples who, at the time of the baptism, had not yet been called. The statement that he saw the spirit descending "as a dove" probably meant that it came suddenly, swiftly coming down like a dove would do and not as a scavenger bird would. Luke, who might not have been familiar with the Jewish use of the dove as representing the spirit, is the only one who makes the spirit come in "bodily form" which might imply an external vision to everyone, but there is no evidence of any awesome following from the crowd.

## THE TEMPTATIONS OF JESUS, p. 16

All temptations are always a testing and they are essentially necessary, because there are options between which one must choose. Jesus was committed at the baptism, so certain questions were bound to arise. How will this ministry be carried out? What kinds of methods should be used to implement his life plan? These temptations were real and Jesus could be tempted and he was! One must never lose sight of the fact that Jesus was a real human being and he was capable of sinning and of refusing to sin, just as we are. Primarily, these three pieces of narrative are representative of him choosing a method for his mission and his decision about that mission. One should never think that these were the only temptations Jesus faced, but rather they provide an opportunity, as he must have told them, for his followers to see his introspection and struggling with the concept of what kind of Messiah he would be – this was vital to his ministry!

The Synoptics indicate that "immediately" after the baptism Jesus was driven (or led) by the Spirit into the wilderness area. The order of the temptations is not really significant, but it is the "Q" material from which Matthew and Luke get the major portion of this information. The Temptation narrative takes the form of a dialogue between Satan and Jesus. The accepted idea that the entire world was permeated by a host of invisible demons led by one called Beelzebub or Satan (and many other names) had developed after the exile and contact with Persian dualism. There are numerous references to this concept in many non-canonical works which must have affected the thought of the first century. (T. W. Manson, *A Companion to the Bible* [Edinburgh: T. and T. Clark, 1950] 340-347) Whatever ones understanding of Satan may be (it is a rather ridiculous escape mechanism to say, "The devil made me do it."), the fact is that temptation comes in many different ways, but it always represents an internal struggle, even though there may be external stimuli. In the first two temptations (according to Matthew's order) the proposition is posed by, "If you are theSon of God." That is what is called in Greek a first class conditional sentence it does not deal with whether the statement is true or false, Here it means that for purposes of this discussion it is assumed that you are. The first of these temptations dealt with whether the Messiah will be a materialistic Messiah, providing for the physical needs. It also related to economic and military logistics. Remembering the intense nationalistic hopes for a military revival and knowing that one of the greater problems of any military maneuver would be the logistics of supply, what a boon it would have been if the leader could just reach down and turn rocks into food. But this would have meant that Jesus would have been exempt from ordinary human conditions? One can readily see that if this wonder man could take up stones and turn them into bread, hungry people would rush to follow that kind of economic Messiah, but that would never change their inner being. Keep in mind that in those few times when Jesus did provide for their hunger, the people immediately tried to take him by force and make him King. (John 6:15) He rejected that option by quoting from Deuteronomy (8:3).

Then he is attacked with another idea. It surely was presented mentally and there is no need to assume that Jesus literally went to the Temple, climbed to the highest point and then decided not to jump. That was an effort to side-track the mission by being presumptuous about God and use sensational and fantastic means to secure the loyalty of the people, Superman style! In the gospel story there were records of some miracles and some sensationalism, cf. walking on the water and certain healings, but Jesus limited them and nearly every time there was a sensational event, it apparently got in the way of his proclaiming the mission. Sensational means probably would attract followers, but in every case they would follow for the wrong reasons. Clearly, Jesus saw his purpose in mission as changing the inner man and signs, wonders, and miracles would never do that.

The last of the ideas suggests another way! Keeping in mind his mission, more than anything else Jesus wanted people to follow him. How is he to get that done? This temptation dares him to use the tactics of satanic methods such as force, power, and manipulation which is what kings have done. To "Fall down and worship the prime forces of evil" is to surrender to that age old concept of control. This is the first narrative which unquestionably shows the subjective nature of these experiences. One should know that Jesus did not stand on the top of a mountain and see all of the continents of the earth jump up and orbit the globe in front of him. It was another mental suggestion that the whole world could be his if he would use evil methods. He knew that such a method would thwart what he really came to do and simply prolong the corrupt methods of control and power which have always plagued the world. He also understood that the choice made here set the course for the long, hard, suffering way. But that was the only way to do the task of changing men internally. Rejection of this temptation shows that Jesus was not seeking just to get followers, but he was trying to transform men into God's likeness. His mind was now set as to how he must proceed, but that temptation would crop up again, probably many more times! In dealing with each of these temptations Jesus responded with quotations from the Old Testament.

If there is any hesitation on the part of the reader to allow Jesus to struggle with sin, then temptation was not really temptation and one must ask were these narratives a farce. It is hard for some to admit, but Jesus could have chosen the wrong way! This is a part of the difficulty of allowing Jesus to be human, but the narratives never allow us to forget that he struggled against evil all through his life. The beauty and truth of the matter is that if he had succumbed to any of these or other temptations then he would not have become the redeeming Suffering Servant, but he did not yield!

## THE BEGINNING OF THE PUBLIC MINISTRY p. 17,18

Soon after the experience in the wilderness Jesus heard that John had been arrested; Luke had given warning about that in an earlier portion of his narrative. We usually suppose that Jesus was around thirty years of age when he decided to leave Nazareth and make his headquarters for his ministry in Capernaum, largely because that was the accepted age for a man to enter his public work. Matthew uses another of his proof-texts, another one from Isaiah, and the reference to people who have been in darkness having seen a great light pictures perfectly what Matthew believed was happening. In that first preaching Jesus used the same inference that John had used, "the kingdom of heaven has come near." Again, the same word with the Perfect Tense indicated the immediacy of the kingdom's arrival. Matthew nearly always used the term "kingdom of heaven" while Mark and Luke use "the kingdom of God." This is probably because off Matthew's effort to connect the Messiah as the Jewish fulfillment and because the Jews hesitated to use the name of God and used substitutes for fear of taking the name of God in vain. The truth is that God is and always was King, but up to the time of Jesus that sovereignty had only been partially recognized. The content of his message is simple - the Kingdom is here, get into it by commitment (which meant absolute surrender) to the King.

Luke places the rejection at Nazareth at the beginning of Jesus ministry while it comes much later in Matthew and Mark. Because of the fact that the narratives existed in isolated units, it is impossible to tell, but Jesus may have spent some time in other parts of Galilee before coming to his home town. As he taught in their synagogues, many must have responded positively to him for Luke indicates that he was "praised by everyone." The procedure that was commonly used in the synagogue had a leading elder inviting a visitor to read the passage for the day and give a short homily. The passage for that day was from Isaiah 61 and dealt with the hope and promise to Israel. When he had finished reading, Jesus applied the passage to himself. But in his home town where he had grown up the response was different from that in other places. He was allowed to read in the synagogue and at first there seems to have been a positive response, but when he applied the passage to himself they responded, "is not this Joseph's son?" Toward the conclusion of the homily, the doubt of the crowd led him to further statements: "no prophet is accepted in the prophet's hometown" (Luke 4:24) and when he used two references to people outside Judaism, the widow of Zarephath and Naaman who was from Syria, being helped by the prophets, Elijah and Elisha, they were incensed and drove him out of town. (Remember that this is Luke's account and keep in mind his universal emphasis.) The very force of his personality may have been the cause for him being able to pass through the crowd and not be destroyed, but he was certainly rejected. The old proverb is true! It is extremely difficult for a native who has grown up in the midst of people to speak any message that counters what they have been and done. There have been many examples which prove that point. How many really believe that someone will turn out to be a great or famous person who is from your acquaintance as a child? People still saw him as the little boy and not the mature, prophetic Jesus. This was the first mention of the times when Jesus was rejected.

## THE EARLY MINISTRY IN CAPERNAUM  p. 20,21

In Capernaum the people were astonished at the teaching of Jesus for he taught with authority. Apparently Jesus did not used rabbinic references to support his message. It was offered with authority. Little is ever said about it but the term authority, *ex-ousia*, has ties with the Greek idea of "out of ones own being." It would suggest that he simply said something because it was true and his demeanor and character was all that was needed to support it. Once in the eighth grade, this author had occasion to witness something of this sort of thing. One teacher was a big strong man and also a football coach, who could have physically turned anyone in the class upside down (and that would have been permitted in those days), but he could not keep order at all and was constantly sending students to the principal, while the other was a little old woman, about four feet and eight inches tall, who did not have strength enough to confront anyone, but when she said "frog" everyone jumped, simply because she had some weird inner authority. Everyone has known people like that and the people of Capernaum met it in Jesus in a way they had never seen it. It was also demonstrated by the healing of a man who was demon possessed. We are not told what kind of difficulties the man had, but nearly all diseases or irregularities were credited to demon possession in the first century and there were many who exorcised demons. Whatever that man's problem was, Jesus commanded that the demon come out and the man was convulsed and healed. It was that commanding authority that awed the crowd!

After Jesus left the synagogue he went to Simon's house and there we get sight of one of the early healings. Peter's mother-in-law was sick of a fever and Jesus was able to heal her so that she immediately began to serve them. Those events created such an impression that Jesus found himself surrounded by those who were brought to him to be healed, indicating once again how acute the temptations were. If he would become a physical deliverer, many would follow him, but for the wrong reasons.. The very next day Jesus left that area and went to another place and as he put it, "Let us go on to the neighboring towns, so that I may proclaim the message there also; for that is what I came to do." (Mark 1:38) One might recall that this parallels one of ideas in the temptations where doing fantastic things was rejected as a tactic for his mission. But wherever he went and performed miraculous cures, great crowds followed him to receive physical help. Did these things get in the way of the mission?

Reference has already been made to an article by a fisherman which can shed great light on many of the fishing narratives. It is a little difficult to harmonize the accounts in Matthew and Mark with that of Luke in dealing with the call of the first disciples. The "L" source tells us that Jesus used a boat which was Simon's, probably for acoustics purposes, and taught the people from it. Then he commanded Simon to put out into the sea and let down the nets. Simon hesitated because fishing had not been good that night, but he did what Jesus asked and they caught an unbelievable number of fish. This narrative represents Luke's telling of the call of the first disciples, Simon, Andrew, James, and John and may give some insight into the response of these four in being willing to leave everything and follow Jesus. It is the climax of this section where this experience is the catalyst which led Peter and the others to leave their occupations and follow Jesus to "catch men."

# CHAPTER IX
## THE SERMON ON THE MOUNT (TEXTUAL CRITICISM) pp. 24-38

Matthew and Luke both give accounts of the material which is in what is called The Sermon on the Mount or The Sermon on the Plain, but while they contain some of the same material they also differ considerably. The major question that this raises is, is the sermon as we have it, particularly in Matthew, a unity? Granted that the narrative is told as if it were a single event, there are more than forty subjects in the sermon and the fact that there is a lack of complete of thorough discussion appears to validate the concept of this being a synopsis of some of Jesus' teaching. Some of those ideas which are barely discussed in the sermon are found in detail in other places. Since there are differences in Matthew and Luke's reporting, the idea that it is a synopsis of some of Jesus' teachings is appealing.

The sermon, as we have it, is a guide for kingdom citizens. It is not an evangelistic sermon. Jesus gave no code by which one, if he obeys that code, is acceptable to God. In fact, he always opposed that legalistic way, which was the way of the Pharisees. Instead this sermon is an outline of the principles of kingdom life. In order to deal with this material a definition of the "Kingdom of Heaven" or the "Kingdom of God" must be considered. Jesus never gave an exact definition of the kingdom, but he talked about it in terms of parables and similes. From those materials it would appear that the kingdom is a spiritual reality of the sovereignty of God in the lives of those who are committed to the Lordship of Christ. It is not of a physical, political, earthly nor of a purely future nature, but is a present reality in the lives of his followers with many implications about how that sovereignty affects the social responsibilities of each participant. On one occasion dealing with the kingdom as present, not future, he said, "The kingdom is within you." (Luke 17:21) There certainly are passages which deal with the future of the kingdom and there has to be a consummation at some point, but those verses in no sense rule out the definition ascribed to here. The theme of the sermon as Matthew presents it seems to be: True happiness is dependent on the inner attitude of surrender. It is not so much what external actions are done as it is whether they derive from proper character. Happiness as it is dealt with here is not a feeling, but the characterization of one who has found the proper relationship between himself/herself and God and how that relates to others in society.

After a short introduction which pulls all the material together, the sermon begins with a series of character traits for kingdom citizens. These have been designated as the "Beatitudes" since each of them described something of the inner happiness that comes from having the type of character trait stated and each one states "Blessed" or "to be congratulated" (*makaroi*), are the following:

The first one, as Matthew states it, is "to be congratulated are those who are poor in spirit, for theirs is the kingdom of heaven." This appears to refer to one who knows or understands his/her spiritual inadequacy or poverty. That is not to create an inferiority complex, but is the basis for a true humility. Other places in the scripture teach that God is never pleased with haughtiness and pride. Keeping in mind Luke's different purpose and his constant emphasis on the problem of wealth, he congratulates the "poor people" and that is also in keeping with Jesus' warning about wealth being a hindrance to many people. It would be difficult to decide in favor of one of these interpretations against the other, since both are compatible with Jesus' thought. However, most scholars have taken the position that the Matthew version is nearer to the original idea.

The second message of congratulations is to those who mourn. This beatitude must deal with those who are so concerned about spiritual conditions that their lives demonstrate that they care. There is no great spiritual value in mourning in itself and every person on this earth, kingdom citizen or not, shares in some experience of mourning. Jesus did not put a premium on mourning over personal general calamities or disasters. However, any real spiritual concern which would produce mourning would be preceded by love.

The third character trait deals with meekness. It is necessary to be very careful about the meaning of this term, for the normal English interpretation equates "meekness" with "weakness" and that is an error! Years ago there was a comic strip in which the main character was Casper Milquetoast. Casper was a wishy-washy kind of person who never stood up against anything. He was pushed all over the place by circumstances and people and they called him meek. He wasn't meek; he was weak. The Greek word used here is *praus* and in some papyri it is seen to refer to a horse that has been broken to the bridle. At no time has such a horse lost its strength, it has simply learned how to be directed. Therefore, Jesus must have been congratulating those who have learned how to be directed by God and are thus "bridle-wise." This meekness presupposes another kingdom-like trait of humility.

The fourth character trait has to do with those who "hunger and thirst" for righteousness. Those two figures are strong language! Sometimes when people are hungry they may be so weakened that they just lie down and die, but usually anyone who is hungry will search until he/she finds something to eat. Thirst always produces action to quench the thirst. During World War II a company of men was training in the summer of 1943 in Arkansas. On the last day of the training a long combat simulated problem was planned and at the end of that hike a hill was to be assaulted. The temperature that day was 117 degrees and each man had a canteen of water to last for the day and some "K" rations for lunch. This author, although trying to conserve, ran out of water about mid-afternoon. We had begun the day with more than one hundred men, but many fell by the wayside and were picked up in ambulances and taken back to the company area. When time came to assault the hill, only twenty six men remained! My mouth was dry enough that I believe I could have struck a match on the roof of it. When we reached to top of the hill we were lined up to get some water. I learned something about myself that day; if anyone had tried to prevent me from getting a drink I could have easily killed him. Thirst drives one beyond the rational level. I was so thirsty that I drank two canteen cups of water before I realized that it was concentrated salt water. Thirst will drive you to get that thirst quenched. So it is with a kingdom citizen and nothing should be more important than development of a genuine inner righteousness, not a legalistic righteousness.

The fifth of these great challenges suggests that those who are merciful are praised and they will obtain mercy. Mercy is another character trait of God and therefore, if one ever senses the tremendous value and nature of God's mercy, she/he will have a goal of becoming inwardly and outwardly merciful. This quality is somewhat like that of forgiveness. When a little later in this sermon the words appear, "forgive us our sins as we forgive those who sin against us," it does not mean that we earn God's forgiveness by forgiving others. It means that if we ever sense the fantastic value of God's forgiveness to us we will become forgiving people. So it is with mercy.

The sixth of the great statements congratulates those who are pure in heart. That does not refer to perfection, but to those who are not attempting to be deceitful before God. It has to do with personal honesty and is again a character trait which is a God-like quality. A little later on in this sermon Jesus said one should let his "yes" mean "yes" and his "no" mean "no." That, like purity in heart, deals with genuine integrity!.

The seventh of the beatitudes congratulates the peacemakers. This is not in the sense of emissaries of a government who travel around and try to make nations live with one another without war. That is a noble undertaking and should be done with diligence, but this refers to those who first attempt to make peace between man, who lives in enmity, and God. Once that peace is accomplished it then becomes possible for there to really be peace among individuals.

The last in this series suggests that those who are persecuted for righteousness sake are to be congratulated. The author once knew of a man who traveled around as a tent evangelist. On one occasion he went to a small county seat town and found that they had a law that no one could use a loud speaker system on the city square. The town officials told him it was perfectly OK to use it at the fairgrounds where his tent was set up, but on the crowded court square it was not allowed. He promptly set up his speaker system on the square and began to preach and they arrested him. When he was thrown in jail he screamed from the second story window of the jail that he was being persecuted for righteousness sake. That wasn't for righteousness sake, it was for stupidity and bull-headedness. There are thousands of instances in the history of Christianity, however, when people have been persecuted because of their faith. This is not about developing a persecution complex and the statement specifically has in it the idea that one is being persecuted <u>falsely</u> and for Christ's sake.

Being a follower of Jesus is a constant matter of becoming, growing in Christ-likeness. These are not traits one must already have to be accepted by Jesus, they are traits that one who has entered the kingdom is diligently pursuing and each of them, with the exception of the last one seems to be a description of character traits that are God's. To become like God in character is the highest goal! (Matthew 5:48)

## THE FUNCTION AND MISSION OF KINGDOM CITIZENS
p. 26

Following the order of Matthew, since Jesus had stated some of the qualities of a kingdom citizen, he now used simple illustrations to show how those citizens should function. The first of these had to do with the normal functions of salt. One must remember that the salt Jesus talked about was not the same as modern refined salt. However, it served many of the same functions. Salt saves from corruption by contact. In a time when preservatives were rather limited, that commodity was vital. There must be some sense in which the character of kingdom citizens has literally saved society. Salt also flavors and in its best moments the church has provided a distinct flavor to the society it serves, such as the many aid agencies sponsored by followers and certain moral influences it has offered. Unfortunately, those representing the church have not always shown the proper kind of character and as a result there have been many times in its history that it has done as much damage to society as it has done good. But according to Jesus salt can lose its "saltness" and when it does, since it had probably come from the Dead Sea area and was unrefined, the residue was a chalky mass which could be used only as we might use ashes for a path. Salt also had the quality of cleansing and purifying whatever it came in contact with. In some cases salt served as a monetary unit, but that appears to have little application in this illustration.

The sermon then used light as a second illustration. In numerous religions light was the usual figure for good or for God. So when Jesus said that kingdom citizens were the light of the world he was showing how kingdom citizens were to function. The purpose of a lighted lamp was and is to illuminate. Perhaps this meant that the Christian community was not to be ascetic and hidden. Light always gives guidance and warning and is never designed to be hidden. In fact, it is nearly impossible to hide light as many have discovered during times of blackouts in wars.

## THE IDEAL MORAL STANDARDS. pp. 26-30

It was necessary for Jesus to clarify his position on righteousness as opposed to the common Pharisaic interpretation. Jesus was not in any sense a legalist and that will be demonstrated in the numerous conflicts he had with the legalism of the day. Legalism can only deal with the external action of an individual and that is part of its downfall. The intense legalism of the Pharisaic community had made extra laws to protect the Law. In order to be certain that people did not violate the Mosaic Law, scribes, Rabbis, and others had created extra prohibitions that would be like a fence around the Law. If one did not violate those regulations, then they would never violate the Law. But the accretions had come to be accepted as being just as important as the Law itself. For instance, the distance one could travel on the Sabbath was precisely stated as two thousand cubits. If one did not go beyond the stated distance from his home, he would never violate the Sabbath by traveling too far and thus working on the Sabbath. But someone suggested that one may take a few possessions and place them in a "camp" which is a little less that two thousand cubits from ones residence and then call that "home." Then on the Sabbath he could travel from his residence to his "home" and then if need be, he could travel two thousand cubits beyond that and never break the Sabbath Day journey law. Cooking on the Sabbath was forbidden; even the building of a fire was a violation. On one occasion an ingenious inventor had discovered how to put reed pipes together to run water into his home from a tank on the roof. Then he discovered that if he made clay pipes and ran them around behind the fireplace, he could have both hot and cold running water. But the Rabbis argued that he could not use that system or any like it on the Sabbath, for heating the water would be working.

> *"The men of Tiberias once passed a tube of cold water through a spring of hot water. The Sages said to them: If this is done on the Sabbath it is like water heated on the Sabbath and is forbidden both for washing and drinking; and if it is done on a Festival-day it is like water heated on a Festival-day and is forbidden for washing, but permitted for drinking." (The Mishnah trans. Herbert Danby* [London: Oxford University Press 1954] p. 102)

Jesus appears to have accepted the Mosaic Law, but not the accretions; he accepted the Prophets, but not the scribal additions and interpretations. So when he stated that kingdom righteousness must exceed that of the scribes and Pharisees, what could he possibly mean? How could the righteousness of kingdom citizens exceed that of the rigid religious leaders? To show how that is to be understood he used six illustrations which demonstrated how the standards of the kingdom are superior to those of the religious leaders.

On murder! The first distinction that must be made is between the terms "kill" and "murder." While the taking of any human life is deplorable, it is possible to kill accidentally, or even in war, without doing murder. Murder, on the other hand, implies an action which is pre-meditated and in some uncontrollable way, destroys a person. Law can deal with that, but only after the act is performed and it should be obvious that throughout the history of humanity there has not been much success by law to prevent murder. What Jesus indicated was that the kingdom citizen must stop what ultimately produces murder by controlling the intent in ones heart (inner being). To show this he used a progression of terms. He indicated that if one is angry with another, that one is liable to judgment and that anger must be controlled and dealt with in this initial stage -stop it there or else face the legal consequences! If the anger is so uncontrolled that it leads to insult (calling one *raca,* which means something like empty-headed or numb-skull), then the action is considered to be similar to the current understanding of slander and it could lead to action by the Sanhedrin. But then he moved beyond that to a more overt action. The problem arises if one gets to the place where he can call the other person *more'*, we often translate that term as 'fool,' but it means much more than that. If one can call another *more'* (fundamentally consider one worthless) he has demonstrated contempt for the very heart and character of a person and in fact, inwardly he has reduced to person to a ZERO. The person has been made to be nothing and all that remains is the actual act. In fact, reducing the other person to nothing is equivalent to "rubbing him out" and the attitude of murder is already present in the inner being. Although the sin is already present when ones attitude reaches this point, to actually do the deed is much worse in its consequences - but Jesus showed that the sin is already inside the person as attitude. He did not suggest that to think a thing is as bad as doing it. What he did indicate was that the progression in attitude is necessary before one can get to the point of being able to make a zero out of another person. Legislation can never deal with attitude, it can only deal with act. One can hate as much as he wishes so long as he does not externalize anything. Therefore, kingdom righteousness goes far beyond Pharisaic righteousness by dealing with the attitude.

There will always be a difficulty in what a soldier does in war when he kills another. Many soldiers have killed out of the necessity of the situation and have never hated the enemy, but the danger is always there that the attitude will also be corrupted and turned into vengeful murder. One day in April during the last days of World War II in Europe, the unit the author was with was pinned down on a hillside and could not advance. A patrol was sent back behind the unit and around through a small valley to flank the machine-gun nest and remove it. When they found the nest, one of the men, (one of the most liked men in the company) stood up, why he stood is a mystery, and pointed to where the machine gun was. He was seen and was shot through the head. Soon the unit was able to move forward and some of the Germans who were captured had John's wallet, watch, rings, and any other possessions that could be taken from him. The entire company was incensed and the attitude of soldiers turned swiftly into an attitude of vengeance. The captives were placed on the ground, face down, and when they were asked a question and raised their heads to reply, someone's foot stomped their faces back down into the ground. Fortunately, someone of rank came along and rescued the prisoners and sent them back as POWs, but attitudes had changed!

On adultery! There is a distinction to be made between adultery and fornication. The term "adultery" deals with a situation where one or both of the parties engaging in sexual intercourse is/are married and not to each other, so that adultery is a violation of a marriage relationship. Fornication is not dealt with in the Ten Commandments! Fornication deals with any sexual intercourse outside the marriage relationship and there are ample condemnations of it in many other places in the New Testament. What Jesus said in this illustration was that sexual sin is also in the attitude. Once again, legislation has a difficult time dealing with attitude. It was Jesus' position that the evil in this case is in lust. Many have tried to define lust and often the term has been dealt with erroneously. It is not just the having of biological instincts or urges and therefore, is not just the thought, for a healthy person probably cannot prevent attraction. It would even be difficult to suggest that sexual fantasies fall in this category, but perhaps holding on to them and nourishing them brings one to the initial stages. That is one problem with pornography for it encourages lust. It would seem that lust deals with the holding and developing the ideas in ones mind so that only such things as the fear of being rejected, the fear of being caught, or the fear of pregnancy keep one from doing the act, and to legalists even the fear of hell. What Jesus suggested with harsh figures of speech was that each person should take the strongest measures in personal discipline to prevent lust. He did not suggest that one should literally cut off his/her hand or pluck out his/her eye. Obviously, that would not stop sex! Incidentally, this discussion was totally from the point of view of the male side of the race, perhaps because few people dared to discuss the subject from the standpoint of females, but the issue is real on both sides of the sexual fence. Human beings are not to be animals who follow their desires or instincts and since human sexual experience involves the deepest of human sharing and commitment it is not something to be done "just for the fun of it."

In a day of great sexual liberty, Jesus' position may sound a bit "old-fashioned" and even unrealistic, but the New Testament holds that sex and its responsibilities should be reserved for marriage. Keep in mind that the purpose of this discussion was to show that in sexual matters, just as in murder, the sin is in the attitude, perhaps using another person as an object to be controlled. It is not to bring condemnation on those who have failed in this area for Jesus always offered forgiveness. And although he never mentioned it, it might even be recognized that within the framework of marriage one might abuse his/her spouse with the wrong attitude.

On divorce! The question of divorce always prompted disagreement. In Jewish history of the idea of divorce there was no protection for women before the time of Moses. Marriages were often arranged and the idea of choosing a partner because of "love" was often foreign. In most cases a woman was a piece of property and while there are evidences of husbands who really cared for their wives, still it was rare that a woman had any rights. When Moses addressed the issue he was offering some protection for the Hebrew women. Of course, in a time of polygamy, if a man decided that he wanted another woman rather than his wife, he could just take her and the rejected wife would have little recourse. So even prior to the time of Moses, if a man wanted to rid himself of a wife, he just did so, but Moses stated that before the divorce can occur there must be a writing of the causes for the divorce. That meant that any complaint would be public and the woman could take the "bill of divorcement" with her and show it, particularly if she needed to show she was not guilty of immorality.

In the first century everyone knew that the two major Rabbinic schools differed about this subject. Rabbi Hillel allowed divorce for various reasons, such as burning the food, but it was still slanted toward the benefit of the males. Shammai, on the other hand allowed divorce only in the case of marital infidelity. These were the only things which were offered as conditions of divorce. Since the husband was the ruler of the house it would have been extremely rare for anyone to consider what is today known as abuse, either sexual or emotional. Although Jesus never defined sin, by studying his discussions and his parables it is rather certain that Jesus considered anything that either destroyed or damaged personality, whether ones own or that of another, was evidence of sin. Years ago in a discussion with a marriage counselor about a situation in which we were both involved this author was told, "You are trying to save a marriage and I am trying to save a person." He was right, and

Jesus would have probably taught that saving a person is much more important than saving what appears to be a marriage.

So this explanation represents another illustration of the wrong attitude being the cause of the external action. It is probably the first of the hints that Jesus considered women more than property. Remember that he did not give laws and there is no reason, even with the exception clause in Matthew, to make this legalistic. It is another illustration of how a wrong attitude destroys a beautiful relationship. Keep in mind that Matthew also said, "anyone who divorces his wife except  on the ground of unchastely causes her to commit adultery" (Matthew 5:32). Of course, if she has already been unchaste, she is already an adulteress, but how does one force her to become an adulteress if the divorce came about because of burning the bread or nagging? (It may offend modern sensitivity but perhaps the only way she could stay alive in the first century might have been to turn to prostitution.  One could say, " I'd never do that," but if that were the only way to stay alive, who knows what she would do?) So perhaps, he leaves her with no other choice and therefore, makes her to become and adulteress.  In a day when many women make their own living in many different occupations, that idea is foreign.  In the account of this story in Mark, the woman also can divorce her husband and that way of dealing with the issue may be because the gospel was written under Roman influence, where women could initiate divorces.

Was Jesus simply using this current debate as one of the six illustrations about how the attitude causes the sin?  If so, we must still affirm that God intended for marriage to be permanent, but there are cases in which divorce may be the only and better answer.  This teaching, even in its setting in Matthew, must be placed in the first century context and a principle must be extracted.  Is it that one must always try to develop the relationships of people so that they produce a better life?  It is extremely difficult to see this area of life as the only one where Jesus would withhold forgiveness, although many rigid legalists do.  At times a divorce may be the only answer to saving the person.

On swearing  p. 29 The old commandment from Leviticus 19:12 ordered that one should not swear falsely, but carry out the vows made to the Lord.  Swearing an oath to tell the truth has always suggested two levels of integrity and that in itself is a violation of  the concept.

People have assumed that as long as they are not under oath, they can tell the truth or not at their own pleasure. That very process is a contradiction to integrity! Often on tests at school a student might be asked to sign a pledge that he/she had neither received or given any help. That has always been peculiar because anyone who would cheat would also lie. Part of what Jesus said in this passage is an illustration of inner integrity and the truth is, you either have it or you don't. No amount of swearing will really make any difference. To suggest that if ones fingers are crossed or if there has been no oath that one is free to lie is exactly the evil that Jesus was concerned about. His statement that one should not swear at all does not prohibit taking an oath in the courts, but rather it indicated that there should be no need for an oath. One either has integrity or else there is deceit and evil in his/her life. When he suggested that your word should either be "Yes" or "No" he was simply indicating that a kingdom citizen has an attitude of truthfulness and that evil comes into play when one has to back up his/her word with some outside entity, such as God or heaven. Integrity is vital to relationships. There can be no trusting or sharing when there is doubt about the integrity of another's character. The simple fact is that oaths do not change a persons character, all an oath can do, even in the civil courts, is to make one liable for perjury and that has no real bearing on ones integrity.

On retaliation  p. 29 The old *lex talionis* came about in order to limit vengeance. An eye for and eye means that one cannot take both eyes or an eye and a leg in order to get vengeance, one can only take what is equivalent to what was destroyed or injured.. So it produced a limitation but did not address at all the basic attitude of vengeance. Vengeance is an unredeemed human characteristic, for each of us is prone to think that we should get back at the one who wrongs us. This illustration goes far beyond that and again reaches to the attitude. It may very well be that the message was given in a time when the end of the age was expected and therefore, to give more than was demanded, a cloak in addition to a coat, would not be as severe as it may sound. But that is not the point. The issue at stake is that kingdom citizens not take vengeance into their own hands. There is a sneaky little idea that comes out when Jesus says, "if one strikes your right cheek." A hefty percentage of the population is right handed and if those people strike your cheek it will be your left one. The only way they will strike your right cheek is to do a back-handed slap. That has for centuries stood for an insult and considering the rest of the paragraph, Jesus was apparently saying that one was not to react to insult, but be bigger than the one doing the insulting. The following statement, "if anyone forces you to go one mile, go also a second mile," bears that out. In occupied Palestine a Roman soldier had the legal right to demand a native to carry his pack for one mile. Imagine the growling and griping as they traversed that mile; no good could come out of that, and at the end of the mile the pack might be thrown on the ground with a "cuss" word or two. But what if, at the end of the mile, the native should say, "This pack is not so very heavy and I don't mind carrying it another mile for you." What has happened to the oppressor in that case? Refusing to be lowered to the level of retaliating, takes away the bitterness and so the teaching is difficult but simple. A kingdom citizen's righteousness is manifested by the control of the "ego" and immediately makes possible better human relationships. Vengeance only begets vengeance, whether one is talking about personal vengeance or national retaliation. Everyone knows the stories of feuds among families. One person does something wrong and to get vengeance someone of the other side retaliates. That in turn calls for retaliation from the first side and soon the whole thing escalates into a long lasting feud, and perhaps many deaths. What Jesus said is a very tough position to take and it has been for many centuries since it was stated and the human family has not yet been able to grasp it. Jesus knew that the medicine of peace was not retaliation but forgiveness! Therefore, the kingdom citizen should have an attitude of forgiveness and not vengeance. However, it is necessary to recognize that there is a vast difference between vengeance and proper legal punishment.

On love p. 29-30 The Law did not state, "and hate your enemy" (Lev. 19:18) but either that was the way Jesus found that the passage being interpreted in first century Palestine or it is the way the early church tradition referred to the problem. It may have come from the numerous accretions, but it seems to exhibit the same spirit that Ezra showed. Jesus did ask for a new approach toward your enemy. The main issue in this passage is Jesus' use of the term *agape* to represent the kind of love one should have toward everyone, enemies included.

Most everyone knows that there were several Greek words used for the concept of love, each having a distinctive meaning. (cf. any good Koine' Greek lexicon) That is not true with common English usage where everything from people to objects is loved. Modern Americans say that food is loved, jewels are loved, automobiles are loved, and people are loved. The term *philos,* which is not the term used in this passage, means a friendship kind of love and it depends on whether there is something in you that I see and am drawn to which makes me like you. That kind of love which is determined by some quality or action that I am drawn to, is highly fickle. Something may be done which changes all of that atmosphere and that kind of love may end. The term *eros* deals with the sexual aspect of love. It is that meaning which seems to have captured the thought in common (American) usage. We often say that people "make love" when what we really mean is they have sex. That term is foreign to the discussion Jesus was involved with in this statement. There is a term which is not used in the New Testament that refers to family love or affection and that term is *storge.* But the nobler term, and the one which is always applied to the kind of love God has for his created beings is *agape.* It is a kind of love that does not depend on any nature or quality of the one being loved, but rather on the one who loves. It is always interested in doing or acting in such a way as to make the best possible things happen for the person loved. It is an indiscriminate love that cares even for the unlovely, the ugly, even those who are devoted to evil. It is almost foreign to the idea of emotion and therefore is never fickle or changing. It may, at times, have to take the form of "tough love" to try to produce the best, but that is never because the essence has changed. It is possible to love someone with this type of love without necessarily liking them or their behavior. That is God's kind of love!

In this illustration, kingdom righteousness is aligned with the God quality of love. God is shown to love all people indiscriminately, just as the rain falls both on the just and the unjust in that same fashion and the sun shines on everyone in the same way. God never bribes individuals to respond to Him. To further illustrate this point, imagine what would happen if two farmers lived side by side, one just and the other unjust. After they have planted their crops, the rain comes, but it only falls on the land of the just man. Then the sun comes out a bakes the dry land of the unjust person. How many crop failures would it take for that man to join the church? That is not God's way and to love for what one can get out of it is not God-like. Jesus indicated that even the tax collectors love that way and to love only those who love you in return is what anyone and everyone does. Kingdom love must surpass that kind of selfishness. *Agape* requires something different and it is that for which a kingdom citizen must strive.

The sentence that is often translated, "be perfect, therefore, as your heavenly father is perfect" probably refers to the concept of being all inclusive in your love, even as God is all inclusive. The term which is translated "perfect" means complete or mature. This paragraph concluded the group of thoughts which show how kingdom righteousness surpasses legalistic righteousness. Kingdom righteousness is always internal and attitude oriented. To be mature in kingdom love one must learn to love as God loves, and to describe that would require volumes.

## THE IDEAL ATTITUDE OF A KINDGDOM CITIZEN TOWARD RELIGIOUS EXERCISE AND DUTY. pp. 30-38

<u>On giving:</u> Valid and sincere worship is very difficult to maintain without finding a bit of hypocrisy in it. Jesus knew that difficulty well for he had probably seen both in the synagogues and in the Temple many times, people "practicing their piety" before men. His basic warning was that in any formal religious gathering there is always a danger of trying to be pious before the people to get their praise. If people do this, he said, they get what they want, but they do not get praise from God. When he said, "when you give alms, do not sound a trumpet (probably another cryptic figure of speech) before you as they hypocrites do" he must have witnessed this mockery many times. He suggests that those who have given to be seen have received their reward in full. The admonition "do not let your left hand know what you right hand is doing" is again one of his beautiful figures of speech suggesting that your giving is not to be done so that people may know about it, but between the individual and God. (Left hands and right hands do not have brains with which to think, so it must be a figure.) There is a Greek word, *apecho,* which is found in many papyri written across bills that have been paid in full. Jesus used that term and with it he was simply saying, they got their human praise and that is what

they wanted, but that is all they received. Valid giving doesn't care about public recognition or acclaim. God's reward comes for honest worship in giving and the best manuscripts suggest that when one gives in secret (between the worshipper and God) He will reward, but the word "openly" is not in the better manuscripts. That not only does not belong there because of the manuscript evidence, but if the term "openly" is added it negates everything Jesus said in this section for his emphasis is that worship is between an individual and God and there should be no concern about recognition.

Another issue must be dealt with when talking about giving. Giving is a worship expression of our love for God and motives for it must never be prostituted. I once heard a man state in a worship service designed to raise money that he believed that if he did not tithe he would lose at least that much money and perhaps more, either on medical bills or some other misfortune. To offer gifts so that God will repay in kind is also to prostitute the motive for giving, The common "success theology" is quite contrary to the spirit of the New Testament and most likely even to the Old Testament. If one feels blessed by God because of his/her faithfulness in economic matters, that is fine, but to give in order to be blessed with gain is foreign to the spirit of the Master.

On Prayer: He opened this discussion with the same admonition that he gave in the section on giving. Prayer is not to be done as a pious exhibition to be heard by men. Apparently, he had seen many pious ones standing out either in public or in the synagogues or on the streets and lifting up their hands so that everyone could see them and know they were praying. He indicated the very same thing in this discussion that we have just looked at. Prayer, like giving, is to be done between a person and God and not for pious show. If acknowledgement is what men want, they get that and nothing more for, "your father who sees in secret will reward you." (again, not "openly") Standard phrases seem empty and certainly God is not interested in long-winded, wordy prayers. In the case of public prayer it is difficult for the one who is leading the prayer to be praying and not making a pretty speech. A very subtle temptation comes with this worship issue and with all worship issues. Each person wants to do well, but the huge question is whether one is doing that for her/his own ego or with the desire to please God. Ministers have that difficulty with sermons. It would be nice to know that people think the minister has done well, but if (way down deep inside) he has done it to get their praise, it is an empty gesture. This author once called on a man to pray in public who had been somewhat of a leader in the church, but he did not ask beforehand if the man would lead the prayer. There was an embarrassing moment when nothing was said, but the man was standing as if to lead. Then he began to pray. The worst prayer grammatically that one can imagine, but soon everyone knew that he was not praying to the crowd, he was talking to God and did not care what others thought. That may have been one of those public prayers which pleased God.

In Matthew's organization of the sermon Jesus told the disciples the issues they should pray about. The prayer is not "The Lord's Prayer" but rather a model prayer. In the Luke account the disciples asked Jesus to teach them to pray as John taught his disciples. We know nothing about John's teaching his disciples to pray, but this model should help us to see what Jesus thought was important. That does not mean that the prayer should not be used in public worship, but it does mean that just saying the prayer is not praying it. These are the issues:

a. In prayer one must recognize that we are addressing a special being. The concept by Eddie Rickenbacher that "God is my Co-pilot" is an admirable one, but God is not just the man upstairs - he is the Holy and Awesome Creator and deserves he highest respect possible. "Sacred, holy, and set apart is His name." The concept "name" in this case stands for His entire being.

b. A kingdom citizen should wish and pray for the kingdom reality to come about. The prayer does not necessarily represent only some hope for the future, it is asking that the sovereignty of God can and will be manifested in the lives of his followers, who will include many many more than these twelve. The kingdom will spread, but the goal of the kingdom is that His sovereignty will be found here in the lives of his people just as it is in heaven. For the kingdom to come will involve aiding the poor and the enslaved. The gospel is an event of liberation even if it is not physical revolution. That asks for a sobering moral reformation among the people. We may not know what we are asking for!

c. Daily needs are important to God and it would be foolish to think that they do not matter. However, there is good reason to believe that what Jesus was really trying to get them to see was that disciples are always dependent on God from day to day. The prayer may actually say, "provide for us today our sustenance for tomorrow." In a time of preserved foods and often bountiful storage of plenty, there is a temptation to forget that we must daily rely on God. Even though modern Christians seldom think of it, still it is a basic truth of the kingdom that God sustains us day by day. Sometimes in the midst of what we call natural tragedies, we are brought back to that awareness.

d. The prayer then turns to a concept that has been looked at before in another context. This prayer did not suggest that if we forgive other people, God is obligated to forgive us. That puts the cart before the horse! Jesus was saying        that we need to be becoming forgiving people because we have come to understand God's forgiveness to us. Forgiveness is a God-like trait and if one, in deepest gratitude, comes to understand it, she/he will want to share that with those who may have sinned against us. If the term "debtor" is used in this translation it may reflect on Jesus' future parable of the unforgiving servant. The same phrase and emphasis is repeated at the end of the prayer.

e. The translations then tell us Jesus prayed that we not be brought to the time of testing. Perhaps the real emphasis is in the second half of the request that God will help and deliver us in the time of trial. For every person, Jesus included, finds herself/himself in times of trial often; they seem to be inescapable.

In the better manuscripts there is no ending to the prayer, however, some late. manuscripts add, "For Thine is the kingdom and the power and the glory, forever, Amen." That was probably added very early when the prayer became something repeated in worship services

On Fasting: p. 32 The last of the issues in which Jesus warns about doing the externals of religion to be seen is fasting. It was probably the one issue which lent itself to "show" more than any other. In many religions fasting has become a sign of piousness and that was also the case in first century Judaism. (In one of the narratives dealing with a Pharisee who boasted about his fasting he proudly indicated that he fasted twice a week.) It had probably become fashionable to look as dismal as one could when fasting, putting ashes on their faces and thus letting everyone know what they were doing. Jesus responded to that "exercise" just as he had with the others, warning that because those "hypocrites" had done their religious deed to be seen of men, they had their total reward. The same term is used in all three of these statements (*apecho*) and means that it is paid in full! Therefore, any fasting, almsgiving, or prayer done to be seen of men has no value except that it was seen. His warning suggested that if fasting was to be done, one should look as pleasant as possible, having washed ones face and anointed ones head, because any religious exercise or duty was to be done for God and not for men. It is interesting that there is no textual addition of "openly" in this discussion. None of these issues is denounced because of any innate problem with the external act itself. The danger is in the show. Many current expressions of religion have minimized fasting but there are times when it may still have value. Certainly, if one gets so concerned about any spiritual issue that she/he forgets to eat or feels little need for eating, that would be valid fasting. So whether it be philanthropy, praying, or fasting it should never be done for the purpose of being praised for giving, honored for a beautiful prayer, or pointed out because of fasting. The temptation to be seen by others is always very strong and if one is not careful it may negate the value of the "exercise."

## TEXTUAL CRITICISM

In the discussion concerning Source, Form, and Redaction Criticism it was suggested that a fourth science would be dealt with later. Several times already a textual problem has been alluded to, so perhaps this is the appropriate place to try to understand the science of Textual Criticism.

> *"Textual Criticism seeks, by the exercise of knowledge and trained judgment, to restore the very words of some original document which has perished, and survives only in copies complete or incomplete, accurate or inaccurate, ancient or modern. If we possessed the twenty seven documents now composing our New Testament exactly in the form in which they were dictated or written by their original authors, there would be no textual criticism of the New Testament. The original documents, however, have long perished, and we have to make the best of the copies which have survived, by howsoever many removes they may be from their ultimate originals."* (Alexander Souter, *The Text and Cannon of the New Testament, 5th impression* [London: Duckworth Press, 1948] 3)

All of the copies from which our current printed texts come were copied by hand, laboriously. Scribes, especially trained to do that task, worked both as individuals and sometimes in team efforts to produce new manuscripts. When the King James Version of the Bible was produced, the only text was the one called *Textus Receptus.* All of those manuscripts which make up that group are late, several coming from the eighth century (E, F, V, Y, and Psi) and some from the ninth and tenth (G, H, and S) and have been through many copying sessions.. It is not possible here to give an in depth history of the development of this study but with the invention of the moveable type printing press it was just a matter of time until the science began in earnest. The honor of printing the first Greek New Testament went to Cardinal Ximines and the printing was completed on January 10, 1514 C.E. but it was delayed for three years because Pope Leo X deferred his permission. Because of that delay, another edition, the work of Erasmus, was published earlier (1516) at Basle in Switzerland. The manuscripts which were the basis of that printing were neither ancient nor valuable, but were a part of what became known as the *Textus Receptus.* Numerous scholars devoted themselves to this new study. As manuscripts were discovered and it became obvious that the received text should be revised, there was opposition, some of it rather fierce. The greatest strides were made in the mid-nineteenth century as archaeologists and others discovered manuscripts before unknown.

Probably one of the most interesting stories relative to those discoveries is that of Count Constantine von Tischendorf. He had dedicated his life to the search for and study of ancient documents. In 1844-45 he was at the St. Catherine Monastery and happened to see in a trash basket several pages which he recognized as probably being from an old manuscript. The monk who was with him told him that the basket had already been emptied several times and the contents burned to start fires. Tischendorf was able to rescue those pages he found, but when he attempted to get the other pages, even though they had shown him the manuscript rolled up in a cloth, they would not allow him to have it. He spent the night laboriously copying the pages he had found. He was later in Egypt and was able to get the curator to send the manuscript there. It turned out that it was one of the oldest manuscripts that has ever been found and is dated from around 375 C.E. Later in the pursuit of other texts one was found in the Vatican library which is from the same period of time, most scholars think it is about a half a century older. When those two agree on a reading, it is some of the strongest evidence available. Most of the manuscripts which are called "uncials" were copied in capital letters and have been given capital letters of the English alphabet to designate them. Obviously, there are many things which go into ascertaining the value of a manuscript. The more times the document has been copied, the more likelihood there is of error. But one also has to determine, when possible, the location from which a work comes and what "family" it represents.

Even though the copyists were trained scholars, that laborious task of copying the material by hand offered many ways in which errors could creep in. Sometimes, if an individual was copying, just a mistake of the eye could make for an error. Sometimes when a manuscript was being read and several scribes were copying, there could be mistakes of hearing. Often, those who studied the manuscripts wrote notes in the margin and when that copy was used as the next document from which others were made, the note got inserted in the text. It is often possible to trace "families" because of the same error being found. (Any professor who has graded papers, especially essay types, and has found the exact same error in two papers must invariably have his/her suspicions raised in terms of copying, especially if it is a misspelling!) One should never assume that this science has made the message of the *Textus Receptus* invalid. "There are more than five thousand available Greek manuscripts in which there are approximately one hundred and fifty thousand variant readings." (R. C. Briggs, *Interpreting the Gospels,* [Nashville: Abingdon Press, 1969] 39) In spite of that, the primary message of the gospels has been preserved even in the *Textus Receptus.*

The term "openly" has been referred to in a previous discussion. It is easy to seen how that term could have been written in the margin of a text and later crept into the text itself. In cases like that two kinds of evidence must be considered. The external evidence is simply the readings from the various manuscripts. Often that is enough to decide the issue, but internal evidence must also be dealt with. In the case of the term "openly" (*en to phanero*) in the Sermon on the Mount, that idea discounts everything Jesus was saying about not doing things to be seen. So not only is the manuscript evidence overwhelming, the internal evidence also helps see the error.

A few other readings will help one to see how this science works. In the older and better manuscripts, as has already been said, there is no ending (doxology) for the prayer that is called "The Lord's Prayer." As has been seen, the prayer was not given to be a poem to recite, but an example of how and what one should pray for. Later when it became a part of the public worship, there had to be an ending, so one was created. In the story of the angels singing at the birth of Jesus the better manuscripts read, "Glory to God in the highest and peace on the earth among men of good will" while the *Textus Receptus* reads, "Glory to God in the highest and on earth, peace, good will to men." One last illustration, and perhaps one which has had more influence is that of the ending of the gospel of Mark. Anyone reading a modern translation will find that Mark ends abruptly at chapter 16 and verse eight. The ending (vv. 9-20) was added in the late manuscripts and is the material from which many get the authority for snake handling and drinking poison. That the ending is spurious is <u>not</u> in debate, but one can only guess how those things got included. Perhaps the story in Acts of the viper fastening to Paul's hand (Acts 28:3) and the fact that he did not die could have been the basis for it.

Whatever the estimate of these critical studies may be, Textual Criticism is not a destructive science in any way, but a restorative one. Some may grab a proof text from Revelation (22:18-19) to support opposition, but attention needs to be paid to two things regarding that argument. The first is that something has already been added to or taken away from the texts involved, therefore, the only thing being done is the attempt to get back to what was originally there. The second would be that The Apocalypse writer was warning against anyone changing the message of that book, not of looking at the various documents (manuscripts) of the entire scriptural material. Textual Criticism is probably the most accurate of these four sciences. Many scholars believe that the best text that has been produced to date is that of the most recent edition of *The Greek New Testament,* (edited by Kurt Aland, Matthew Black, Carlo Martinin, Bruce Metzger, and Allen Wikgren, 1983) It, like the same kind of work by Eberhard Nestle, has been through several editions as new materials impact on the readings.

> *"Until the invention of printing with movable type in the fifteenth century the text of the New Testament - and, indeed, the text of every ancient record - could be transmitted only by laboriously copying it letter by letter and word by word. The consideration, therefore, of the processes involved in the making and transcribing of manuscripts is of utmost importance to the historian of ancient culture in general and to the student of the New Testament in particular." (Bruce M. Metzger, 3rd ed. The Text of the New Testament, [New York Oxford: Oxford University Press, 1992] 3)*

# THE IDEAL ATTITUDE OF A KINGDOM CITIZEN TOWARD GOD

## ON SINGLE HEARTED DEVOTION pp. 32 - 33

One Treasure: A kingdom citizen must understand that God is the whole object of his devotion and any deviation from that causes a substitution for his 'Pivotal Value." The first evidence of this in the discussion is that of treasures. Single hearted devotion means that the only treasures which are of fundamental value are those which deal with spiritual things. All earthly treasures are temporary, and in a sense are a stewardship. To give that which is temporary the status of the permanent is to short circuit and misplace ones values. In other places Jesus shows that material things can stand between a person and God in that they can take the most prominent place in ones system of values. When that occurs, they become her/his God even though there may be a profession otherwise. So it is fundamental that God be God. Wherever one places his supreme loyalty, that is where his major interest and dedication is. As Jesus put it, "Where your treasure is, there your heart will be also."

One Priority: This issue is illustrated with the concept of the sound eye. Again the thrust of the discussion is that of no diversion. For an individual who has difficulty with the eyes giving double images, this illustration is vivid. Since one sees two objects, it may be impossible to know which is the real one on which one should focus. Even with two good eyes, anyone can demonstrate this problem to herself/himself by placing a finger on the side of the eyeball and pressing until there are two images. How can there be a decision about which is the proper one to choose? Since the concept of light represents God (and good) so it is again plain, if one does not make God her/his PRIORITY ONE then darkness, or a lack of God, fills that life. There is an urgency to understand that it would be a absolute impossibility for God to tolerate any other being or thing as a primary loyalty in the life of his follower or even to think that one could have two Gods

One Master: The last phase of this "single hearted devotion" states what is almost repetitive and should be obvious. There can be only one PRIORITY ONE! Is it impossible to have two masters of equal importance. One must be supreme and since he has placed so much emphasis on the danger of material substance, Jesus' statement, "You cannot serve God and Wealth" (Mt. 6:24) strengthens the argument that only God can be God. A divided loyalty cannot be tolerated!

## ON WHOLE HEARTED TRUST  pp. 33 - 34

One of the things humans have difficulty with is trust in God. That seems to be so foolish, but it is extremely difficult to believe in God's concern and care, especially when things go wrong. Being concerned about His existence and working diligently to understand it is not evil in itself. However, Jesus seems to say to us that if we just look around, we can see God's care of his whole creation and if we believe that mankind is the crown of the creation, and the Bible seems to order things that way, then we should know he cares intensely. One is reminded of a science experiment where students try to create a closed and balanced system. Either there is not enough oxygen produced by the plants or the problem lies with the carbon-dioxide. Trial after trial has produced failure, yet God sustains the balance of our planet (it still continues to function) even though humans have done and continue to do great damage to it. Clothing and food are important and the Bible never encourages indolence, but they, like all stuff, are just stuff, and even in the midst of drought and famine, we should not lose sight of His concern.

Of more significance than that is the folly of anxiety. The King James Version did not do justice to what Jesus said. He did not say "take no thought" in the sense of not being concerned about life. But what he did suggest was that we should not have anxiety about it. This writer must confess that this is one of those places where it may be only about twelve inches between ones head and her/his heart, but it is a lifetime journey. That God cares and will care for us is primary to our trust in Him, but it is hard, especially when things do not turn out as one thinks they should nor as quickly as it seems they should. Doubtless each of us knows that worrying, not being concerned but worrying, does not do one bit of good. In fact there is evidence that it does a great deal of harm and it may be necessary to ask, is anxiety evidence of our lack of faith? If it is, then worrying is sin! No one is in a position to "preach" on this without also admitting that worry is a besetting difficulty for most of us.

His whole thrust in this section has been that we should have undaunted confidence in God and that if we seek his sovereignty in our lives everything will be taken care of. It almost suggests the old cliché: Work like everything depends on you and exercise your trust because everything depends on God. It may sound a bit too mystical to modern man, but Jesus believed it was so. Therefore, "Seek first the sovereignty of God as PRIORITY ONE and all other things will fall into place." That does not mean that kingdom citizens will become wealthy, nor does it mean that everything will go as humans think it should, but it does mean that success, in the best sense of that term, belongs to God's people.

## THE SOCIAL PRINCIPLE OF THE KINGDOM  pp. 34-36

<u>Against Censorious Criticism:</u>  So often people seem to have misunderstood Jesus when he said (as translated) "Judge not, so that you may not be judged." That is not all that he said, and certainly one who has warned us about making good decisions cannot mean that we should never make judgments! Rather what he says is that ones judgments must be just and exactly the kind of judgment one would want made against him. When one is placed in a position of responsibility, judgments on the work of others is a necessity. (In fact, the very next section demands that we use the power of discernment properly, and that requires judgment.) All that Jesus wants his followers to do is to first look inside and inspect ones self and then it will be possible to look at others. Jesus often used vivid exaggeration to get his point across and there must have been a little speck of humor in the statement, "How can you attempt to dig out the little tiny speck that is in your brother's eye when you have a telephone pole sticking out of your own?" (Paraphrase is the author's)

Having warned us about censorious judgment, he then turned to what the *Gospel Parallels* call, "Profaning the Holy." Two humorous illustrations again show the somber importance of the use of the power of discernment. One should not take the elements of the Eucharist (Lord's Supper) and present them to dogs. They wouldn't know anything to do with them except gobble them up. Or what if your place a Bible before a dog. More than likely he will tear it up. Dogs cannot use "holy" things as they are supposed to be used, they will prostitute those things to another use. In the same fashion, placing a beautiful strand of pearls in the pig trough is a foolish thing. Corn maybe, but not pearls! The pigs would destroy the pearls which were certainly never meant for hogs. So if Matthew had any reason for placing this section in this place (immediately following the statement on judging) it must be to show that if the God given power of discernment, which human beings have, is not used properly it is another case of God given gifts being prostituted.

These are tough words and challenges. Knowledge about how to use God's gifts will come as prayer is exercised. To be sure, there are hundreds of cases in the history of Christianity where men have prostituted their gifts, but if there is hope, it will come through the confidence that God knows how much leadership is needed and he will provide it to those who exercise faith. Since the human family is in a degraded and corrupted world and even kingdom citizens do not have perfect "followship ," there will be abuses and mistakes. So it takes confidence in God to hope gifts will be used properly. A crucial point of belief is that God knows what His followers need and He will provide and lead, if those followers allow Him to do so.

Then, according to Matthew's arrangement, he gave the highest principle! In some senses this short statement sums up everything Jesus laid out as the social principle of the kingdom. The essence of this statement is not unique to Jesus, but that does not affect its value! It had been stated before by Confucius, Plato, and others down to the Rabbi Hillel. To be sure it is often stated in the negative, but that does not change its essence, only its direction.

The book of Tobit (4:15) states,

> *"And what you hate, do not do to anyone."*

In the Letter to Aristeas quoted by R. H. Charles,

> *"As you wish that no evil should befall you, be a partaker of all good things, so you should act on the same principle toward your subjects and offenders, and you should mildly admonish the noble and the good." (The Apocrypha and Pseudepigrapha, vol. II [Oxford: Clarendon Press, 1913]Verse 207, p. 113)*

> *Hillel's statement was, "What is hateful to you, do not do to your neighbor; this is the whole law; the rest is an explanation of it."*

> *Immanuel Kant's Categorical Imperative (quoted by W. T. Jones), although coming after centuries of Christian History, also lays the same foundation for moral behavior. I am never to act otherwise than so that I could also will that my maxim should become universal law. (Kant and the Nineteenth Century, a History of Western Philosophy, 2nd edition* [New York: Harcourt Brace Jovanovich, Inc.1975] 75

## THE CONCLUSION OF THE SERMON (Matthew 7:13-29) pp. 36-38

There is a warning to his followers not to take the way of least resistance. This summary is difficult, the words are difficult, and therefore the temptation to water it down and take the easy way has always been present. Jesus indicates that following him and his teaching is a deliberate choice and as he pointed out in Luke 14:25-33, it is both demanding and strenuous. He showed once again that making judgments about the validity of those who teach is a necessary deliberation, testing what one says by what he/she is. Fruits are the natural outgrowth of what one is in character, regardless of appearance or what one may claim. In the same way he offered a sobering thought that it is even necessary to guard against self deception in regard to ones commitment.

The sermon, as Matthew concludes it, suggests that a kingdom citizen will be successful in her/his life to the extent that such a life is built on the principles set forth in the sermon. In the insightful parable of the two builders, probably from the "Q" source since both Matthew and Luke (in what is often called "the Sermon on the Plain") used it to sum up his teaching, he contrasted the foolishness of rejecting this message as a basis for life and the wisdom of accepting the stability it offered.

Once again, Matthew reminded his readers that Jesus taught with a unique authority and that the people who heard him were astounded at what he said. That was not just true about the words of this sermon, but about all of his teaching.

## WAYS OF INTERPRETING THE SERMON:

It is no wonder that Christian teachers throughout the generations have struggled with these hard and challenging sayings. The warning even seems to suggest that with all the emphasis on Pharisaic legalism everyone needs to be aware of how easy it is to "become a Pharisee."

Some of the ways teachers have looked at the Sermon:

This cannot be an exhaustive accounting of the ways the Sermon has been interpreted, but it may help to see some of the different ways of approaching the material. There are those who believe that the Sermon is something that needs to be taken literally and applied universally. That view would almost make the Sermon a new Law, but even those interpreters suggest that some passages contain a symbolic element. Others, apparently attempting to deal with some of the rather radical ideas, suggest that Jesus taught with hyperboles and used exaggeration to emphasize his challenges. Their position is that if those commands should be taken literally social life would be impossible. Still others have concluded that Jesus meant to give general principles to teach basic truths through illustrations. Some, like Schweitzer, have insisted that Jesus himself believed that there would be an immediate end to history and he proposed the radical ethic for the interim period. These interpreters seem to believe that his ethic was only for the short period between the time he spoke and the end of the age. There are others who suggest that the Sermon sets forth the absolute will of God; it is what God demands of men at all times, but its complete fulfillment cannot come until the Kingdom comes. (That requires a different definition of the Kingdom from what is proposed in this work.)

Perhaps there is a bit of truth in each of these and other views which may be held. But the position taken here is that Jesus was giving the fundamental principles which should govern the behavior of kingdom citizens as they live in a secular society. The teachings should be taken as the basis of kingdom life, and (even though they may be difficult) a kingdom citizen will strive to reach these standards. They really emphasize the fact that all are sinners and fall short of God's righteousness, but they still point out how one should live. One must also struggle with the figures of speech and especially, the hyperboles. Who can make the claim that they have never had a mean, vengeful desire or a selfish, lustful thought?

# CHAPTER X
## THE HEALING MINISTRY(THE APOSTLES CALLED)

**pp. 38-41**

Immediately after the placement of the Sermon on the Mount, Matthew spoke of several healings. There can be little doubt that Jesus saw the healing ministry as a part of his Messianic work, but he would not heal or do anything material for the purpose of proving that he was Messiah.

> "*The healing ministry of Jesus, considered in this chapter, was a first century phenomenon, and the gospel accounts describing it were written by first century writers. This means that the world view of the first century permeates the records.*
>
> *The basic assumptions of that day concerning nature differed from ours. These should be called pre-scientific. Modern conceptions of natural law and of an established order in the universe did not exist. All causality was regarded as free, direct, and immediate.*
>
> *This world view placed a high value upon miracles. Rather than presenting a problem in interpretation, they were welcomed*

> *as evidence of the presence of God. Religious functionaries were expected to perform signs and wonders. These provided heartening examples of divine power, and indicated God's victory over evil, demoniacal agencies, which were believed to have control over the lives of men. From this standpoint miracles had to occur if a religion were to attract a following.*
>
> *The healing ministry of Jesus must be approached with this background in mind.* (Charles M. Laymon, *The Life and Teachings of Jesus,* [New York: Nashville Abingdon Press, 1952] 149)

Leprosy was a dreaded disease and those with leprosy were considered as outside the reach of first century Judaism. Perhaps that was because many believed, rightly or wrongly, that any disease was due to being under the judgment or a curse from God. In Leviticus there is a long and tedious discussion regarding the treatment of lepers. (Leviticus 13) Life must have been miserable for those who contracted the skin diseases which were under the umbrella of leprosy. boils, scaly spots, infections, exema, acne, impetigo, and the dread terminal leprosy were included. Fear and often despair surrounded the disease. If one has seen the movie "Ben Hur" or read the story, there are two scenes which have probably indelibly imprinted themselves on the memory. The scene of the chariot race was a vivid one, but the leper scene has also probably made a lasting impression, That showed some of the religious, ceremonial and even family defilement. There was to be no interaction in the synagogue, the Temple, civic affairs and even with ones family. It has been suggested that a leper, if not in a banned community, must cover his/her mouth, cry out "unclean, unclean," should live with hair disheveled, wear loose and ragged clothing and stay away from everyone. Alfred E. Edersheim and others have written that, if the wind were blowing from the leper toward another person, a distance of one hundred paces should be kept between them, while if the wind were blowing from the clean person toward the leper the distance might be decreased to five paces. (*The Life and Times of Jesus the Messiah,* [New York: Longmans, Green, and Co. 1910] 495) Sherman E. Johnson has said that the leper probably came to Jesus outdoors because the very entrance of a leper into a house would have polluted everything in it especially since there was even the belief that leprosy could contaminate clothing and walls of houses. ("Matthew," *The Interpreter's Bible,* vol. 7 [Nashville: Abingdon, 1952] 338)Perhaps the most remarkable thing about this healing is that Jesus actually touched the man! Under most conditions that would have rendered Jesus unclean but that almost goes unnoticed in the story. Jesus did not usurp the priestly function but told the man to go and show himself to the priest for recognition of his cleansing and for his restoration to society. The atmosphere in the story changes from the time Jesus first met the man and just before he commanded him not to tell anyone. In Mark's account Jesus is said to be angry or at least he threatenly enjoined the man that he tell no one, *embrimesamenos.*

All the Synoptics emphasize the command that the man should not tell anyone but when the he paid no attention and went out, proclaiming his healing, that produced such notoriety that Jesus could no longer freely enter the towns. (According to the theory that Mark held to a "Messianic Secret" theme, this may be a part the desire to conceal the Messiahship until later.) Matthew then moved to the story of a Roman centurion whose servant was in a state of paralysis and the request that he be healed. Luke indicated that the centurion was highly regarded by the people and they felt that he deserved help. (that high regard may be because there are inferences that sometimes centurions even built synagogues.) The centurion himself demonstrated great humility and did not even feel worthy to have Jesus enter his house. Apparently, because he saw great faith in the man, Jesus indicated, in what may either refer to the group called sinners or to the people of the Gentile world, that many outsiders would share with Abraham, Isaac, and Jacob in the kingdom while those who should be heirs would be left out. (He used the graphic figure of speech, "outer darkness.") He did not go to the home, but the servant was healed. According to Matthew all of these healings fulfill another Isaiah proof text, from one of the Servant poems in the second half of Isaiah, "He took our infirmities and bore our diseases.

The narrative concerning the raising the widow's son at Nain is unique to Luke. A burial procession came out of the city and apparently, without any request from the mother or the mourners, Jesus touched the bier. (Another sign that he did not pay any attention to the taboos of clean and unclean.) Once again the people acclaim this as the action of

God. The Matthew account then gives an experience with two "would-be followers" of Jesus while Luke, in material that primarily agrees with Matthew, adds a third. There must have been many who at first, before they knew the cost, professed a desire to follow him. The first of these volunteered that he wanted to follow, but was told that there would be no security, if he did so. Jesus indicated that he had no permanent place where people would be comfortable. To the second Jesus offered an invitation, "Follow me." (Luke 9:59) When the invitation was made the man replied that he had a duty to perform for his parents. One mistakes the situation if it is thought that the parents were already dead and that Jesus could not wait for just a short while. The custom was that the eldest son was expected to stay near the parents until they died and were buried and then he would be free to leave. It is this prolonged wait that Jesus indicates is unacceptable. The statement "let the dead bury the dead" obviously cannot apply literally to dead bodies burying other dead bodies, but it must mean that the responsibility for burying the parents can be carried out by those who have not responded to the life challenging invitation. Waiting until they die would be an indefinite time and Jesus' call was urgent. In Luke's account the third man wants a similar delay. Going home to say farewell was also not something which would take a few minutes or even an hour. It would require a prolonged period and again, the call is so urgent that any waiting is not acceptable. Mid-eastern customs, even to the present day, reflect this prolonged way of greeting and saying good-bye. Years ago a missionary to the Pakistan area indicated that one day he received a notice that there was some material for him in a Post Office in a city some distance from where he was and that he needed to come in person to get it. When he arrived, he was greeted by what we would call the Postmaster and was offered a cup of very strong coffee. Although the Postmaster had never met him he inquired about the welfare of his parents, his immediate family, and others. That took nearly an hour and then the man told him that he needed to go to another government office and get permission to take the material. When he arrived at that office he went through the same greeting, (parents and all) and another cup of the thick coffee. That also had consumed about another hour and then he was sent back to the first man and went through the same greeting and drinking of coffee (the whole procedure) that he had been involved with before! That process took the entire day to do something that should have taken a couple of hours. So Jesus emphasized the fact that he could not wait for those long postponements, that discipleship was urgent. Just why that was so is left to our imagination, but in one sense any idea to put off following Jesus is a kind of refusal.

The story of calming the sea is a transition to going over to the Decapolis side of the Sea, a predominantly Gentile area where swine were commonly herded. The calming of the storm again shows how awed the disciples were of Jesus and what he did. But the big issue had to do with the healing of the demon possessed person or persons. Both Mark and Luke stated that there was one man in Gergesa while Matthew tells of two, and Matthew gives the site of Gadara (there are a few manuscripts that "correct" this to Gergasa), but the incident must be the same. From the story in Mark, abbreviated a bit by Luke, the description of the man indicates someone who was insane. People were afraid of him and he seemed to have almost superhuman strength, breaking chains and shackles, but the fact that he lived among the tombs did not help his sanity. The people of the first century attributed everything like this to demon possession, and the victims appeared to have lost control of themselves. In this case the demons, using the voice of the man, ask to be allowed to go into swine. Efforts have been made to explain this phenomenon and it just may be that the frantic movements of the man (men) stampeded the swine and when the man sits, now completely sane, and the pigs are running wild over the cliff and choking, the assumption was that what had been causing the man to be wild was now in the swine. In any case Jesus did not command the demons to go into the swine, but allowed them to. If he had so ordered them, he would have been destroying the property of others and that would create a moral problem. In any case, the owners of the hogs were so upset that they wanted Jesus out of their country. It is not surprising that they were more concerned more about their economic loss than they were about the man being healed. Demon possession was a familiar designation for illnesses to the people of the first century. There were many professional exorcists and apparently they had some success.

The issue of demons is a very complicated one but it must be addressed by any interpreter. The first concept which is contrary to the way modern man thinks, is that the entire world is saturated and under the control of invisible demons. Since there was a totally different approach toward the problem of sickness, it is not surprising to find not only mental illnesses, but also some physical problems attributed to demons. In fact, it is evident even in this modern age that the mind has a great deal of control and influence over the body. There have been occasions where paralysis has been the result of some kind of mental block and when the mental condition was removed the paralysis also departed. In the first century that concept that illnesses, nearly all of them, were the result of demon possession, made exorcism a flourishing occupation, if that is a proper term. In both Matthew (12:27) and in Luke (11:19) Jesus indicated that exorcists were working among them and they also cast out demons. From some ancient burying places there have been skulls found which have been trepanned. A very small hole had been bored into the skull to allow a demon to escape. (The same was probably done in the case of toothache.) These things were done without anesthetics and with what the modern world would call crude instruments and must have produced great pain. But the belief was so strong that people endured the pain to get the relief. The result of such a strong belief was, that if a person was convinced that a demon had taken possession of some part of his/her body physical symptoms would usually follow. So as long as a person believed that he/she was demon possessed, no cure was possible. Barclay has summarized the situation in this fashion:

> *Two questions will immediately arise. First, is there any such thing as demon-possession? Is demon-possession a reality or is it a complete delusion? There are those who are not so willing to dismiss demon-possession as nothing but an ancient superstition . . . . There are, for instance, types of epilepsy in which there is no morbid pathology of any kind; that is to say, there is no discernible physical reason either in the body or in the brain for the illness; and there are those who wonder if it may not be that there is such a thing as demon-possession after all. But the fact is, in thinking about the miracles of Jesus, the reality or otherwise of demon-possession is really irrelevant. The one quite certain fact is that the sufferer himself was completely convinced that he was so possessed. . . .*

*Second, did Jesus believe in demon-possession? To that question there are two answers. It is not in the least likely that the medical and scientific knowledge of Jesus was in any way in advance of his age; all likelihood is that Jesus did so believe. Further, even if Jesus did not believe in demon-possession, even if he knew that it was a superstitious delusion, it was absolutely necessary for him to assume the patient's belief before he could effect a cure.* (Barclay, 73,74)

The Jewish historian, Josephus, tells of knowing a man of his own country, whose name was Eleazar, releasing people from demon-possession by taking a ring and placing it in the nostrils of the sufferer, apparently the ring was split, and then he drew the demon out and ordered it not to return again, reciting incantations which would prevent that. (*Antiquities,* VIII 2. 5.)

If one couples all of that thought with the concept that sin and suffering were inextricably entwined, it would have also been necessary to assure the ill person that his/ her sins had been forgiven. Until the sufferer had that assurance, nothing could cure him. Twentieth century thought would relegate much of what is called demon possession to the realm of psychiatric disturbance. The narratives may present difficulty for moderns, but any effort to understand just what took place must deal with the strength of the personality of Jesus and his deep compassion for people in bondage.

## THE HEALING OF A PARALYTIC pp.42-43

Matthew indicated that the story of the paralytic took place in Nazareth, "his own town" while Mark places it in Capernaum. The fame of Jesus had spread so much that the crowds thronged the place where he was and no one could get to him. In a remarkable demonstration of determination, the men, according to the account of Mark and Luke, could not get to Jesus in a normal way, but they climbed to the flat roof and made a hole through which they let the man down. The main issue in this healing lies in the first century belief that sickness was the result of sin and therefore, no one could be healed    unless his sins were forgiven. Jesus had stated that the man's sins were forgiven. That did not mean that he accepted the  normal interpretation of the cause of sickness, but he used this event as an opportunity to teach that he had the authority to forgive sins and that was blasphemy to the scribes. (cf. The case in the Fourth Gospel of the man born blind in which he refuted the idea that the blindness was the result of sin.) When the man was able to pick up his pallet and walk away, according to their own theology, his sins had to have been forgiven, therefore Jesus could forgive sin!

## THE CALL OF LEVI p. 44

It is extremely difficult to get any chronological order in dealing with the call of the first disciples. All of the writers agree that there were no disciples until after the story of the temptations, but Mark puts the calling of Simon. Andrew, James, and John very early in the ministry. The call of Levi (Matthew) is presented by the Synoptic writers as the next addition to the disciple band. Levi was a tax collector, a *mokhes*, a hated custom's house official, and he was at his job collecting tolls as the caravans came by. According to the Jews he would have been a thief and a traitor, therefore, (to them) he had no standing before God. The apparent position of the Jewish community was that one must get good and then come to God - for sinners must reform first. Jesus seems have said something like, "Come to God and He will help change you." For Jesus, God was interested in receiving sinners. Levi appears to have given a dinner and invited some of his friends who, obviously, were not of the Pharisees since no Pharisee would ever eat with "publicans and sinners." (Who could his friends have been except some who were sympathetic to his work?) It immediately put Jesus against the Pharisees who saw the publicans as being grouped with sinners. Their concern, whether sincere or not, was that Jesus ate with unclean people. When he overheard their criticism Jesus replied with a parabolic statement, "Those who are well have no need of a physician, but those who are sick." (Mk. 2:17) That did not mean that the Pharisees had no need, but rather that those who were outcast were the ones Jesus was interested in. Then some disciples of John asked why Jesus and his disciples did not adhere to the fasting like they and the Pharisees did. This confrontation is a first glimpse of the fact that John had expected a hope for a reform of Judaism, but Jesus' teaching was new! His reply indicated that fasting should come at times of sorrow and regret and not at times of joy, like a wedding feast. There would be time enough to fast when Jesus was no longer with the disciples. So he offered two little parables, the first seen in the presentation of his teaching. There was no pre-shrunk cloth in Jesus' time. When a patch had to be made new cloth would serve well until it had to be washed, then when it had shrunk and pressure was put on it, say either on the knee or the seat, since it was stronger it would tear out the surrounding old cloth and the situation would be worse than before, so no one was stupid enough to patch an old garment with a new piece of cloth that had not been shrunk. In like fashion, when new and unfermented wine had to be placed in wineskins, new, un-stretched skins were used. No thinking person would ever put new wine in old skins from last year that had already stretched to their limit and become dry and hard. Anyone who did that would soon find that as the new wine fermented and gave off gases, the old skins, which could no longer stretch, would burst and everything would be lost. Coming immediately after the discussion about eating with unclean persons and that of fasting, both of these little parabolic statements appear to suggest a break with the old religious structure and that the new teaching will not fit into the old legalistic patterns and forms..

## THE SENDING OUT OF THE TWELVE  pp. 47-50

Even though to this point in the narrative there had been no discussion about the calling of the rest of the twelve, Matthew indicated that Jesus found a need to expand the ministry. His statement that "The harvest is plentiful, but the laborers are few," indicated that need, so after he had given the twelve authority, they were sent out. The lists of the names vary  but except for Mark and Matthew giving the name of Thaddaeus while Luke gives Judas son of James,  there is little difference.

| Matthew 10: 2-4 | Mark 3:13-19 | Luke 6:14-16 | Acts 1:13 |
|---|---|---|---|
| Simon (Peter0 | Simon (Peter) | Simon (Peter) | Peter |
| Andrew | James | Andrew | James |
| James | John | James | James |
| John | Andrew | John | Andrew |
| Philip | Philip | Philip | Philip |
| Bartholomew | Bartholomew | Bartholomew | Thomas |
| Thomas | Matthew | Matthew | Bartholomew |

111

| Matthew | Thomas | Thomas | Matthew |
|---|---|---|---|
| James (Alph) | James (Alph) | James (Alph) | James (Alph) |
| Thaddeus | Thaddeus | Simon (Zealot) | Simon (Zeal) |
| Simon (Canan) | Simon (Canan) | Judas (James) | Judas (James) |
| | Judas Iscariot | Judas Iscariot | Judas Iscariot |

The instructions Jesus gave were very simple in Luke. They were to go in pairs and proclaim the kingdom of God and to heal. Only in Matthew did Jesus say "go nowhere among the Gentiles and enter no town of the Samaritans." (That part must have come from the "M" source.) The proclamation is essentially the same in both Matthew and Luke so it probably comes from Mark. Since they are going among their own people, the general instruction is that they can depend on daily sustenance from those to whom they minister, so no money or extra baggage is needed. This is not a decree to all who serve in missionary capacities, indicating that they should not have support. It is a specific piece of instruction for a specific task among ones own people. There is to be no excessive pleading, just the greeting and if that is returned with hospitality they were to stay there but if the greeting is rejected they are to "shake off the dust from your feet," a rather vivid visual object lesson.

Jesus warned them that they would not necessarily find a warm acceptance, Instead, they are warned that they would be mistreated, opposition would come (possibly even from ones own family), and even imprisonment. There is, however, one phrase in Matthew 10:23 which needs examining. Mysteriously he told them to move to the next town if they were persecuted for "you will not have gone through all the towns of Israel before the Son of Man comes." It is obvious that there was some sense of urgency in this challenge, so it is important to look at some the possible interpretations. The enigma in this verse is simply the meaning of the "coming of the Son of Man." Albert Schweitzer, the famous missionary-doctor, believed that this referred to the end of the time and apparently, Jesus was mistaken about that, so this instruction is for that particularly very short time between when he spoke the command and the end time and therefore, very urgent. It is strange though, that Jesus would offer something like that and then indicate later that neither he nor even angels nor anyone else, knew when the end would come. (Matthew 24:36) A second interpretation has been that the phrase points to the coming of the Holy Spirit. It is true that there is some connection to be seen between the coming of the Spirit and the continued presence of Jesus with the disciples, but there does not seem to be any particular urgency in that meaning. A third way of looking at the phrase is that it relates to the destruction of Jerusalem. This is a passage peculiar to Matthew and if the suggestions made in this work are correct, that calamity (the War of 66-70 A.D.) was in some sense a consequences of the message of Jesus being rejected. This would have excited all of the old hopes about a political kingdom which would bring about the ultimate destruction and judgment. That appears to have great urgency! If they could convince the Jews about Jesus' message, it might be possible to avoid the coming war. Jesus sensed that there would be rejection and warned the disciples that "if they have called the master of the house (which would refer to Jesus himself), Beelzebub, how much more will they malign those of his household." They are immediately consoled in verses 26-33 with the idea that God cares for them and they need not fear anyone. Jesus knew that his message, although it initially received a positive response, would bring about persecution, family divisions, and controversy. The phrase, "Whoever loves father or mother more than me is not worthy of me; and whoever loves son or daughter more than me is not worthy of me" is a essentially the same as Luke's narrative in 14:26-27 where it is said, "Whoever comes to me and does not hate father and mother, wife and children, brothers and sisters, yes, and even life itself, cannot be my disciple." That passage from Luke cannot be taken literally in the light of Jesus' commands that we love one another, but it does mean the same as Matthew's statement means, that any loyalty that comes between one and Jesus makes his Lordship (discipleship) impossible.

The concluding thought in this passage regards "taking up ones cross and continuing to follow Jesus." (All stated in the Present and thus linear action tense) That must also be looked at in the light of what his first century hearers would have understood. So often in current thinking the taking up of the cross is interpreted as carrying a burden. All kinds of things have been called "crosses," from sicknesses to disasters to persecutions. But in the first century to any one who heard it a cross would have meant death, much like being a victim of capital punishment would mean in the modern world. If a distinction can be made between "literally" and what is figuratively accurate, the passage means that one must die (put an end) to the old conception of running or controlling his/her own life and from the decision point on, the life belongs to the Lordship of Jesus. As St. Paul said, "Don't you know that your body is the temple of the Holy Spirit, which you have from God and you are not your own? For you were bought with a price." (I Corinthians 6:19) Jesus concluded the instructions with a discussion that no one will lose their reward, if they use their gifts even to do as small a thing as offering a cup of water in the right spirit. But one must be warned that the idea of doing something in order to gain a reward is foreign to Jesus' thought.

Reward is incidental! Then following Matthew's order Jesus resumed his own preaching.

# CHAPTER XI
## JESUS RELATES TO JOHN THE BAPTIST (CONTROVERSIES) pp. 55-56

The narrative proceeded to the dilemma of John the Baptist who was now in prison. John had already been in prison for some time, some suggest as long as six or seven months. He could not have helped but wonder why the one who was coming had not done something to straighten things up. John had looked for immediate judgment, "his fan is in his hand," but judgment was not happening. His descriptions of the Messiah and his work did not seem to fit. When he heard the things that Jesus was doing it prompted him to inquire as to whether Jesus really was the one whom he had hoped for or should they look for another who would come. Doubt and uncertainty are not inconsistent with even great religious figures, for questions are a part of the lives of even the greatest stalwarts. (Consider the statement of Mother Teresa regarding her own questioning.) John's problem most likely stems from the concept he had of the Kingdom of God. If one had been looking for deliverance in the sense of restoring Israel to its former power, Jesus had not done that; instead he fitted a Messianic picture which was strange to them, that of the Suffering Servant. So John's disciples were told to report what Jesus had been doing. All of his powerful works indicated the activity of God in the ministry of Jesus. But the very inquiry from

John and evidence of uncertainty prompted the possibility that people might lessen the value of John's work. So Jesus indicated that John the Baptist was "more than a prophet." The statement that no one has risen to a greater height than John emphasizes that praise. But then the little phrase, "yet the least in the kingdom of heaven is greater than he" screams for interpretation. It must mean something like, John stands at the highest peak of those who looked and waited for the kingdom, they had not yet shared it.

Therefore, anyone who enters into the kingdom stands automatically on a higher plain of understanding than they. This statement has nothing to do with the ultimate sharing of John, Abraham, or any other Old Testament figure in the eternal blessings of God, it simply states that the current level of understanding is higher. So, John has been told to keep faith, for he was the messenger who was to come." (Malachi 3:1) Jesus then offered another hard saying. Evidently he was trying to show that the concept of the kingdom had been distorted because men have continually tried to force the kingdom into their own political concepts, what they want it to be, and it is not that! Nothing seemed to please them and they were acting like children. Note the little parabolic statement, "It is like children sitting in the marketplaces and calling to one another, 'We played the flute for you and you did not dance; we wailed, and you did not mourn.'" Does it show that John stood at one end of the spectrum (almost hermit like) and they did not accept him, and Jesus stands at the other end, participating somewhat in society, and they refuse to accept him? In the supreme event of history they could not see it as the crisis of first magnitude. They were "fiddling while Rome burned." Apparently, nothing would convince them?

## WOES, GRATITUDE, AND CONTROVERSY pp. 57-61

Because of their lack of response, Jesus warned the cities in which he had preached. His suggestion was that pagan cities like Tyre and Sidon would have repented, had they heard the message. Because of this a principle of judgment appears - those who have greater opportunity also have greater responsibility! Even the land of Sodom, which had stood for many generations as the symbol for evil would find more favor than the respected cities of Galilee. He then offered, once again, the challenge of taking his yoke and bearing it. It should always be remembered that a yoke united two oxen and therefore, the figure of the yoke must represent the idea that a follower united himself with Jesus. There are contradictory ideas in the accepting the yoke of Jesus and both are true! His indication in this passage that the yoke is easy is quite different from the notion that one must be willing to give up everything else in order to follow. All that is required to assume the yoke is submission, no great work, nor great position, simply surrender. That sounds easy, but the other side of the coin is a reminder of what took place in the story of the evil in the Garden of Eden. Fellowship with God was easy, but it required that Adam and Eve understand and agree to the "god-ness" of God. That was the essence of the disobedience which doomed them and can doom all humanity. This has been amply demonstrated. Someone has said, and I agree, that the antithesis of belief is not unbelief but disobedience. Dietrich Bonhoeffer, using the story of the rich young man who came to ask Jesus, "What must I do to inherit eternal life?" (Matthew 19:16-22) (The entire chapter in Bonhoeffer's work dealing with "Grace and Discipleship" makes this explicit.)

> *"Moral difficulties were the first consequence of the Fall, and are themselves the outcome of "Man in Revolt" against God. The Serpent in Paradise put them into the mind of the first man by asking, "Hath God said?" Until then the divine command had been clear enough, and man was ready to observe it in childlike obedience. But that is now past, and moral doubts and difficulties have crept in. The command, suggests the Serpent, needs to be explained and interpreted. "Hath God said?" Man must decide for himself what is good by using his conscience and his knowledge of good and evil. The commandment may be variously interpreted, and it is God's will that it should be interpreted and explained; for God has given man a free will to decide what he will do.*
>
> *But this means disobedience from the start. Doubt and reflection takes the place of spontaneous obedience. . . . The only answer to his difficulties is the very commandment of God, which challenges him to have done with academic discussion and to get on with the task of obedience. Only the devil has an answer for our moral difficulties, and he says, "Keep on posing*

> *problems, and you will escape the necessity of obedience." But*
> *Jesus was not interested in the young man's problems; he was*
> *interested in the young man himself. He refused to take those*
> *difficulties as seriously as the young man did. There is only*
> *one thing which Jesus takes seriously, and that is, that it is*
> *high time the young man began to hear the commandment*
> *and obey it. Where moral difficulties are taken so seriously,*
> *where they torment and enslave man, because they do not leave*
> *him open to the freeing activity of obedience, it is there that*
> *his godlessness is revealed. All his difficulties are shown to be*
> *ungodly, frivolous, and the proof of sheer disobedience. The*
> *one thing that matters is practical obedience. That will solve*
> *his difficulties and make him (and all of us) free to become*
> *the child of God. Such is God's diagnosis of man's moral*
> *difficulties." (The Cost of Discipleship,* [New York: Macmillan
> Publishing Company, Inc.1963] 79-81)

It almost appears that the Pharisees were lying in wait everywhere to trap Jesus and his disciples. Evidence of that comes in the narrative about the disciples shredding the heads of grain as they walked through the grain fields. Keeping in mind the laws about gleaning, there is no difficulty except that this was done on the Sabbath. The rigid Sabbath laws, as they interpreted them, forbade any work like reaping and threshing grain on the Sabbath, the amount did not matter. Jesus defended the disciples by showing that everyone had accepted the story of David and his friends eating the Bread of the Presence (I Samuel 21:1-7), which was unlawful, and therefore, they had accepted that violation of the proscription as permissible. He also used the fact that the priests regularly break the Sabbath law by working in the Temple and no one accuses them. Evidently the principle of "necessity" was dominate as He proclaimed their guiltlessness and then made the startling claim, "The Son of Man is Lord of the Sabbath."

Luke's narrative moved to another situation and he indicated that again it is the Pharisees, lying in wait to find some accusation against Jesus, who question the legitimacy of healing on the Sabbath, in this case a man whose hand was withered. Jesus showed that they themselves break the Sabbath law in regard to saving a sheep and certainly a human being is of more value than a sheep, while they certainly would have said that the man could wait another day. But then He deliberately healed the man! At this point the Synoptics each give evidence that because of their fury there is a movement to destroy Jesus. (In the accounts in the Fourth Gospel, that attitude was reached early in the ministry of Jesus.) Jesus then continued to heal and cast out unclean spirits and Matthew used another proof-text from the Servant poem in Isaiah 42 to show that this work was in keeping with the prophet's expectation and that the passage indicated that the work of God would continue among the Gentiles.

## THE WOMAN WITH THE OINTMENT AND THE MINISTERING WOMEN p. 69

There are several accounts of anointing in the gospels and it is very hard to determine whether they are doublets or whether anointing occurred more than once. The account in Luke (7:36-50) differs somewhat from that in Matthew and Mark and serves another purpose. It has already been noted that Luke has an interest in the poor, in injustice, and in the position of women. This account will be discussed separately from that of Matthew and Mark, not only because of the chronological arrangement but also because of the reason and significance of it. Perhaps there were those of the Pharisees who were interested in Jesus and perhaps even followers, for he was invited to eat with them on more than one occasion. In this case, there must have been an almost public meal, perhaps in an outdoor situation, patio like, near the street to which bystanders had access. The story indicates some criticism of Simon (the Pharisee) because he did not provide the usual amenities for a visitor. He did not provide water for washing the feet nor did he offer a kiss as a greeting. The woman involved is, in all probability, a prostitute, since she is described as having unbraided hair with which she wiped the feet of Jesus. She was also known as "a woman in the city who was a sinner." It is not possible to identify her with certainty, Some have felt that she was Mary Magdalene, because Mary was described as one out of whom Jesus had cast seven demons and that seems to imply she had been about as bad as she could have been. That has led to the assumption that Jesus had rescued her from prostitution and that she became a devout follower after that. Such could certainly be the case, but no positive or certain identification can be made. What can be determined is that at some point, either before the event described here (which would require some previous contact with the woman at which time her sins had been forgiven) or at this time Jesus had cleansed her life. If there had been a previous meeting, the love which the woman demonstrated could easily be understood. But if the forgiveness comes either at the same time or after the expression of love, the expression of her devotion remains as a tribute to her. Whatever may be the case, this ointment was a very precious and expensive offering, and the difference in the love she showed and that which may have been absent in Simon offered Jesus an opportunity to use a little parable to drive home the point that her sins were forgiven and her expression of unselfish love demonstrated that.

Simon is required by a question to decide which servant would appreciate (or love) more, one who had been forgiven a debt equal to five hundred days wages or one who had been forgiven a debt of fifty days wages. Obviously, there are factors which could enter in to alter the conclusion. For instance, if the man who was forgiven the greater debt was not in any need and the man who was forgiven the lesser debt was in dire straits, then the forgiveness might mean more to the second man. But in the normal application of the story, the man who was forgiven more was more grateful and the Pharisee host concludes that. In either illustration, the person who appreciates what has happened more seems to love more. So it teaches that the woman, who was a sinner and desperately knew her need, was more overwhelming in expressing her love than Simon, who (perhaps as a self-righteous Pharisee) did not feel the same need. But the primary teaching, once again, that awed those present was that Jesus could forgive her sins! None of the other narratives relating to anointing carries that kind of teaching. In the one which is in the context of the Passion (Matthew 26: 6-13 and in Mark 14: 3-9) Jesus interprets the event as dealing with the woman making a sacrifice preparing for his ensuing burial.

In Luke's immediate contextual construction, the people with Jesus are the twelve and several women, the first of whom is Mary Magdalene. That context may indicate why so many have felt that the woman in the previous story was Mary Magdalene, and it is an intriguing suggestion, but certainly not capable of proof, especially since the context may have been created by the author. These women provided for Jesus and the small band out of their substance.

## ACCUSATIONS AND CONFRONTATIONS pp. 70-72

Mark indicated that the family of Jesus did not understand him and thought that he had lost his senses, and they went to restrain him. Those of the family who felt that way are not named, but we are forced to wonder if some "pondering" was still going on in the mind of his mother, Mary. (Without diminishing the importance of Mary we need to admit that such a "holy aura" has grown up around her that few would dare to suggest any vulnerability in this area.) It has already been seen that the religious leaders had decided that something had to be done about Jesus, but for the present they seemed to simply try to link Jesus with the forces of evil rather than the power of God. In his defense, if it can be called such, Jesus showed that it would be utterly foolish for any kingdom, even a satanic one, to divide and fight against itself. It was at that point that the discussion leading to what people have called the "unpardonable sin" arose. But that discussion has led to many incorrect interpretations. The position taken here is that what we are dealing with is not an act but a condition. Notice that the "blasphemy" is against the Holy Spirit. Nearly all Christendom has agreed that the initial work of the Spirit has to do with conviction of sin. It must be kept in mind that the people to whom Jesus addresses this hard saying are still alive, so it cannot mean that they are dead and therefore cannot be forgiven. Once, this writer was attempting to deal with an unmarried woman who had a child. When she was asked to commit herself to Christ for forgiveness and salvation she said, "I wish I could, but I cannot because I have committed the unpardonable sin." As I discussed this with her I found that some preacher had told her that there was a passage (Deut. 23:2) which said that no bastard shall enter the congregation of Israel. She knew that the little boy out in the yard was not responsible for the "illegitimacy" and therefore she was convinced that she had committed that which was unpardonable. I was not able to change her mind. What an injustice that misinterpretation produced for it created a condition in which she believed that her sin could not be forgiven! It must be kept in mind that this blasphemy is not against Jesus, but against the Holy Spirit. So we are left trying to see what Jesus meant. It has already been stated that this is a condition, not an act. I have always hesitated to identify any living person as having gotten into this state, but perhaps someone who is dead, might be an example. For instance, it would seem highly unlikely (even impossible) to have convinced Adolph Hitler that what he was doing to Jews and others was evil. He had gotten into such a frame of mind that nothing could convince him. (This discussion is not talking about forgiveness being impossible because he is dead, but that during his lifetime he had reached a condition in which he would not think of being convicted and therefore, since conviction of sin is a prerequisite to forgiveness, his sin was and is unforgivable. That denies the initial work of the Holy Spirit.) How many are in that condition it would be foolish and dangerous to hazard a guess, but Jesus seems to imply that it happened and he may have felt that the religious leaders had turned their minds into concrete so that they could not see any truth different from what they had already accepted. That is one danger of dogmatism! It is not murder - Paul was forgiven that; it is not adultery - David was forgiven that (as have many others); it was not denial of the Lord- Peter was forgiven that; it is not even suicide (for the only way suicide is unforgivable is if salvation comes by works and not by faith and assumes that one does not have the time to repent if he/she takes their own life. That is not to say that suicide is not wrong, it simply recognizes that there may be many problems to which the individual cannot see any other answer, and that would be forgivable.) Nor is it any other act or deed! Anything can be forgiven, if man can be convicted. So none of Jesus' followers, or anyone else, can pronounce judgment on anyone for having committed that which is unpardonable - none can know! Judgment is an awful thing and it would appear that to Jesus what a person is inside (character) is that which determines her/his destiny. This is one of those hard sayings of Jesus that many could wish the gospel writers had given a little more light on. Perhaps it is enough to say that such blasphemy indicates that the person had destroyed his ability to discern his evil!

Many questions could be answered if only signs could be given which would prove for mankind what they want to hear, but it would probably negate the issue of faith. In the discussion about the Temptations, we saw that Jesus rejected doing fantastic things to prove he was Messiah. (Jump off the Temple pinnacle) Jesus indicated that no sign would be given except that which was the sign of Jonah. Luke's use of that passage implies that the sign of Jonah was his preaching. (Luke 11:30) However one interprets that Old Testament narrative, one thing is certain, the only thing in the story that the people of Ninevah saw or heard was his preaching. "Repent, or else!" That was the only sign that Jesus offered - his proclamation of the truth. The parallel of "three days and three nights" became for Matthew a kind of proof text, after the fact of the tomb, and it came after the effort of the scribes and Pharisees to get a sign, so for Matthew it was a sign after the fact. Jesus then said much of the same thing he had said about Capernaum, Bethsaida, and the other cities, that the people of Nineveh and the queen of "the south" (who came to listen to Solomon) would condemn the current generation because they had repented at the preaching of Jonah and something greater than either Jonah or Solomon was in their presence, and they did not recognize it!

Self righteous reformation will be of little value in the long run. When an evil spirit has gone from a person and nothing replaces it, that person, now illustrated by a house, is empty. Because nothing has been put in its place the evil in the person becomes magnified by the figure of seven other spirits and the condition is worse than when it began. This appears to suggest that unless a life is filled with something better, the final difficulty will, be worse than at the beginning. Does this imply that the emptiness allows something like pride or arrogance at what has been accomplished to enter and that grows in the life and destroys it?

There had always been a problem that Jesus had with his own family. Perhaps it is a little like the "prophet is not without honor except among his own household." Jesus' mother and brothers are bothered by Jesus. We cannot tell whether they are worried about his own safety or whether, as was stated before, they thought he was out of his mind and the mission made no sense to them. We do know that it was not until after the death/resurrection experiences that at least James became a disciple. Perhaps they were disturbed about a possible clash with the authorities. There are evidences that they did not understand this strange man who had grown up in their midst and they may have believed that the kingdom that he was talking about was a political one for at least once they suggested that he should go to Jerusalem and make himself known (Luke 7:3-5), which might have urged him to pronounce himself king. Whatever may have been the cause of this issue it gave Jesus an opportunity to express the greater truth that there is a closer kinship among like spirits than in simple physical heritage. That did not mean that Jesus had renounced his brothers and mother, but rather that some who were following him were closer at that point than they. Perhaps many of us have discovered such a closeness with certain other disciples that they are nearer in spirit than those of out own physical kinship.

# CHAPTER XII
## THE FUNCTION OF PARABLES AND JESUS' USE OF THEM   pp. 74-80

Parables have always been a distinguishing characteristic of Jesus' teaching. The Synoptics place the parables in a group although, Jesus had previously used a few short parables or parabolic statements. The primary writer, Mark, felt the need to explain their use, but it is important first that the need for them be understood. Whenever people are confronted with a new teaching or one which necessitates a change of mind or a correction, they tend to throw up any kind barrier of defense that they can. There are ways to overcome those barriers, and each of them has value, but often they also carry damaging consequences.

Many have known of those who have had the power to simply force their position on others. Many a CEO or College President has used this technique and either the underling agrees with it and continues in relative peace, or he/she opposes it and is often fired. In either case, the point at hand may be successfully won, but the hearer is lost. Socrates and many others have used irony to overcome this opposition. In the dialogues one can watch Socrates as he discusses the issue with an opponent and he often pretends ignorance or appears to concede a point, but after some while the opponent has been led "out on a limb" and it gets sawed off and he looks stupid. The argument is successfully won, but again the opponent may be so embarrassed or humiliated that he is lost in the process. The parable is different, but it too has some drawbacks. The use of a parable simply asks the one hiding behind a barrier to listen to a story. It may be either factual (taken from a real life experience) or it may be fictional. The story then gets into the mind of the hearer and stays there.

Parables act like delayed intellectual time bombs. The amount of time before they "explode" varies, but either immediately or eventually, the story illustrates the discussion and the listener must answer for himself the question at issue. The difficulty with a parable seems to be several-fold: either the listener may not really hear the parable at all (he simply enjoys a good story, but he makes no application), or the parable may be misinterpreted and the wrong lesson drawn, or the parable may be turned into an allegory.. But when it does succeed, and with Jesus that was very often, it wins both the argument and the hearer. For the hearer it means "draw your own conclusion" and as he makes the answer for himself, he saves face, and probably agrees with his antagonist.

That being said, a parable is a story placed alongside either an abstract idea or a practical truth to make it plain. It is not an allegory, although many have been so interpreted, but it primarily illustrates one point. Sometimes people have defined a parable as an earthly story with a heavenly meaning. That may serve for some parables, but it is not applicable to all of them and therefore, it does not adequately serve as a definition. At times there may be several other lessons which can be drawn, but most often it is possible to get at the primary truth. It is an ingenious teaching device and whatever one thinks of Jesus, he was a master at using the parable.

Before discussing this series of parables which Matthew uses to illustrate what the kingdom is like, it is important to look at the material from Mark and try to make some sense out of what is said about why Jesus used parables. The material, for which Mark is the primary responsibility, appears to indicate that Jesus told parables to confuse people. That, on the very face of it is absurd, for what teacher would want to waste his time confusing the hearers? The Marcan account is translated as follows:

> *"To you has been given the secret of the kingdom of God, but*
> *for those on the outside, everything comes in parables; in order*
> *that 'they may indeed look, but not perceive, and may indeed*

listen, but not understand; so that they may not turn again
and be forgiven.'" 4:11,12)

That very plainly says that Jesus taught in such a way as to keep
people from seeing and understanding. An answer may to be found
in the fact that Jesus probably spoke in Aramaic and the gospels were
written in Greek. In translating from the spoken language to the
written there was some confusion. At the risk of being tedious, but also
because it is necessary, we need to look at that problem. In the Aramaic
(Targum) the passage has the particle "de" which may either introduce
a relative clause or a purpose clause. That means that the clause may
either mean "who see, but do not understand" or it may mean "in order
that they may see but not understand." The Greek text as it stands
in our manuscripts is translated properly and the latter is the way the
passage reads because Mark used "hina" (meaning "in order that" and
introducing a purpose clause) instead of "hoi" (which means "who" and
introducing a relative clause).

> *Now in the Aramaic the particle, "de," which is used in the
> Targum here, can be used to introduce either a relative or a
> final clause: it can either mean "hoi" or "hina." The conclusion
> to be drawn is, I think, that the form in which the words were
> spoken by Jesus approximated to what we find in the Targum,
> and that the Marcan version rests on a misunderstanding of the
> Aramaic due mainly to the ambiguity of the particle "de." We
> may conjecture that what Jesus said was: "To you is given the
> secret of the kingdom of God; but all things come in parables to
> those outside who 'see indeed but do not know and hear indeed
> but do not understand, lest they should repent and receive
> forgiveness'" where the last words would seem to mean; 'for
> if they did they would repent and receive forgiveness'.* (T. W.
> Manson, *The Teaching of Jesus,* [Cambridge: The University
> Press, 1948] 78)

That would mean that we could paraphrase the passage as A. M.
Hunter has suggested, "To you, my disciples, is revealed the secret of
God's reign, but the parabolic method must be used with the multitude
who, as Isaiah also found, are lacking in spiritual insight." He also
stated, "In private Jesus explains the reason for parables. But his words,

as they stand in the A.V., read as if he used parables deliberately to blind and befog the common people. This is absurd." (*The Gospel According to Saint Mark* [London: SCM Press Ltd, 1955] 55)

With that in mind, we must always try to find what the main point that Jesus was attempting to illustrate was and then illuminate our thinking by applying that story to our own experience. Remember, Jesus used parables to teach spiritual (abstract) truth. These were not necessarily new stories nor was it a new method, but his application is peculiar to his own purposes: He used them because moral and spiritual truth demanded it. These lead to further understanding where there would normally be no further interest. Remember also that the purpose of a parable is to illustrate one point. There may be side lessons, but violence is done to a parable when the effort is made to find some hidden meaning in every word that he spoke.

## Parables of the Kingdom: The Sower: p. 74

This is a simple story and is probably the result of observation that Jesus and everyone else had made. In ancient Palestine, with rather primitive farming methods, the soil was plowed with crude plows and therefore, in a very shallow fashion. When the ground had been prepared the seed was sown "broadcast" style. That simply meant that seed would fall in a lot of different places, in this story the seed falls on several types of soil. Many interpreters believe that the story is really about the reception the gospel gets as it falls on the ears of various hearers so that this would teach about the labor of Jesus and the results he had. Others suggest that it is a story illustrating the preparation God had used to bring the Kingdom to fruition. (If the Kingdom was a present reality in Jesus' thinking, the preparation would have been in the past.) C. H. Dodd has said,

> *Similarly in the parable of the Sower the wayside and the birds, the thorns and the stony ground are not, as Mark supposes, cryptograms for persecution, the deceitfulness of riches and so forth. They are there to conjure up a picture of the vast amount of labour which the farmer must face, and so to bring into relief the satisfaction that the harvest gives, in spite of all. The parable of the Sower leads to the judgment that in agriculture, much labour may be lost and yet a good harvest may be reaped.*

(*The Parables of the Kingdom* [London: Nisbet & Co. LTD, 1948] pp. 24-25)

May this then mean that while many were claiming that the kingdom could not come until all Israel had repented, everything had been done by way of preparation that was needed? This would show that some work had been lost because the seed had fallen on three kinds of soil (ears) which ultimately did not produce any harvest, for various reasons. Jesus had seen seed fall on the path which did not provide for germination since it was hard and beaten and the seed never had a chance. The soil described by "stony" probably refers to the fact that just under the surface there were many places where a ledge of stone was barely covered and the seed which fell there could not get moisture for growth when the thin layer of soil dried out, no matter where the little roots tried to find sustenance. The seed which fell in the thickets simply had no chance to produce because of the thorns and weeds. That does not translate into an idea that seventy-five percent of the teaching goes unused, it simply describes that the kingdom does have a harvest and the quantity of production is not important, although it runs the gamut from thirty fold to one hundred fold - there is a harvest.

Each of the Synoptics gives an allegorical interpretation to the parable. One cannot help but wonder if this is evidence of the early church's interpretation being added to the oral material. In that allegorical interpretation the seed is the word and the birds represent Satan who is able to destroy some of the seed before they have opportunity to germinate. The stony ground deals with those superficial hearers who seem ready to receive the seed, but persecution, which is represented by the stony ground, causes them to fall away. The thorny thicket represents the materialistic cares which crowd out the seed and nothing is harvested. One can hardly argue with the truth of those ideas, but probably they are not the primary teaching of the parable.

### The Seed Growing Secretly: p. 78

This little story is another taken from observation of agricultural methods. Sowing is done and mysteriously, there is germination, growth, maturity, and harvest. One does not examine the sprouting seeds and re-plant them, the process goes on without the farmer intervening. Only when the harvest is ready does he enter the scene and reap the crop. This story may illustrate the power of self development in the gospel. It may also show that Kingdom character develops over a period of time. Dodd seemed to think that it represented the fact that the crisis that Jesus produced was the consummation of the long process of preparation. It certainly appears to imply that the harvest time had come.

**The Weeds or Tares: p. 78**

This parable belongs to Matthew alone. It may emphasize the statement "The harvest is come" and showed the immediacy of the kingdom. One cannot help but wonder whether Jesus had seen this very thing happen when ones enemy tried to contaminate the crop of another. The weeds are really "black wheat" which would look almost the same as good wheat while they were growing. The only problem is that when harvested and ground up, the grain produced a fine black substance which destroyed the value of the good wheat.

The desire of the servants to remedy the situation is seen by the master to be fruitless and dangerous to the entire crop. Apparently, if left to mature, the black wheat could be separated from the good wheat in the reaping process.

This story may teach that good and evil will exist, side by side, throughout history, but it also may suggest that kingdom reaping will not be delayed because there are weeds in the crop.

It is a realistic story of agricultural life, told vividly and naturally. Attention is fixed upon the moment at which the farmer becomes aware that there are weeds among his corn. The spiteful act of his enemy is a part of the dramatic machinery of the story and has no independent significance. He (the owner) regrets the weeds, but is quite content to leave things as they are, knowing that the harvest will provide the opportunity for separating the wheat and the weeds.

*Now we have seen that in the parable of the Seed Growing Secretly Jesus may be supposed to have referred to the work of God as manifested in the growth of true religion before his ministry, and particularly referring to the ministry of John the Baptist; and that in the parable of the Sower, He is explicitly answering an objection; the Kingdom of God cannot be here yet, because all Israel has not repented. The parable of the Tares might fitly be a reply to a similar objection. There are many sinners in Israel; how can it be that the Kingdom of God has come? The answer is: As little as the farmer delays his reaping when harvest-time is come because there are weeds among the crop, so little does the coming of the Kingdom of God delay because there are sinners in Israel.* (Dodd, 184-185)

Dodd may be right! If Jesus saw the Kingdom as present reality (cf. "the Kingdom is in your midst"), then there can be no delay regardless of the condition of Israel or of the world.

## The Mustard Seed: p. 78

The usual interpretation of this parable has been that it describes the very small beginning of the kingdom (in world history) and the extensive growth that it enjoyed, coming from the smallest seed and producing a large plant. The parable probably means much more than that. It may mean that the time has come for the blessings of God to be available for all people. That would be a logical outgrowth of the concept of Monotheism. As has already been seen quite often the Gentiles were called "birds:" and "dogs" by the Jews and therefore Jesus may have meant that the plant has grown so that there is inclusion for the birds to lodge in its branches and that the kingdom is universal. Luke, whose purpose has been described as promoting the universal idea, places this parable in a different setting (13:18-30) and at the conclusion of that discussion he alone adds, "Then people will come from east and west, from north and south, and will eat in the kingdom of God." (Note that the "red-letter" editions which propose that they identify the words of Jesus, are just late human efforts to identify those words and are not in any sense a part of hallowed scripture.)

## The Yeast: p. 79

First century cooks had no prepared yeast, but they did their own leavening of the meal. A lump of leaven (yeast) was placed in the barrel of meal and left there and as a result all of the meal became leavened. When Jesus likened the kingdom to that process, it again seems to be that he was describing the process of the kingdom is for all and therefore affects all men. It is true that wherever the message of the kingdom has been proclaimed even when there are distortions, it permeates all society and flavors it.

The Gospel of Matthew then proceeds to interpret the parable of the weeds by means of an allegory. One of two possibilities is open to the reader: either one must assume that these rare allegorical interpretations of some of these parables are due to the early church tradition or else conclude that Jesus used these same stories at different times, some as parables and some as allegory.

## The Hidden Treasure and The Pearl: p. 80

One must always be aware that the morality of the story of the parable is not necessarily commended. Jesus may have known of an occasion like the one in this story. Many have heard of stories of someone finding valuable resources on the property of another (in stories about the last century wild-west, oil was discovered on the property of a widow) and the evidence concealed. Then the evil person buys the property at a price less than he could if the real value were known. That is immoral, but the morality in the parables does not affect its teaching. (The same problem will be discovered in the story of the unjust steward.) Jesus did not commend the greed and dishonesty, but he used that to teach that the kingdom was ultimately of more value than anything and everything else.

The story of the pearl merchant teaches the same truth but does not have any ethical problem attached to it. The merchant simply finds that he is willing to sell everything he owns in order to buy that most valuable pearl which he has found. That simply illustrates, like the Hidden Treasure, that the kingdom is more valuable than anything or everything else.

## The Net: p. 80

A story that everyone, certainly all the fishermen, of the first century would have understood had to do with the fact that anytime one is fishing with a net (and that was the method that was used) he catches both edible and inedible fish. Therefore, when the catch is evaluated, there are some fish which are of no value. This must infer that there is a process of selection (not Calvanistic) which operates when the message is cast out. We have already seen some who appeared to respond to

Jesus, but when the demands of the kingdom were explained they stopped following. This may also reflect the same idea that the Parable of the Tares taught, that the ultimate judgment belongs to God.

Then those who heard were asked, "Do you understand? Jesus did not question their answer, but simply indicated that they needed to use every bit of information they had in order to serve as scribes in the kingdom.

# CHAPTER XIII
## KINGDOM MINISTRIES - JOHN'S EXECUTION    pp. 83-85

It has already been shown that the performing of great deeds often produced such responses that Jesus had difficulty doing any teaching. However, as he came back into Galilee (Mark and Luke have placed the cleansing of the demon possessed man in Gerasa at this point while Matthew discussed it earlier.) he was met by a leader of the synagogue named Jarius. The fact that he is a leader of the synagogue does not necessitate that he is anything more than a local lay person, but it does indicate that Jesus had numbers of Jews who at least reverenced him. At the initial point of the story the little girl is severely sick, so when Jairus pled with him, Jesus began the journey to his house.

But there was an interruption! The crowds were pushing around him and in that process a woman who had had a hemorrhage for twelve years came behind him, touched his garment, and was healed!. Mark is a little harsh on the medical people suggesting that she had spent all that she had and was no better but rather grew worse. Luke's language is a little softer and simply suggests that she had spent everything and no one was able to help her. Could that softening be because Luke was a physician himself? (Col. 4:14) Regardless of that, Jesus indicated that he had felt something go out from him, some power, because someone touched him and in Luke's account it appears that Peter felt anyone could have done it because of the throng. But the woman, in great fear confessed to Jesus that she had been the one who touched him and Jesus stated that because of her intense faith she had been healed.

While all this had been going on, some people came from Jairus' house and told him that the girl had died and that it was useless to trouble the teacher. But Jesus continued on his way with an urging, "Do not fear, only believe." A crowd of mourners, Matthew seems to describe them as the professional mourners (flute players and others), was already at the house and when Jesus said the little girl was sleeping, they laughed at him, Luke says it was because they knew she was dead. Most interpreters think that Jesus was simply using a euphemism and that the girl was really dead. Only Peter, James and John went into the house and witnessed the event. Jesus addressed the girl and told her to get up and she did. The parents were overcome with amazement and they were told not to tell anyone what had taken place, but as appears to be common with these events, Matthew suggested that a "report of this spread throughout that district." There is a great distinction between the resurrection of Jesus and these stories of restoration to the previous life condition. This same restoration is seen in the experience with the widow's son at Nain, the one dealing with this girl, and that of Lazarus (given in the Fourth Gospel).

But if the people of Nazareth had heard of what he had been doing, it made no difference. The barrier that the people of Nazareth faced was due to the fact that they had known him all his life; they knew his parents, they knew his brothers and sisters. The brothers (James, Joses, Simon, and Judas) are named and his sisters are mentioned. The general position of the Roman Catholic Church has been that these were not children of Mary. That appears to most Protestants as an effort to impose a church doctrine of perpetual virginity on Mary, implying that for some reason she and Joseph never had a normal marriage. There is nothing evil about God's creation, including sex, and to most people it does not lessen Mary one iota, to have her as the real mother of those children. From the language used, it would seem that the marriage was normal. (The NRSV translates the passage in Matthew 1:25 as, "but had no marital relations with her until she had borne a son; and he named him Jesus.") The Greek text used the normal way of stating sexual relationship by says that "he did not know her until she had borne a son."

However one wishes to deal with that, the identification of Jesus with the family and the fact that they had known him all of his life, created unbelief and prevented him from doing much. No one knows anything about the childhood of Jesus, except that he is said to have increased in wisdom, stature, and in favor with God and man. If he had been just a normal boy to these townspeople it should not be surprising that they could have had difficulty in seeing anything great about him. One must always keep in mind, that his brothers did not believe in him until after the resurrection.

## HEROD AND THE DEATH OF JOHN pp. 87-89

All of these reports of what Jesus was doing reached Herod Antipas and he assumed that Jesus was John the Baptist returned from the dead. There were other rumors about who Jesus was, but apparently this fear of Herod's gave opportunity for the Mark source to narrate the death of John. John stirred the wrath of Herodias. Before she married Herod Antipas she had been the wife of Philip, Herod's brother, and John had addressed that evil. So it is not surprising that with a grudge against John, Herodias was looking for some way to get vengeance against him.

> But Herodias, their sister was married to Herod (Philip), the son of Herod the Great, who was born of Mariamne, the daughter of Simon, the high priest, who had a daughter, Salome, after whose birth Herodias took upon her to confound the laws of our country, and divorced herself from her husband while he was alive, and was married to Herod (Antipas), her husband's brother by the father's side; he was tetrarch of Galilee. (Josephus, *Antiquities of the Jews*, Bk. XVIII, V, 4, trns. William Whitson [Philadelphia: Henry Coates & Co.])

Now some of the Jews thought that the destruction of Herod's army came from God, and that very justly, as a punishment of what he did against John, that was called the *Baptist*; for Herod slew him, who was a good man and commanded the Jews to exercise virtue, both as to righteousness towards one another, and piety towards God, and so to come to baptism; for that the washing (with water) would be acceptable to him, if they made use of it, not in order to the putting away (or the remission) of some sins (only), but for the purification of the body; supposing still that the soul was thoroughly purified beforehand by righteousness. (Josephus, *Bk XVIII, V, 2*)

A banquet, which Herod gave on his birthday at the prison fortress of Machaerus must have provided that opportunity. Most commentators believe that at that banquet, Salome performed a dance. (Mark gives the name as Herodias but even in that account she is called Herod's daughter, so the name in Matthew is probably correct ) It is suggested that she danced (what moderns might call a "strip-tease") a "dance of the seven veils" removing the veils one at a time. She did such a "superb" job pleasing Herod and the crowd of Arab chieftains that Herod made a foolish vow, giving her, according to Matthew, anything she wanted. Mark goes further and says that she might have as much as half of the kingdom. Both accounts state that she was prompted by her mother, Herodias, to ask for the head of John the Baptist on a platter. (Imagine a sixteen or seventeen year old girl making such a request when she had the opportunity at this point to gain great wealth!) That must have not been what Herod expected, for both accounts indicate that he was grieved, but found himself in a position where he could not refuse the request and save face. So John was executed and his disciples buried his body.

According to the account in Mark, Jesus and the disciples tried to get away from the crowds for a while. There may have been several reasons for that retirement. If we can dare try to reconstruct an order for the events, there was a need for meditation and rest. By that time the disciples had returned from the mission that Jesus had sent them on and a critique dealing with that journey was needed. It is almost certain that Herod Antipas harbored some jealousy and suspicion regarding Jesus and there was a growing hostility of the religious leaders. Perhaps the fanaticism of some of the followers in Galilee also led him away so that there could be a cooling off time. If we can refer to the Fourth Gospel, Jesus constantly put off confrontation and said that his time had not yet come. But those crowds anticipated where Jesus was going and went on foot ahead of him and when he disembarked, he saw them and was concerned for them and began to teach them. Since the time of day had become late the disciples wanted Jesus to send the crowds away so that they could get food. But he saw no need for them to go away and told the disciples to give them something to eat. They seem to have been astonished that he would give such directions, because it would take the wages of two hundred days to feed the crowd and they had only five loaves of bread and two fish! Luke records that there were about five thousand men in the crowd in addition to the women and children. But Jesus took what they had and fed the crowd! The account of this miracle in the Fourth Gospel gives some additional information about the little boy who had the lunch of five loaves and two fish and it also adds at the conclusion of the section that they saw this sign and interpreted it as a reference to "the prophet who is to come." The temptation to be an economic Messiah was just what Jesus wanted to avoid and when he realized that the people were about to try to take him by force and make him king, he again withdrew. (John 6:1-15)

There is reason to suspect that the disciples were part of the instigating force in the move to make him king, because the first thing Jesus did was to have the disciples get into the boat and leave. If they were the movers in the event, getting them away would then allow him to dismiss the crowd. We would like more information about this crisis, but none is available. Even though the disciples were trying to cross the sea, an adverse wind was preventing them and early in the morning he came to them.

Midnight is not the most frightening time of the day. The hours just before dawn when there is not enough light to see clearly, but yet enough to be able to see just a little are the spookiest ones. This author experienced that during an event in World War II. The unit I was with captured a small village just before dusk and immediately began to make defense preparations. I cannot remember what I was assigned to do, but I did not dig any of the perimeter foxholes and therefore did not know their location. Someone had made the foxhole that I found myself in as comfortable as it could be with an overstuffed chair. My hours of guard duty were from ten to twelve p.m. and then later from four to six a.m. The first tour went off without a hitch. I was well armed, with a light machine gun, a regular M1 rifle, and a forty-five caliber pistol. Just before dawn, I heard guttural noises that to me sounded like Germans talking under their breath. I eased up over the edge of the foxhole and saw crawling up the hill in front of me what looked like a hundred men. I had been taught that especially in dim light if one will look directly to the side of one of the objects, if it is real it will still remain, but if it is imaginary it will disappear. Sure enough, as I looked to the side of it, one of those objects disappeared. That must have gone on for forty-five minutes or an hour. I started to fire at them, but they were making no progress, so I waited. Finally, dawn came and with it enough light to see clearly. When it did, just to the front of the hole I was in and to its right about five or six yards (I have no idea why those foxholes were dug so close to each other.) a man climbed out of another hole and vomited. When he had finished, he turned to me and said, I ate some canned cherries we found last night and my stomach has been growling and giving me fits for the past hour. There were my Germans!

So when the disciples saw something coming on the water, they thought it was a ghost and were afraid! It is useless to ask how Jesus could do some of the things that are reported. There have been those who have tried to suggest that Jesus was walking on a ledge of rock alongside the boat, but there is no valid evidence for that. Others have said that he was probably walking in the surf, but that certainly does not account for the account of Peter's action. On that night something unique happened, just as it did when he fed the multitude, and the disciples, who were fishermen and knew the sea, never forgot it. Mark's account does not tell the story of Peter's failure when he got out of the boat to go toward Jesus. (Perhaps this is another place where Peter's exuberance and then lack of faith was an embarrassment to him.) But Matthew preserved it and the whole experience astounded the disciples!

## ABOUT DEFILEMENT pp. 92-93

A confrontation with the Pharisees occurred because Jesus' disciples did not follow the Jewish practices, the tradition of the elders, of ceremonially washing their hands before they ate. Jesus responded by quoting from Isaiah a passage which indicated that the people were following human precepts as if they were true doctrines. (29:13) He showed that even though they had the commandment, "honor your father and mother," they used another of their precepts to avoid doing their duty. The issue of Corban is a little difficult to explain, but it would appear that children, or anyone, could say that some of their substance was dedicated to God and could not be used for their parents or any other purpose. Whether it could be reclaimed later for their own use is debatable, but there are statements in Leviticus that suggest offerings may be reclaimed but one fifth has to be added to it. That certainly avoided the responsibility for parents. Then Jesus used that as an opportunity to show what really defiles people. It is again back to the message of the Sermon on the Mount when he said that evil comes from the attitude. Externalisms such as what one eats cannot defile for that which defiles is spiritual and has its source on the inside. Peter and the others needed an explanation and he elaborated that evil intention comes from the inside. Murder, adultery fornication, theft, false, witness, and slander all come from the heart, the inner being, and that is the defiling thing, not what or how one eats. This narrative has nothing to do with the hygiene of washing ones hands before eating, it only deals with the ceremonial. In this passage Mark adds an interpretation, "Thus he declared all foods clean" (Mark 7:19)

## THE SYROPHOENICIAN WOMAN  pp. 94-95

According to the source from Mark, Jesus left the area of Galilee and went to the Phoenician territory of Tyre and Sidon. Even there he could not escape the fame that surrounded him and that is evident as the woman whose daughter was afflicted by an unclean spirit asked for his help. Mark points out that she was a Gentile (Matthew calls her a Canaanite) and that Jesus seemed to hesitate by suggesting that "it is unfair to take the children's food and throw it to the dogs." At first glance that seems to be a harsh and "un-Jesus like" statement, but the word Jesus used softens the statement somewhat for it means "little puppies." Keeping in mind that Gentiles were often called dogs by the Jews, she did not take offense, but simply asked for the scraps which fall from the master's table. This story must illustrate the temptation to turn from the Jews and go to the Gentiles. The conclusion would be that at this time a ministry to Gentiles would not become primary, but only incidental. Jesus had already indicated that the kingdom was for all people, but one must remember that his ministry was to his own people, the base must be laid, and the expansion to the rest of the world would take place later.

The ministry then returned to the site of Galilee and Jesus continued to heal many, including a man who had a speech impediment and that probably also included a hearing problem. This provoked great awe from the people even though such things had occurred before, but there was still an atmosphere of reverence among those who witnessed the healing.

A second narrative of feeding a crowd occurs both in Mark and Matthew. It is difficult to know whether this is a doublet or another event much like the first. There are differences in the narrative as Alfred Plummer points out,

> *"It must remain doubtful whether the narrative of the feeding of 4,000 people is merely a variant of the feeding of the 5,000, or represents a different miracle. In favor of there being only one miraculous feeding are the similar details, the fact that numbers frequently get changed in tradition, and the improbability that the disciples would express a difficulty about feeding the multitude, when Jesus had fed a still larger one only a few weeks ago. But, if there were two miraculous feedings, many of the details would be sure to be similar, and the differences in the numbers occur not only as to the crowd, but as to the loaves and baskets. Besides these differences, the attendance on Christ for 'three days' is peculiar to the 4,000, meaning that they had been with him 'since day before yesterday'; so also is the diminutive ichthudia for the fishes, and it evidently means 'small fishes' (RV.). Above all there is the different word for 'baskets. All four Evangelists use kophinoi of the 5,000, and both Mt. and Mk. use sphurides of the 4,000; and this distinction is observed in referring to the two miracles afterwards (xvi. 9.10; Mk. viii. 19.20). (The Gospel According to S. Matthew,* [Grand Rapids: Wm B. Eerdmans Publishing Company, 1956] 218-219)

The site of this miracle has not been established since Matthew uses Magadan and Mark uses the district of Dalmanutha. It is evident that this location proved a concern for the copyists for there are four different readings in the various manuscripts. (*Dalmounai, Melegada, Magdala,* and *Magedan*)

## THE PHARISEES AND SIGNS pp. 96-97

One cannot help but wonder what more the Pharisees wanted for a sign. Healings of all kinds, dead people being raised, and many other things should have convinced them, if they were genuine in their request. Jesus indicated that they were experts in discerning the signs of the weather, but they could not sense the "signs of the times." Matthew and Luke (in a somewhat parallel passage) both repeat that the only sign which will be given is that of the prophet Jonah (which must be his preaching) but they do not repeat the idea of "three days and three nights in the fish." Mark simply stated, "no sign will be given."

This led Jesus to warn his disciples about the teaching of the Pharisees and Sadducees. In this passage he called it the "yeast" and the disciples did not understand but thought that he was talking about actual bread. He alluded to both feeding miracles, and then Matthew stated that they finally understood that he was talking about their teaching.

In spite of the fact that no sign was to be given, Mark's account deals immediately with a blind man. It was "some people," not Pharisees nor Sadducees, who brought this man to Jesus. The fantastic restoring of the man's sight was done in stages as Jesus put saliva on his eyes and then touched him once again and his sight was restored. As was typical of his actions in some other instances, Jesus told the man to go home and not to go into the village.

# CHAPTER XIV
## THE SHOCKING REVELATION (THE GREAT CONFESSION) pp. 99

A fourth withdrawal took Jesus and the disciples to Caesarea Philippi. Caesarea Philippi was in what has been designated as Northeast Palestine and was on the lower part of Mount Herman. The time had now come for a more forth-right and startling revelation. The question which prompts the confession had been implied earlier and when Jesus asked in both Mark and Luke, "Who do men say that I am?" Matthew used the term "Son of Man" in this context and so links Jesus with the Old Testament concept from Ezekiel and perhaps Daniel. The question draws out the answer which had been heard before in the discussion of the death of John the Baptist, but here they replied that some see him as John the Baptist, some as Elijah or Jeremiah, and some are saying he is one of the other prophets. The question was probably designed to lead up to the personal question, "But what do you say?"

It was at this point that all three Synoptic writers link Jesus with the Messiah in Simon Peter's great confession. The confession does not imply that Peter understood everything about Jesus and his mission. In fact the following discussion indicates that he did not understand. Perhaps this little band has come a long way, but learning is often slow. They had seen Jesus reject signs and even the physical kingdom, and they still followed! But this introduced a special passage from Matthew which has been the source of diverse interpretations.

> *"And I tell you, you are Peter, and on this rock I will build my church, and the gates of Hades will not prevail against it. I will give to you the keys of the kingdom of heaven, and whatever you bind on earth will be bound in heaven, and whatever you loose on earth will be loosed in heaven." (16:18,19)*

There have been three prominent possibilities suggested for the meaning of this passage:

1. The basic position of the Roman Catholic Church is that at this point Jesus proclaimed Simon Peter as the foundation of the church and that this made Peter the first Pope and gave to him the powers which are listed in these verses. That position was solidified by Pope Leo I in 450 C.E.

2. During the Reformation Martin Luther proposed another solution. He indicated that Jesus used his hands to demonstrate what he meant. When he said, "You are Peter" he pointed to Simon Peter, but when he said "on this rock" he pointed to himself. The primary passage Luther used to support his position was: "other foundation can no man lay than that which is laid, Jesus Christ, the righteous." (Ist Corinthians 3:11) One may very well agree with Luther that the church is founded on the Christ, but, without video cameras, to prove it by means of trying to guess where he pointed is a very weak position.

3. There is a distinct difference in the Greek words which are used. In the application of the name "Rock" to Peter the word is *petros,* which is a masculine word which would have to be used for the man Simon, and is often translated as a stone or even a pebble, while the second usage, "on this rock" uses the feminine form *petra* which mean a ledge of rock. If that difference is applicable, the first one gives Simon the title of being a stone in the building while the second would have to refer to the event which had just occurred, that is to the faith

which Peter voiced in the confession. Faith, *pistis,* is a feminine word. That would in effect say, "Peter, you are a stone in the building of the church but the foundation of the building itself is the faith commitment which you have just made." Some have tried to refute this argument by saying that Jesus spoke Aramaic and the word *kepha* (translated Cephas) would serve both the masculine and feminine forms, but he may also have spoken in Greek.

One might almost hazard a guess that if the development of the church structure which claimed Peter as Pope had never arisen, the passage might not have been so difficult. Later in the New Testament the church is said to be built on the foundation of the prophets and apostles. (Ephesians 2:20) However, the entire statement is a figurative way of speaking for the church is not a literal building and for some to say that it is absurd to think that Jesus said, "You are Peter and I, the builder, will build the church on myself" is to forget that figurative idea. An absolutely certain interpretation of this passage is probably not possible, but each reader will need to choose from these possibilities and perhaps some others.

The following statement gave to Peter, and later in Matthew 18 to all the disciples, the keys of the kingdom. That must represent, again in figurative language, the conditions of entrance into the kingdom. Those conditions must be personal faith commitment to Jesus as Christ and Lord. Moreover, the translation, "What you shall bind on earth shall be bound in heaven" is probably not correct. What it literally says is, "I will give (future tense) to you the keys of the kingdom of heaven and whatever you shall bind on the earth shall be as already having been bound (future passive) in heaven and whatever you loose on earth shall be as already having been loosed (future passive) The issue is: Where is the initiative, on earth or in heaven? The position taken here is that whenever the church speaks consistently with what is God's Intentional Will, it agrees with that will and whatever the issue is, it is bound or loosed (rabbinic figures meaning permitted or prohibited). However one interprets that statement, the same authority was given to all of the apostles as well as to Simon. (Matthew 18:18) That St. Paul certainly never saw Simon Peter or any other single person as the ruling authority over the church is obvious in the book of Galatians. (2:11)

It must have been a calculated risk on the part of Jesus, for just after the high experience of the confession he "sternly commanded" them not to tell anyone about him. (Matthew states not to tell anyone that he was the Messiah.) One must emphasize that at this point, for the very first time, Jesus positively linked his concept of Messiahship with that of a suffering servant. So from this point on he introduced them plainly to the what would have been a radical idea that he would have to suffer and be killed at the hands of the religious leaders of the Jews. But he also told them that even though he would die, after three days, or on the third day, he would be raised. Imagine what a shocking idea that would have been. All hopes had been on him as the deliverer and more than likely most of the people, including the disciples, believed that the conquering moment was not far off. And at this point he stated that it was all about to end in his death. In retrospect, it is easy to find elements in the Old Testament, particularly in Isaiah, which indicate that the Messiah would be a suffering servant, but it would take some time for those early apostles to make that connection.

So it is not at all surprising that Simon Peter felt that it was necessary to take Jesus aside and rebuke him. It is difficult for present day disciples to conceive of Peter or anyone else rebuking Jesus, but one must remember that the Christology which makes Jesus the divine Son of God developed in their minds after the event of the resurrection (which was also beyond their imagination). Apparently, Simon's concept of what the Messiah would be and do was quite different from what Jesus had just said. We do not have the words of Peter's rebuke, and no one knows exactly what his concepts were, but he must have said something like, "You don't know what you are talking about. Everybody knows that the Messiah is to be a conquering hero sent from God. We have just expressed our confidence in you that you are the Christ (Messiah) and now you say you must die? That can't happen to you. That is absurd!"

Whatever words Peter may have used, Jesus, who had just commended him for his profession of faith that Jesus was the Messiah and even indicated that such confession had been revealed from God, now identifies him with satanic purposes. It is not necessary to think that Jesus actually called Peter "Satan." It appears more likely that he saw in Peter's attitude the same old temptations to avoid the Suffering

Servant approach to the Messianic task coming forth again, just as they had in the early temptation experience, and that was satanic!

Whatever the actual situation might have been, Jesus saw their lack of ability to accept the idea of suffering as a stumbling block to his future ministry and in the light of this shocking revelation it was necessary that they begin to try to see things God's way rather than from the human way. Both Mark and Luke imply some little time between the Caesarea experience and the fresh statement of the terms of discipleship by indicating that the crowd was also involved in that challenge. Matthew seems to limit this one to the disciples and while it is certain that Jesus did address the same challenge to the people as a whole, perhaps it makes sense that he would have first pressed his closest followers to understand the call. That very next challenge to the disciples, needs some careful examination. Jesus never offered an easy challenge. He always showed those who were interested that responding to him meant a radical challenge and change. In this case he stated three parts of the offer. One who comes to him must denounce the right to rule his own life. That is the meaning of "deny themselves." (It has nothing to do with denying ones-self things.) To deny self reaches back to the story of the first problem recorded for the human family. However one interprets the story in Genesis, as a literal event or as a parabolic statement, the significance of it must be that, while the original fellowship was beautiful and satisfying, the disobedience of the Adam and Eve characters (male-kind and female kind) denied God the right to be God in their lives and because of the assertion that they would run their own lives as they pleased, the beautiful fellowship was broken, destroyed by their choice. That reveals several things:

a) Human-kind refused to trust God. Listen to the challenge once again, "Did God say?" That implies that God either did not know or for some other hidden reason was not stating the whole truth.

b) Most likely it implies that those early beings, and everyone else who has followed, refused to follow God's Intentional Will to become all that they could be. Now Jesus restated the claim. In order for one to follow Jesus, then and now, one must renounce the right to rule his/her own life and actually make Jesus ones Lord!  The second phase of that challenge talks of taking up ones cross.  It has already been stated, but must be reaffirmed here, that taking up ones cross does not mean bearing a burden.  In the first century the term "cross" meant death, not just hardship.  It may be true that some who follow may have to bear hardship, but first he/she must die to self control over his/her life.  St. Paul stated it in the most graphic way, " I have been crucified with Christ." (Galatians 2:20)  That is a figure of speech, but it means that my personal god-ship over life must be destroyed if I am to be a follower.  Otherwise He cannot be Lord!.  The last part requires that one should continue following.  It never has been the old idea, "I got salvation and now I can go my way."  Clinging selfishly to ones life destroys the potential of that life and whatever one gains by that is meaningless in the ultimate sense of value.

Then all three of the Synoptics give another of the 'tough to understand sayings' of Jesus.  It should not surprise anyone that the disciples thought Jesus was talking about some kind of immediate climactic event.  What could the verse, "I tell you, there are some standing here who will not taste death before they see the Son of Man coming in his kingdom," possibly mean? (Matthew 16:28)  Be reminded that some contemporary interpreters who believe that Jesus expected such a literal event in the immediate or near future certainly have grounds for their position.  But that is only correct if the kingdom is totally future!  If the kingdom was a present reality as well as something to be consummated in the future, there may be another meaning.  Perhaps it refers to something like the coming of the Holy Spirit at Pentecost, most of them were still alive and witnessed that.

## THE TRANSFIGURATION  pp. 101-102

After two such a jarring experiences, the rebuke to Peter and the hard demanding statement about following him, there was a definite need for some reassurance and the Transfiguration vision provided that.  Only the three (Peter, James, and John) were witnesses to that event.  That it was a vision is supported by Matthew (17:6) and there is no need to think of an actual physical experience of a reappearance of Elijah and Moses. (Who could have recognized them anyway- there were no paintings or photographs?) Moses had been the one who received the Law he had long been used to represent the Law and Elijah held the revered place of being representative of the Prophets. The Law and the Prophets were the two divisions of the Hebrew scriptures at that time. (As has already been stated, the Writings did not become canonized until about 90 C.E.) It would appear that as this vision unfolds what Jesus was teaching Peter, James, and John was that the accepted Hebrew Scriptures agreed with the identification of the Messiah with the Suffering Servant concept. Luke gave some of the content of the experience as Jesus conversed with Moses, the Law, and Elijah, the Prophets, about his "departure" obviously, meaning his death, which he was about to accomplish at Jerusalem. (9:31) The narrative indicates that the three disciples had a hard time staying awake, but they saw the close of this vision. This is a mysterious event, and it has some of the same elements in it as the Baptism narrative. (The saying, "This is my Son, my Beloved; with him I am well pleased; listen to him!") We need to re-emphasize that the necessity for and the content of this experience was to document the idea that the Old Testament scriptures (Law and Prophets) supported the Suffering Servant concept. (Mark 9:12) It is a little strange again that Jesus asked them not to talk about this vision until after his resurrection, even to the other apostles. There was a prevalent idea that Elijah would return, literally, before the coming of the Messiah, and Jesus took this opportunity to identify John the Baptist's work with that idea.

## THE HEALING OF THE EPILEPTIC BOY pp.103-104

Mark again gives a much longer account than either Matthew or Luke. That indicates once again that Matthew and Luke both used Mark and edited his work according to their needs. Normally when a work is an expansion, the narrative of the event might be longer, but in this case the story shows evidence of reduction in the works (Matthew and Luke) that are themselves longer. The progress of the narrative indicates that this event began while Jesus and the three were gone and when they returned the crowd immediately besieged him. One man, brought his son to Jesus and pled for healing. His plea for help was preceded by the statement, "If you are able." That again, like in the temptation narratives, is a first class conditional sentence and it is stated in such a way as to mean something like, "If you are able, and for my plea I accept that you are." Jesus does not allow that statement to even slow him down, but indicates that to one who believes there are no limits to what can be done. In the narrative the problem is attributed to demon possession, but in modern terms, even from the story itself, it is plain that the boy was an epileptic. The description of what happened to the child is exactly what many of us have seen, if we have witnessed and epileptic seizure. The first time I witnessed a seizure occurred during ROTC training while I was in high school. I had no clue that one of my fellow students had epilepsy, but one morning he said he felt funny and he was allowed to go over and sit on a wall which surrounded the football field. The upper side of the wall was about a foot and a half high, but the on the lower side it was nearly ten feet. As he sat there, suddenly he fell over, fortunately on the foot and a half side, and began to squirm around and to foam at the mouth. Someone placed something in his mouth to keep him from chewing his tongue, but since I had never witnesses a seizure, I thought that he was dying and it was a harrowing experience.

It is not difficult to understand the constant stress that this parent had when he stated that the seizures came on the boy at unexpected times and he was in personal danger because of them, and particularly since the only explanation for what was happening was that an invisible demon had seized the boy. Much had occurred since the disciples had been sent out with directions to cast out demons and heal all manner of diseases. That journey must have been a successful one for Luke tells us that they "returned with joy, saying, 'Lord, in your name even the demons submit to us.'." (10:17) Yet, for some reason now they could not help this man and his son. One cannot help but wonder if they became a bit arrogant and had forgotten that whatever power they had came from the Master. Whatever may have been the problem, after the boy had been healed, the puzzled disciples asked why they were not able to cast the demon out. Jesus rebuked them and said it was because of their lack of faith. Probably using a figure of speech again, ""If you have faith the size of the mustard seed, you will say to this mountain, 'move from here to there,' and it will move; and nothing will be impossible for you," (Matthew 17:20) Jesus tried to teach them that great and marvelous things, which may have been beyond their imagination, could be done if they had faith and that those things were only possible through prayer. In Luke the illustration of what could be done had to do with a mulberry tree being transplanted into the sea, but it served the same purpose. Some of the late manuscripts (Textus *Receptus)* add "fasting" to the concept of prayer being the necessary element in casting out the demon, but that clearly has little manuscript support.

The gospels all agree that Jesus, at least for a second time, tried to get the disciples to understand his coming death, but they could not comprehend it. Not only did they not understand, but they were distressed so much that they did not dare ask him to explain what he meant. Perhaps they remembered the sharp rebuke Peter received when that idea was first presented to them. Modern students can scarcely appreciate the difficulty that these early disciples faced in accepting the idea of the Suffering Servant. Everyone knew that the Messiah would be a conquering hero! Old established concepts are nearly always hard to dislodge. Remember that everyone, probably including some of his crew, thought that Columbus was an idiot who was about to fall off the edge of the earth into oblivion. Many, including the leaders of the church, who had always accepted the Ptolemaic theory that the earth was the center of our solar system, denounced Copernicus for daring to say that the sun was the center. When dealing with that proposition by Copernicus, even Martin Luther rebutted it by saying, "Any fool knows that Joshua commanded the sun to stand still." As late as the middle of the last century, many believed that Werner von Braun was out of his mind when he suggested that if we could shoot a missile into the sky at a fast enough speed, it would orbit the earth and not fall back. To the disciples and the people of the first century, Jesus' statement was ridiculous and untenable! There is an often overlooked term in the account in Matthew 17:23 which may subtly imply that some of the disciples were so puzzled that the band may have been fragmented. The term *sustrephomenon* at least indicates that it was necessary for them to reassemble in Galilee, whatever may have been the cause for their separation. It is difficult to state the struggle that these men were going through with this "new" approach of Jesus, but if the context is correct he continued to show them the oncoming conflict by suggesting that he would be delivered (betrayed) into human hands and then be killed!

## THE TEMPLE TAX p. 105

Every Jewish male above twelve years of age was expected to pay the tax to support the Temple. This was not a Roman tax collected by the publicans! The half shekel tax was like a voluntary church-rate; no one could be compelled to pay it. (Plummer, 244) The inquiry implies that those who were collecting the tax knew that Jesus did not always conform to Jewish practices. Peter's answer to them was, "Certainly." Some have suggested that Jesus' instruction to Peter was to go catch a fish and sell it to pay the tax, while others follow the narrative literally. The purpose of the little two line parable must have been to teach that the children of the kingdom are free from the responsibility of the Temple Tax, but he acquiesced just so that unnecessary offense might not be raised.

## GREATNESS, SERVICE, AND RESPONSIBILITY IN THE KINGDOM pp. 106-108

The disciples were not able to rid themselves of the thought of a physical kingdom and the important positions that such a kingdom would have. There was some dissention among the disciples as they walked along the way about who would be the greatest. Jesus was aware of their selfish ambitions and took their argument as an opportunity to teach a fundamental principle of the kingdom. Everything is inverted! The great ones in the kingdom are those who forget about greatness and become servants. The issue of becoming like little children taught that humility is fundamental to being a kingdom servant. Again, the issue goes to attitude, and all worldly ways of measuring greatness do not apply. That battle in the lives of followers of Jesus has never been easy to deal with. The church always looks to the leaders as the important ones and those who receive the most publicity are considered great. The point is not whether one leads the largest congregation, or preaches the most persuasive sermons. The issue is, what kind of servant has one been. An unheard of backwoods mountain preacher in a small community may have been a great servant even though he has gained no publicity. Human estimates are hard to avoid, but Jesus clearly stated, "the least among all of you is the greatest." (Luke 9:48) In effect Jesus had said that one should forget about greatness and focus on service to all. That was hard for the early disciples and it is still hard for modern followers.

We should not despair when we cannot get people to see great issues, for apparently Jesus did not succeed in getting this idea about greatness across; the same conflict crops up later, if we trust the contexts.

Can there be those who do not conform to expectations and do not follow the accepted group who are genuine followers? Jesus forbade the disciples to discriminate against some who "cast out demons" in his name just because they did not join the group. Genuine service in the name (or in the spirit) of Christ, even the smallest kind, is not without value and should not be forbidden.

The vivid illustration of having a large millstone tied around ones neck and being cast into the sea, indicated how important it was, and is, that one not become a cause of stumbling. So much gets lost as cultures change and the millstones concept is one of those. They were of various sizes, even as they were a century ago in the United States. They would have weighed several hundred pounds and would have sunk immediately and drawn anyone under who had one tied about the neck. Of course, throwing the stone into the sea would have been an Olympic size feat, but this was another of the great exaggerations that Jesus used to make the lasting impression. The Master knew that occasions for stumbling would come among his followers, differences of interpretation and understanding are inevitable, but each one must understand the heavy responsibility of his/her influence. The graphic figure must not deter one from exercising his/her talents, but Jesus' teaching is permeated with figures, such as cutting off ones hand/foot or gouging out ones eye, which indicate the severe and awesome responsibility followers have.

## THE LOST SHEEP  pp. 109

There are a number of parables which teach that God loves and cares, but probably the most familiar is that of the lost sheep. Picture the first century method of tending sheep. After a long day of leading the flock of sheep through dangers to pastures and to the streams of water, the shepherd must have been tired. So he brought his sheep home to a common sheepfold or corral. As his custom probably was, he counted the sheep as they entered the gate and discovered that one was missing. That meant that either the one lost was just written off or that the shepherd must re-trace the day's steps and try to find the lost one.

Any good shepherd would want to find his sheep rather than to leave it where wild animals might attack it and kill it. So, weary though he might have been, he went out. When he found the sheep, he threw it over his shoulder and with a new spring in his step, he returned to the sheepfold, rejoicing for all to hear. The statement, "He rejoices more over it than the ninety and nine that never went astray," does not mean that the shepherd did not care for the sheep that were safe, but that because of the recovery, he was extremely happy. That parable teaches that the return of one "that is lost" is an occasion for great joy. Luke's implication that there are those who need no repentance should not be taken in a literal way. It simply emphasizes the great joy over one who is rescued.

## ON REPROVING A BELIEVER pp. 109-110

Since the church was a relatively new concept, no church discipline had been developed. Jesus, at some point, helped the disciples to know how to deal with an erring member. This may not be an instruction on church discipline as such but may deal with one who injures another. It is a simple three stage process, which makes sense, but it may be very difficult to apply. The object is to maintain the fellowship; to produce a restoration of that fellowship. When one sins against another, the first step is to try to deal with it between the two, alone. Sometimes that would be all that was needed and if done without condemnation, it may produce an apology, a solution, and forgiveness. However, for various reasons that would not always have been successful, and so the issue needs to be dealt with in the presence of witnesses. That would mean that the erring member would have the situation carefully explained to him/her and the two or three witnesses could corroborate the entire discussion. If it worked, good! As a last resort, the grievance and the offender needs to be brought before the church. If the offender still will not listen to the corporate judgment, Jesus said that he should be as an outsider. It is interesting that this is a Matthew passage and, as a tax-collector himself, he points out that an obstinate person is estranged from the warm fellowship of a church and is as an outsider, and as an ostracized tax collector. Assuming that the authorship has something to do with Matthew. he would have certainly understood how that felt.

That did not specifically say, exclude them, but it may suggest that the guilty one has excluded himself/herself.

Church discipline has always been a problem, but most of the time churches have not followed the directions Jesus gave. Years ago I was the pastor of a rather strong church located in a community about ten miles out of Jackson, Tennessee. I had been in the community for about five years when a man that I did not know died. His wife had been a very faithful member, so I knew her. While I was talking with some of the people someone said that the man was probably one of the better Christians in the community. I indicated that I was surprised at that, since he had never darkened the doors of the church and even when I went to the home to visit, I never saw him. Then I got a startling story and to make certain of the facts I had the church clerk to go to the bank vault and get the old church records.

The story turned out this way: At some point more than fifty years before the death of this good man, there was a party for young people in one of the homes of a church member. During that party, which was heavily chaperoned, the young people played a game that I had never heard of and no one that I know has ever known of it either. It was called "picking up potatoes" and I gather it was some sort of square-dance game. At any rate, the next Sunday one of the men of the church stood and made a motion that all of the young people who had been involved should be excluded. During the discussion, all of the girls who were involved came forward and whether they felt they had done anything wrong or not, they all promised not to do it again and begged not to be taken off the church roll. All of the boys, perhaps a little more stubborn, said that they knew they had not done anything wrong and they refused to "repent". As a result, all of the boys were excluded. When I read that narrative and I also discovered that the man who made the motion that Sunday morning had also been involved in making the same motion about several other people. I also found that after the recent death which led me into this discovery, there was only one of those men now left alive. I had met him and his faithful family, but had never been able to get him to come to church. I had assumed it was because of his physical problems but now I knew why.

I began to talk with some of the people and asked if they thought the church could ever make a mistake and if so, what should be done about it. Unanimously, they agreed that the church did make a mistake and that we should try to correct it, if possible. I was given the privilege, although at the time I thought it was a dirty job, of going to that one man and telling him that we believed the church had erred and the church would like to ask him to allow his name to be restored. The old man was in a wheel chair as the result of a stroke and was paralyzed on one side. When I told him what the church wanted, I have never seen such joy. He reached out and pulled me over, bumped my head hard against his and wept like a baby. It was one of the most joyful times of my life. But I was saddened that so many others had died without that joyful restoration. I know that it did not make any difference in their salvation, but it made a drastic difference in earthly fellowship. I have wondered many times, as I have read church history and other stories of ex-communication, just how many times has eagerness to apply the last part of Jesus' teaching in this passage resulted in personal tragedy without even trying to use the first two.

At this point, Jesus gave the same promise to the entire group that had been given to the disciples earlier (Matthew 16:19), about whatever they bind on earth shall be as having been bound in heaven. One needs to continue to be aware that the initiative is with God and not on earth. Contradictions in church positions throughout history should prove that not everything the church has opted for has been harmonious with God. The entire passage concludes with an emphasis on meeting and praying in Jesus' name. That phrase must mean, just as the promise about praying in other passages, that what a group or an individual does or asks for in exactly the same spirit and attitude that Jesus had, will be accomplished, for it will be the will of God. It does not mean that anything one asks for in prayer will be granted.

## ON FORGIVENESS p. 110

Matthew continued the restoration theme by telling of Simon Peter's question, "If another member of the church sins against me, how often should I forgive? As many as seven times?" It must be noted that Peter had gone beyond the usual Jewish tradition which suggested three times, and which used Amos 1:3,6,9 and Job 33:29 to justify that idea.

> *The Talmud of Babylon says, "When a man sins against another, they forgive him once, they forgive him a second time, they forgive him a third time, but the fourth time they do not forgive him."* (Broadus, 390)

That raises a hard question! Can there be genuine forgiveness if one counts the times and continues to hold the grudge? The injured man who endeavors to reclaim his injurer must, of course, have forgiven him in his heart: otherwise it would be hopeless to seek reconciliation. He does not, for his own sake, seek reparation, but for the wrong doer's sake, to win him back from evil. To the impetuous Peter that seems to be a difficult saying, and he desires an explanation. Surely there are limits to this kind of forbearance. Is one to go on forgiving forever? Will not seven times be a generous allowance?

> *The man who asks such a question does not really know what forgiveness means. When an injury is forgiven, it is absolutely cancelled so far as the injured person is concerned. It is not to be kept in abeyance, to be reckoned against the offender, if he offends again. Christ's reply is to the effect that there must be no counting at all. Ten times the limit suggested by Peter will be far too little. Multiply that again by seven and it still will not be too much. The meaning is that there should be no limit.* (Plummer, 255)

One must always be aware that forgiveness and forgetting are not the same. Often people remember what they wish to forget and they forget what they would desire to remember. Forgiveness means that one treats the issue as if it no longer matters.

Matthew, masterfully, then placed another parable in the context to drive home the point of forgiveness. In that parable Jesus told of a servant who was threatened with being sold along with his family, and all of his possessions to satisfy a monster debt. The servant pled for compassion, saying if given time he would repay the debt. He owed ten thousand talents! A talent was worth about $1,000 before inflation of recent times and would be worth much more currently. That means he owed somewhere in the neighborhood of $10,000,000! That is impossible and must represent another of Jesus' great hyperboles to drive home the point of his hopelessness. If one takes the average days wage as 20 cents, it is easy to see that paying this debt would require about 500,000 years, assuming nothing was used for living expenses. Various estimates have been offered by numerous scholars, but all of them reach a preposterous figure that indicates the impossibility of the debt. How could one even get that deeply in debt?

Because the master of that slave had compassion, he wiped out the entire debt. How grateful and relieved that slave should have been because that burden was lifted? But in Jesus' story that servant went out and found a fellow servant who owed him one hundred days wages. That was a payable debt, but the "wicked" servant decided to put the man in jail until he paid his debt. The other slaves tattle to the master about the wicked servant - who would blame them? And then the master called that slave back and he discovered that his humongous debt had been re-instated. The teaching of the parable is that when one receives forgiveness and understands its fantastic value, he becomes a forgiving person. Anything short of that implies that the complex completeness of forgiveness has not occurred, for forgiveness offered must also become forgiveness received and that is what changes the character of the one forgiven. Simon Peter had just received the fantastic lesson about limitless forgiveness and the implication was, and is, that if ones character has not changed because of that forgiveness offer, he has not received it. Sometimes people say that they can't forgive when what they mean is they won't forgive. Maybe they are confusing forgiveness with forgetting. A shocking lesson, but vital!

# CHAPTER XV
## LUKE'S SPECIAL MATERIAL

**THE SEVENTY SENT OUT: pp. 112-113**

Luke gives the story of another mission in which seventy are sent out. The instructions are almost identical with those which were given to the twelve and the results are much the same. The messengers are to be dependent on the hospitality of those they serve with no extra provisions. They are to proclaim, again with the verb in the Perfect Tense signifying completed action, that the kingdom has already come to them. The same warnings were given to those people and towns where the messengers were not welcomed, as in the earlier report. It is clear that they are His messengers and rejection of them is rejection of Jesus.

When they returned they came with the same joy that the first group had shared, for they had been victorious over demons. Jesus then offers a perplexing statement: "I watched Satan fall as a flash of lightening falls from heaven." That either refers to a passage in Isaiah 14:12 or it was a simple recognition that in the ministry of Jesus the end of powers of evil had come. In the Isaiah passage the reference is to Canaanite religious understanding that the Morning Star tried to ascend the heights of heaven only to fall defeated. Since it is apparent that the people believed that the world was under the control of evil, in either interpretation, Jesus indicated that the coming of the kingdom ended the satanic control. One may question whether he was correct or not, for even though nearly two thousand years have passed and there is still evil around. Yet faith demands that the followers of Jesus understand that it has ultimately been defeated.

Snakes and scorpions were considered to be half demonic so the idea that one could tread on them with immunity must deal with the notion that in the mission just completed there was evidence that spiritually nothing could touch them. It cannot mean that there would be no physical difficulties for many of these were persecuted and even slain. One cannot help but wonder if this statement may not have been another possible contributor for the spurious passage in Mark. (16:9-20) The entire passage dealt with the idea that although the evil spirits were under control, the important thing was that his followers shared in the eternal blessing. He used the figure, "Your names are written in heaven."

## WHO IS MY NEIGHBOR? pp. 115-116

According to Luke, a lawyer came purposely to test Jesus. This event is used much later on in the narrative by Matthew and Mark, but it is either a scribe or the Pharisees who are involved. Luke has preserved for us another of the confrontations which led to a unique parable. The lawyer asked what he must do to inherit eternal life. He was used to a religion of works rather than one of becoming. He knew what was written in the law - it was absolute total love for God which spilled over into dealing with ones neighbor. Jesus stated that if the man followed this he would share in eternal life. And that brought up definitions! If one can restrict the definition of neighbor narrowly enough, he can avoid many of those demanding confrontations. So Jesus told a story. It may have been a fictitious story, but it was set in a realistic situation. The road from Jerusalem to Jericho was dangerous and thieves often set upon travelers, and for that reason travelers most of the time moved in caravans. This traveler was assaulted, robbed of everything, and left for dead (Jesus said half dead).

Then two men, a priest and a Levite, who were a part of the religious establishment passed by. Even if, in interpretation, they are given the best possible treatment, suggesting that they were going to Jerusalem to serve in the Temple and did not want to become religiously defiled, their actions do not change the fact that they did not stop to care. Luke then indicated that a despised Samaritan came by and became the hero. He not only bound up the man's wounds but took him to the nearest inn and paid an amount equivalent to two days' wages to the inn keeper. Readers may be thinking that is not much for a days wage was only twenty cents, but translate that into the current economy and even taking the minimum hourly wage and multiplying it by eight and then doubling it, the man must have left $100 to $150 for that care. The lawyer himself must now answer, "Which man was neighbor?" Obviously the Samaritan was the only one who showed a caring spirit, perhaps even paying no attention to his own safety. Caring is a God-like quality and anyone who really cares exhibits a character quality that is God-like.

I cannot help but recall that one Sunday evening my family and I were returning from our church to our home in Louisville, Kentucky. I had just that morning preached a sermon about this Good Samaritan. Suddenly, we came upon a man, standing on the side of the road with a hand to his head, bleeding and trying to get someone to stop. To be honest, my first reaction was to pass him by because of the safety of my family. Then the parable "exploded" in my head and I stopped. We got five or six people in our new car, which the bank really owned, and took them and this bleeding man to the hospital. The next morning I found the man's blood all over the door of my car, and in the days of cloth upholstery, the stain would never come out. It was a constant reminder to me of how close I came to piously hearing the story the Master told, but not hearing its message.

## ARE TEMPORAL CONCERNS PRIMARY? p. 116

Any wife who has awaited anxiously the first visit from her new mother-in-law can appreciate the problem in the Mary-Martha tension. (No visit like this should be like a military inspection.) There is no reason to assume that these two sisters are any other than the sisters of Lazarus, although he is not mentioned here. Martha was frustrated because she was concerned about the external, mundane things, and in that frustration and tension she lost sight of what was important and blamed her sister for being unconcerned. Jesus attempted to get Martha to see that the visit was not for a sumptuous meal. She had missed the point of the visit and Mary had seized the opportunity to hear Jesus! All that was needed was a little sustenance. Any country minister of the last generation could testify to the abundance of food when he had been invited to the home of an excellent but perhaps overzealous cook. It is not clear exactly what Jesus was saying ("there is need of only one thing"), but it would appear that he was showing Martha that only one dish was necessary for sustenance.

## THE TEACHING ON PRAYER: pp. 116-117

Luke placed the instruction about prayer as a response to the disciples wanting to learn as John had taught his disciples. The Model Prayer served as the springboard for that instruction and the material Luke used primarily taught two things: The need for persistence and the fact that God is interested in what is needed and best for his children It would be an error to take the story of the friend who was inconvenienced and did not want to get up and help his friend as a teaching that if one pesters God long enough he will give what is wanted. That obviously is a part of the story, but that is not the purpose for which the parable was told. To be sure, the man is described as already having made all the preparations for the night; the children are in bed with him, probably all sleeping in the same area and more than likely on pallets on the floor. Perhaps one can even imagine that a small, crying child has just gotten to sleep and then there comes the loud rapping at the door. No wonder there is consternation! But because of the persistence, the man finally responds to the need of his neighbor. Luke coupled that parable of persistence with the statement that one needs to keep on asking; keep on searching; and keep on knocking. (Each of those verbs is in the Present Tense and in the Greek language it means continuous and linear action.) He also used that opportunity to show that often what humans want is not what they need. The parallel between God and human parents pointedly shows that human parents want to provide for their children, even though they sometimes do not know what is best. If that is true about earthly parents in their weakness, how much more must it be true concerning God? Nearly all kingdom citizens have had the experience of wanting something, even praying for it, and as they later look back on the experience they know it was not best or needed.

The attitude of praying in the same spirit and for the same purposes as Jesus did (literally "in His name") has not always been present. Shortly after I had returned from service in World War II I was called to be the minister of a small half-time church. The church had services only on the first and third Sundays of the month. It had been a rather successful though short tenure when an opportunity came to go to another church which had services on the second and fourth Sundays. I thought what a blessing from God and as I prayed about the coming event I felt most certain that this was under God's direction. The day came and the visit to the church went extremely well and I was almost certain that I would receive a "call" from that church. But I didn't! They did not call me! I wondered about my misinterpretation or misunderstanding and was a little perturbed about it. Then almost our of the blue, the deacons of the little church we had been serving began to talk about going to a full time schedule, and we made that change. It was successful beyond all my hopes and I became convinced that in His own mysterious way, God knew what He was doing. That inevitably brings up the issue of God's will! One of the better works on the will of God, and one which is easy to understand is that done by Leslie Weatherhead. Weatherhead discussed the Will of God under three sub-divisions. He suggested that one needs first to see the Intentional Will of God. That has to do with what God wished from the very beginning and it would have been that which was perfect. But when He created persons who had freedom of choice and the subsequent responsibility, it became evident that the Intentional Will would not be followed. That reached back into the Genesis narrative of the Fall. The consequence of that in all the history of humanity is that mankind is found in the condition of finding what Weatherhead called the Circumstantial Will of God. God is not desirous that men should sin; he is not desirous that they should have trouble, he does not desire that they should be ill or suffer calamity; he is certainly not in the position of wanting them to wage war and inflict punishing suffering on each other, or to ultimately perish, but those things have been and are a reality! Is there anything that a completely good God could possibly will under those circumstances?

*We may make the matter (of the circumstantial will of God) clearer by restating an earlier illustration and thinking of a father planning his boy's career, in co-operation with the boy himself. The will of both may have been, let us say, that the boy should become an architect. Then comes the war. The father is quite willing for his son to be in the armed forces; but a Navy, Army, or Air Force career is only the father's interim or circumstantial will for his boy, his will in the circumstances of evil which the war has produced. It would only be confusing to speak as if the father's ideal intention and original plan for his son was that the latter should spend valuable years of his life in the armed forces.*

*Now in the same way there is an intentional purpose of God for every man's life; but because of human folly and sin, because man's free will creates circumstances of evil that cut across God's plans, because our oneness with the great human family means that the evil among other members of it may create circumstances which disturb God's intention for us, there is a will within the will of God, or what I call "the circumstantial will of God." (The Will of God,* [Nashville: Abingdon Press, 1944] 21,22)

The last phase of Weatherhead's analysis dealt with what he called the Ultimate Will of God, and it indicated that when all of history is over, everyone and everything will be involved in doing exactly what God wills at all times. That will mean that the course of the Circumstantial Will has been run and all of those circumstances which short circuit what God wishes will be over. Perhaps the Ultimate Will is identical with heaven.

It should be evident that it is not always easy in this life to find the will of God, but one of the primary beliefs of the Christian faith is that God leads those who attempt to follow Him through the Holy Spirit, one step at a time. Often, in genuine humility, searchers must make the best choices possible, trying as hard as possible to eliminate the ever present problem of self will. With confidence that most of the time the will of God can be found, one needs to look back after a period of time and then it will probably be clear when the will of God has been followed and when it has been missed. Many things that are claimed by the church and by both ministers and lay people as being the will of God, clearly are not, but one thing concerning the will of God should be evident - whatever that will is, it will always be consistent with the character of God as revealed in the Incarnate Christ.

Again, it must be emphasized that God created mankind with freedom to choose to fellowship with him or to reject that opportunity. The concept of worship would be an impossibility if response to God should be coerced. It is only through free individual choice that genuine worship can occur and that necessitates the opportunity for man to reject God's offer. But a humanity which wishes to follow God must understand that praying "in the name of Jesus" means to pray just as he did and want the sovereignty of God to rule in ones life, even as it did in his. That may, at times, not follow what men want, but as Jesus put it, "not my will but Thine be done"- that is what is important.

## AGAINST PHARISAIC LEGALISM: pp. 120-124

Both Luke and Matthew indicate that at some point Jesus must have reached a point of no return. His stern denunciation of the practices of the Pharisees became even more pronounced toward the close of his ministry. Matthew places this series of "woes" in chapter twenty-three, which is very near the end of Jesus' life. It is not possible to determine exactly where it belongs, but it certainly escalates the inevitable conflict. In Luke's account, there are seven criticisms of Pharisaic behavior. 1) Jesus saw the ceremonial washing of the hands as an externalism which never touched the inward evil. He compared that action to washing the outside of cups and dishes, but leaving the inside filled with old dried, crusty food, and that even though they obeyed the ceremonial regulations, those only had to do with externals and inwardly they were filled with greed and wickedness. From the beginning of recorded history, selfishness and greed have dominated even the best of humanity. Every economy thrives on greed and most often abuses against the human family are fed by that problem - it was and is not just a Pharisee problem. 2) Ritualistic and rigorous tithing had become one of the main items of the religion. It is correct that the Old Testament principle of offering back to God one tenth of ones gain is a part of the command. Jesus did not speak negatively about that, but he did argue that other things, which should have been much more significant, had been neglected, and that was evil! 3) Positions of importance and prestige have always been a subtle temptation, perhaps as much in religious circles as with any other phase of society. On several occasions Jesus pointed out that danger (in the discussion about greatness), even among his disciples. It seems to be a part of human nature to want recognition and importance, but uncontrolled desire for publicity destroys *koinonia*. 4) His awareness of these evils caused him to point out with a rather nasty figure the inward corruption and the outward show of respectability. They were compared with graves, which may be made to look very nice, but everyone knows that inside the tombs there is only decay. How many objections were raised, we cannot know, but at least one of the lawyers indicated that he saw Jesus' statements as a harsh insult. 5) Teachers of the law always face the difficulty of imposing weight and burdens on the people. Jesus was concerned that multiplying legal demands had done nothing to help the common man. 6) All through this section there is the hint of hypocrisy, but at this point it became more than a hint. There is a grave contradiction in honoring the prophets of old by building monuments, but approving the actions of ones ancestors who rejected and killed those same prophets. 7) Jesus was convinced that the first century religious leaders had actually hindered the common people from understanding God's purposes by "taking away the key of knowledge." It is hardly surprising that there was hostility in the minds of the leaders and they began to try to trap him. Jesus was convinced that ultimately no hypocrisies could remain hidden! He also saw that being consumed by fear regarding the future accusations was unnecessary. He probably did not mean that one should never prepare a defense, but rather that one should not be consumed by those fears. The idea that the Holy Spirit will teach you what to say does not prohibit studying and preparing for leading worship.

## THE RICH FOOL: p. 124

Someone wanted Jesus to become an arbiter over the family inheritance. The desire for "stuff" has often destroyed family and other relationships and greed eats away at the very meaning of life. The parable of the rich fool was designed to show that selfish focusing on the false security that comes from material things is ridiculous. In this parable, it is not the fact that the man has wealth that makes him a "fool," but the idea that these things have consumed him and in a sense have become his god. The man had presumed many things such as the idea that he controlled his destiny and that the things he possessed were really his. Much earlier Jesus had said, "man does not live by bread alone" and that principle underlies this parable. The teaching of the parable is that one must recognize that the total stewardship of life involves talents, possessions, and the awareness that all material things are a temporary stewardship.

## WATCHFULNESS AND FAITHFULNESS: pp. 126-127

Luke placed the materials which dealt with watchfulness at this point in the ministry, while Matthew reserved them until later. Here several short parabolic sayings emphasize the importance of preparedness and expectation. The first deals with servants who are on the alert for the return of the master from a wedding banquet. They have no idea when the master will return, but those who are alert and waiting will be ready to serve the master whenever that return may come. The second suggests that one must always be prepared for the thief, since no one can know when the break-in will occur. The third dealt with a faithful manager whose action, although he does not know when the master will return, does not depend on knowing that, but he is he is faithful at all times. The fourth of these dealt with a servant who only served correctly when the master was present and when he was not there all kinds of evil treatment of other slaves went on. The harsh judgment that the servant received occurred because the master returned without warning and "caught" the servant being unfaithful, as he constantly seems to have been. These short sayings demonstrate that one must be prepared at every moment because the time for the coming of the Son of Man, whatever one understands that to mean, is unknown and when that time does come those who have greater ability or talents will find that more has been expected from them. The conclusion of these statements suggests that each person will receive exactly what he/she deserves, and that those who have great opportunities have much expected from them.

(For humans, fair and absolute judgment is always difficult to attain. Through many years of teaching and evaluating students I have often believed that there were some students who had great ability but used only a small part of it, and were still were able to make "A" grades while others who had limited abilities sometimes worked very diligently and were barely able to make average grades. If I were able to evaluate as God can, I believe that often those who received an "A" would get less and those who did the best they could but only received a "C" would probably deserve an "A.")

## ON DEMANDING A CHANGE OF MIND: p. 128

The discussion of the people Pilate had destroyed, mingling their blood with their sacrifices, points out that such calamities did not come about as the result of them being greater sinners, nor do accidents, such as the deaths of those who were working on a tower and it fell on them, show that calamities are the result of punishment for sin. But just having said that, Jesus indicated that unless the people changed their minds they too would perish. That, since it is followed immediately in Luke's ordering of things by a warning parable, seemed to point to Jesus' concern that the Jewish people were not producing any fruit and therefore, unless they changed their minds they would find themselves destroyed. That may have been much more of a warning about the coming rebellion against the Romans (because of the wrong idea about God's Kingdom) than it was in regard to repentance for personal sins. Whatever the application may be, Jesus suggested that ample warning had been given and unless fruit is borne soon, the tree would be removed.

## SABBATH CONTROVERSIES: pp. 128 and 133

There were numerous times when Jesus saw a need on the Sabbath and he responded, regardless of the day. There is a story of a woman who had been crippled for eighteen years, apparently with some arthritic problem or curvature of the spine. (Luke 13:10-17) Jesus immediately healed the woman and the leader of the synagogue criticized him for healing on the Sabbath, saying that the healing should wait until another day. Jesus responded with the illustration that they had no qualms about taking care of the needs of an animal on the Sabbath, but they were not willing for mercy to be shown to a fellow human. The event focused on the characteristic of Jesus' teaching which made compassion a very dominant feature. The illustration silenced the criticism and many in the crowd rejoiced because of the restoration of the woman.

Then there were some Pharisees who warned Jesus concerning Herod, suggesting that Herod was trying to kill him, but Jesus appeared to be unconcerned suggesting that no prophet would be killed outside of Jerusalem. This seems to have indicated that he believed he would die in Jerusalem and it gave an opportunity for a heart-felt lament concerning the city, its rejection of his message, and his desire that repentance should occur.

In much the same kind of conflict, Jesus entered the home of a Pharisee to eat on the Sabbath. There was intense scrutiny as a man appeared in front of him who had dropsy, a disease where accumulation of fluids causes severe swelling. Jesus asked the teachers and Pharisees if it were lawful to heal on the Sabbath. Healings had already occurred on the Sabbath and when he got no response he used the same kind of argument that he had used before, suggesting that if there were an emergency either with a child or an animal they would rescue it. They gave him no reply.

One of the great character traits for which Jesus gave praise was humility. That has always been a difficult trait to acquire and even more to keep it for about the time one thinks a person has attained humility he/she can become so proud of the humility that it is lost. His instructions involving the highest seats at a feast teach that one should not have exalted thoughts about his own importance, but rather should give place to others. He seemed to suggest that if a higher place was deserved, the host would take care of that. Then he instructed the host that people should be invited who could not repay the favor. The implication was that when one traded social favors there was no charity being shown, but when one invited those who could not return the favor, then real service had been performed. Following that piece of advice, Jesus then told a parable which taught that the feast would go on whether there was proper response or not. He believed that the invitation to enter the kingdom was being met with excuses, none of which were valid. Three different excuses were offered for refusing the invitation: a) One man indicated that he had bought a piece of property and had to go inspect it. Certainly, no one would buy a piece of land without going to inspect it first and then decide whether he wanted it or not. This excuse was simply that, it was not a reason. b) The second man had bought oxen without checking whether they were fit or not.

Having already bought them, he was now proposing to go and "try them out." In modern experience that would be like buying a used car and after the settlement making a decision to go see if it would run. It was obviously, a lame excuse. c) The third excuse had to do with a man who had just married. Perhaps his excuse was closer to a reason than the others, but each of them would have been much more honest if they had just said, "We don't want to come." The teaching of this parable was that outsiders, who would have not been offered the first invitation, were now joyfully entering the feast. It is a fairly pointed lesson and probably meant that the religious leaders and maybe the Jewish nation had rejected the invitation of Jesus and therefore the outsiders (the sinners, tax-collectors, and Gentiles) would share in the feast of the kingdom.

## THE COST OF DISCIPLESHIP: pp. 133-134

Jesus never offered easy challenges to those who heard him, whether they were the immediate disciples or just part of the crowd. Some of the demands made in this passage had been made in other situations, but Luke repeated them with special emphasis. Once again, one must examine what Jesus said, in the light of first century culture and social responsibilities, and also sense (by the use of vivid figures of speech) that Jesus would never have literally asked anyone to hate another person, how could he when he so pointedly advocated love? When he said that one must hate his parents, his wife, his offspring, his siblings, and even his own life, he must have been trying to get them to see that if one is to be a follower, all other attachments would appear as hatred by comparison and no attachment can stand between the disciple and the Lordship of the Master. No family filled with hate can produce healthy personalities, especially in its children! I am reminded of a Seminary companion, Leon Chow, whose parents were not at all sympathetic with his interest in Jesus. He had traveled to Hong Kong and talked with missionaries but his parents told him if he did that again then he was no longer their son. He made the choice to accept the Lordship of Christ over his love for his parents. He never talked about regretting that and I was very grateful that I never had to make that kind of choice. The figure of bearing ones cross has already been discussed and must mean that one must die to the principle of running his/her own life as they please and must surrender that life control to the sovereignty of God, not just bear up under some adversity..

No person should ever be invited to the kingdom without being informed about the seriousness and consequences of that call. It may be true that everybody ought to love Jesus, but that is not enough of an explanation about the invitation. Two parabolic illustrations point out how foolish it would be even in daily pursuits for anyone to disregard the cost he/she was facing. Building a house without considering whether one can finance it would be absurd, as has often been seen when economies falter. Years ago in a large southern city, a group had a noble idea of building a hospital, but they had no adequate resources. After they had finished the shell, they ran out of money and the hulk sat empty for a long, long time, testifying to their lack of wisdom. Jesus' second illustration showed how stupid it would be for a king to try to wage a war when the odds were so stacked against him that victory was impossible. No sensible ruler would ever do that! That was not an approval of war, but an illustration about lack of vision! Responding to the kingdom call without understanding that the lordship over ones life must be forfeited is just that absurd. If Jesus literally meant that everyone must surrender all of his/her possessions, the early church never understood that, for they had possessions and, at least among the early disciples in Jerusalem, those possessions were used in a beautiful expression of community stewardship. It would probably be incorrect to propose that Jesus was demanding a "pauper's oath" for every follower, even though some great disciples like St. Francis of Assisi have done that. But if everyone forfeited everything there would be no one left to finance the missions. However, one must never lose sight of the fact that the call to discipleship is a call to total surrender, regardless of what that cost may be.

## THE LOST ARE FOUND: pp. 134-136

Luke placed a trilogy of parables (The Lost Sheep, The Lost Coin, and The Lost Boy) together to demonstrate God's caring nature. The setting of the parables showed that as Jesus dealt with tax collectors and sinners, the Pharisees and scribes grumbled about such concern and the fact that he ate with those people. The primary difference in Jesus' conception of God's nature and that of the Pharisees lay in the fact that

He saw God as a tireless searching being and not someone who marked off the unfortunates, the poor, and those without social standing and ostracized them,  Matthew had used the parables concerning the lost sheep in a different setting earlier, but it taught exactly the same thing. Some have suggested that strict Jews classified shepherds with sinners, but that did not prevent Jesus from using the familiar figure of a caring, concerned shepherd to demonstrate the endless love of God. (Connick, 220)  The shepherd is depicted at the end of the day discovering that one of his flock of one hundred sheep has strayed away.  This sheep was lost through wayward straying and perhaps a bit of carelessness, but the teaching lies in the fact that the shepherd, although tired from the day's work, knew that the lost sheep was helpless and was in great danger, so he re-traced the path he had traveled throughout the day until he found the lost sheep.  The tireless search paid off and when he came home there was great joy among his friends because that which was lost is now found.  The second parable dealt with a woman who possessed ten coins which probably were a part of her head-dress and may have represented her dowry. It was not to be laid aside even in sleep. (Joachim Jeremias, *The Parables of Jesus, revised edition* [New York: Charles Scribner's Sons, 1963] 134)  The coin was probably a drachma and represented a value of about sixteen cents, close to the amount of a day's wage, so the purchasing power would have been fairly significant. One of the coins got lost and frantically she searched the house until she found it.  Some have felt that the loss of the coin might have meant the loss of her claims in the marriage much like a marriage license currently. The same joy was expressed by the woman and her neighbors as that of the shepherd story, and the searching demonstrated the desire of God to search out the lost and outcast.

But one of the most familiar parables is that which is often called the Prodigal Son.  It is easy to see why that name got attached to the parable, but in the light Luke's placement and of the two previous parables a far more likely title would be that of the Lost Boy or the Caring Father. A most intriguing discussion of the possibilities which lay behind and in the story has been done by Helmut Thielicke and he suggested that the story, although there is much about the boy, is really not about the boy at all, but about the father. (*The Waiting Father,* Trans. by John Doberstein, [San Francisco: Harper and Row

Publishers, 1958] 17-39)  An impudent and not very worldly wise boy pled for his portion of the inheritance.  Many psychological things may have underlain his desires.  He may have felt, as youths often do, that he was tired of the "old man" telling him what to do.  Whatever may have been the reasons behind his request and it being granted, the foolishness put the boy  in a position of "wasting his money" and he found himself in such severe need that he was willing to herd pigs, quite an unusual thing for a Jewish boy, and eat from the carob pods that they were fed.  (Carob pods are not to be looked on as "slop", but rather as a good source of nourishment., even if not very elegant)  It took a while for the boy to come to a point of repentance, for he must have "hit bottom" and had to come to a point of knowing that he had no other choice and must "eat crow,"  but finally that time dawned and he went home, hoping that he could find security as one of the hired personnel.  Then the story shifted to the real point of its being told.  The father was waiting!  We are not told what he had been doing, how often he had looked down the dusty road, how much tension and worry had consumed him, but there he stood looking, staring down the road and wondering.  It was no accident that he happened to see the boy "while he was yet a long way off," neither was it an accident that he quickly forgave the wayward son, even before the boy was able to get all of his prepared repentant message out of his mouth.  The entire parable taught that God is waiting, eager to forgive and bring about restoration of fellowship.  Genuine forgiveness is a character trait of God and He offers it with joy.  The same great joy over one who returns is seen in the lesser stories regarding the sheep and the coin.

But having taught that, the story was not over!  The second phase of the parable almost reads like an allegory and who can say that Jesus never used that type of figure?.  Whatever may have been his fears and concerns, the elder brother, who still had his part of the inheritance, was angry and totally negative about the return of his wayward brother.  The older son who stayed at home, may  have been more in a "far country" attitude-wise than the prodigal, and he is the one who stated that his brother had wasted his money on prostitutes.  One wonders what led Jesus to characterize him in that fashion or how he knew that his brother has wasted his money that way, since he was not there.  Or was that what he would have done had he been in the same situation?

The contrast between the loving attitude of the father and the rigid, unforgiving position of the older brother clearly paralleled the contrast between the attitudes of Jesus and that of the Pharisees toward the outcast tax collectors and sinners. The teaching must have been so obvious that the religious leaders were chagrined and repulsed.

## THE UNJUST MANAGER p. 136

There are numerous parables which would give us pause if the parable approved every action of the characters in it. It must be kept in mind that parables are designed to illustrate one primary thought and even if the characters are unscrupulous or immoral, the story still serves to point out its truth. This is not the only parable in which the major person or persons have definite character problems. One could look at the story of the unjust judge, the man who found a hidden treasure and covered it back up so that he could buy the property at a discount price and this unjust steward as examples of such characters. In neither case did Jesus approve of the actions or attitudes, but he used the stories to vividly drive home a point.

> *We must understand that Jesus was accustomed to choosing his metaphors and comparisons with a grand and sovereign freedom. It is a matter of indifference to him that he should use even such a dubious figure as the dishonest steward to point out a truth about the kingdom of God. The person who takes offense at the fact that Jesus never depicts anybody with a halo, but employs as models even sham saints, even the dregs of humanity, in order that their very darkness may permit the divine truth to shine more brightly, that person does not understand him at all.* (Thielicke, 94)

In this parable, although he constructed it and told it, it is not Jesus who commended the unjust steward, but the steward's master. The parable deals with the wise use of money and opportunity, even though in this case the servant was less than honest. As the story was told there are other issues to deal with which may help explain why the steward acted as he did. There were accusations against the steward, but he never had a chance to defend himself, the master simply announced that he had heard the charges and even though he said, "Give an account of yourself," the immediate announcement was that the man was to be removed from his post. There were not many options for the steward. Since he stated that he was not strong enough to do manual labor and was too proud to beg, he searched for another way to ingratiate himself with those who owed the master and he took advantage of it. Kingdom citizens are not instructed to act immorally but to act wisely and take advantage of their opportunities. In our translations the term "shrewd" does not have to imply evil, it may simple be a synonym for "sharp." The conclusion of the parable simply instructed them to use their money (unrighteous mammon) to make friends and their faithfulness in that stewardship will prove that mammon is not their master, but it is a tool to be used in service to fellowmen and to God. In Luke's work Jesus often appeared to disparage wealth, and at other times he proclaimed the responsibility of using it for good stewardship. Again, apparently it was not the possession of wealth which Jesus saw as evil but the dominating control it could exercise over mankind. Jesus' position was not that of the Gnostics who claimed that material substance itself was evil. Material substance is not evil, but materialism is.

## THE RICH MAN AND LAZARUS  pp. 137-138

In this parable the fact that Jesus gave a name to the poor man should not make anyone think that the name Lazarus referred to a real person, it is probably just a common name Jesus used for the man in the story. The narrative indicated that a very rich man had lost all concern for others and in his riches he thought only of himself. The poor man was in desperate need, but no one cared for him. Incidentally, Jesus may have seen this kind of situation many times. It has been seen before that Luke often depicted the attitudes of the rich as a major problem, but the man was not condemned just because he had possessions, but because he had a "rich man" attitude. Likewise, there is no great innate value in being poor. If this parable says anything about life after death in the spiritual realm, one of the things that torments the rich man is his memory. (Whether one should understand memory as a part of the torment of the condemned regarding lost opportunity, may be open to debate.) At any rate, the concern that someone be sent from the realm of the dead to warn the man's family, was rejected on the grounds that enough information already existed in Moses and the prophets to give them sufficient guidance and some kind of miraculous "other worldly" return would not serve to convince them. If Jesus was trying to give any hint about the next realm, he posed a separation, not necessarily geographical, but a real and permanent division in which some sort of chasm divided the two realms and prevented any passage. It is not easy, perhaps not even possible to know when the thought of the Hebrews began to include a life after death. We do know, however, that in many of the ancient religions there was such a concept, for in Egypt mummies were carefully preserved and the parts of the body which would decay were placed in sealed jars, with the idea that if all the parts were present in the next age, life could be re-constructed. (A. H. Sayce, *The Religions of the Ancient East* [Edinburgh: T. & T. Clark, 1902], 50-68)     By the time of Jesus, the prevailing belief looked something like this: There was an all inclusive realm of the dead which was called Hades. It contained both the realm of those who were "approved," which was called Paradise, and the realm of those who were "rejected," which was called Gehenna. These are represented by the following chart:

| | | |
|---|---|---|
| | **H** | Paradise (Eternal Fellowship) |
| Temporal | **A** | |
| | GREAT **D** GULF | |
| Life | **E** | |
| | | Gehenna (Lost Opportunity) |
| | | **S** |

It has already been stated that to speak about anything it is necessary to use symbols and that is even more accurate when one it talking about the spiritual realm. There are no ways to communicate spiritual realities other than by symbols. Be reminded that a symbol, as it is used in this work, is a figure that points beyond itself to something else but in some mysterious way it participates in what it represents. Symbols are not meaningless, "mere" symbols, they are essential communicative tools. Two of those are used to represent Gehenna (Hell) and if they are taken literally and in a physical sense they are mutually exclusive, but taken as symbols they portray fantastic truths. The first of those comes from the first century awareness of what the Valley of Hinnom was used for. It was a garbage dump - not a modern landfill - in which both human sacrifices to the Canaanite deity, Moloch, had been offered and filth was burned! (Robert Young, *Analytical Concordance to the Bible,* [McLean, Virginia: MacDonald Publishing Company, {no date}] 484) Anyone who is old enough to remember those dumps will be aware that they constantly burned and smoldered. The driest garbage burned and gave off both heat and light and the wet garbage was alive with maggots, worms and often rats and other vermin. Where the wet garbage came in contact with the dry it did not burn well and gave off terrible odors and smoldered and smoked all the time. When we think of great personages such as Joan of Arc and many others who have been burned at the stake, probably nothing causes a human being to shudder more than thinking about being burned alive. There is no torment that seems more horrible; so "fire and brimstone" became an almost perfect symbol for the torment of permanently lost opportunity and memory of what was wasted.

The second fantastic symbol is darkness! In order to emphasize the tragedy of darkness, I cannot help but recall an experience which occurred early in my life. My father was the High School Principal and basketball coach in Monticello, Kentucky. That is a karst area and it is honey combed with caves. Because of the position my father held, I knew many of the teen age boys in the little community, even though I was only about five or six years old. I kept noticing that often on Saturday mornings some of those boys would go by our house carrying what I now know were torches to be lighted later and they disappeared - they never came back that way - but they came back down the road late in the afternoon. One day I ask my Dad about that and he told me that there was a cave in the field right behind our house and those guys went down in the cave, crawled through a small opening in the side of the cave wall and through tunnels until they came out at the fairgrounds. Later they would come back down the road. Then Dad said to me something like what God said to Adam and Eve, he said,

"Don't let me ever catch you trying to go down in that cave." There was enough curiosity and I guess sinful meanness in me as a little boy that I began to plan to do what Dad had forbidden. One day I sneaked off from the house and went down in the field and I found that monstrous hole in the ground. As a child I did not know to take any light, but I crawled down in that hole and in the dim light, filtering in from the opening, I saw some unbelievably beautiful stalactites and stalagmites, glistening with moisture. As I eased deeper into the cave I could barely see a small hole and I knew that was where the boys went and that if I crawled through that hole I would be at the fairgrounds. (Have you ever taken a child on a long trip only to hear her or him say after just a few miles, "Are we there yet?") Well, I crawled through the hole and found myself in pitch black darkness, but I also discovered that I must have been on a board for it wiggled up and down like a diving board. I could not see a thing, not even my hand in front of my face! I not only experienced the darkness, but pitch black darkness weighs in on you and it can be felt. I almost panicked and tried to back out but then my feet hit something and I could go no further. About that same time, even though there was no television to tell the story, a man, named Floyd Collins, had been inside a cave up close to Mammoth Cave and he was trapped by a cave-in and the rescuers could not get to him. He died! I don't know whether I had heard my parents talking about that or if I had heard it on the primitive radio that my Dad had made, but I knew about it. I suddenly knew that the same thing had happened to me and that I would never get out! I can't remember how it all worked out, but I finally discovered that what my feet had bumped into was a huge boulder that I had not noticed before and someone had used it to put on the plank to hold it in place. I got out of that cave in a hurry and I told my Dad about it when he was seventy-two! Does it need to be said that that was one of my sins that I told God about? I have not been abnormally harmed by that experience with darkness, but I shall never forget how terrible and frightening it was.

If light has long been used as a symbol for goodness and God, darkness has been just the opposite and while I am convinced that hell is primarily the inability to have fellowship with God, who (or which) is the only option that there must be in eternity, what I sense in the symbol of outer darkness can never approach the hopelessness of whatever that separation is. At the beginning of this discussion it was stated that literally and physically these two things are mutually exclusive and fire gives off light. No torment can ever be described or symbolized, even with these two graphic ones, in its completeness. Lest someone should think that the fire has been taken out of hell, the real spiritual thing (whatever it is) is far worse than literal consuming fire. That is Gehenna!

The other side of the picture, that which represents the condition of Lazarus, is just the opposite. For years the hope of the Messianic Feast had been described as being hosted by Father Abraham. When the little children's song says, "Rock a my soul in the booz of Abraham" it is being true to the picture of a feast. People in the first century lay on couches for formal feasts, and whoever was in the couch next to the host was "in his bosom." When Jesus hosted the Last Supper, one of the disciples, described as the one Jesus loved, was reclining on his bosom. (John 13:23) So the first part that paradise figure or symbol deals with is a sumptuous feast which few of the average people of that time had ever shared. Many descriptions have been used to attempt to get people to feel the beauty and joy of being in the presence of God. The New Jerusalem, which is described in The Apocalypse, represents Heaven as a place of perfect light. ("Place" is not a good word, for that is a geographical symbol and what we are dealing with is a spiritual realm, but the term "place" is about all that can be used.) There is no need for sun nor moon for God is its light. It has been represented as a realm of perfect security. To a modern, the idea of city walls is foreign, but for the ancients those walls were security. God is its security with four gates on each of the four sides of the "safe haven", so that no one can be shut out. The description also indicates that it is a place of perfect sustenance, for there are trees that bear their fruits during all seasons of the year and a river runs through the city so that no siege could ever threaten to cut off its water supply. It is also described as a sphere of perfect beauty with sparkling gems, gates of pearl, and streets of gold. (Once a student, a farm girl, said to me that she would much prefer warm mud on a spring day squishing between her toes.) That almost reminds one of efforts in the movies to show a sparkling, gem laden city in the desert which is of incomparable beauty. It is also a place of perfect worship and God is ever present, face to face (another great symbol).

In fact, nothing is wanting and it is also described as being without any pain, suffering, sorrow, evil, or want. It has absolute harmony. The perfect presence of God and perfect worship and fellowship are beyond human understanding.

Although the source of the idea is probably unknown, Saint Paul said, "What no eye has seen, nor ear heard, nor the human heart conceived, that is what God has prepared for those who love him." (I Corinthians 2:9) That may reflect Isaiah 64:4 which states, "From ages past no one has heard, no ear has perceived, no eye has seen any God besides you, who works for those who wait for him." Or it may reflect a non-canonical work where, while talking about wisdom, the writer says, "It is he who created her; he saw her and took her measure; he poured her out upon all his works, upon all the living according to his gift; he lavished her upon those who love him." (Sirach 1:9-10) Whatever it refers to it certainly implies that no one can know or imagine the fantastic new order that awaits those who are committed to God. So the symbols attempt to portray something far beyond their capability.

Geography, science and every concept that relates to the material world should be seen as temporary. It would be radically foolish for anyone to claim to know what the metaphysical realm would be like, but the struggle of the human mind forces many of us to postulate something about the unseen reality; (At no point in any effort to convey ideas to others have I felt more incompetent than in dealing with these ideas.) The following is in no sense proposed with any finality or certainty. This may not happen to trigger any agreement from others at all, but it is offered after years of effort and struggle and with an awareness that all of its basis lies in a woefully inadequate understanding of the philosophy of existence.

It is my conclusion that there is only one ultimate reality! From what can be gathered from both ancient and modern studies of cosmology, it would appear that the entire, unimaginable vast horde of galaxies (et. al.) has been an expanding phenomenon. At some point that "system" most probably must run out of energy and what will happen at that point is anybody's guess. My conclusion is that all matter is temporary and while it possesses a kind of reality, it is not permanently real. Yet something (and "something" is not an adequate term, but it is the best I can do) must be eternal, whether it goes by the name of Plato's realm of Ideas or the Hebrew-Christian concept of God. So humor me in this speculation.

There is nothing ultimately real except God and the spiritual realm! I have no claim that I understand what that means, but as I see it, that is all that there is! Somehow in the "created in the image of God" concept the inner being of man (call it spirit, personality or whatever) is man's eternal essence. What each individual becomes in personal character passes over into the non-geographical, non- spatial concept. The entire emphasis of St. Paul on the "spiritual body," which incidentally contains two incongruous terms and which, incidentally, I believe (though I cannot prove that) came from Jesus, is a kind of vague attempt to state that in the eternal sphere one retains his/her personal identity. That essence has the capacity for fellowship with the Eternal One and that capacity depends on character likeness to that which has been revealed in the Incarnation. Since it has no geographical or temporal element, it must be entirely spiritual. To be like Him (and remember that all sexual references are limited to this finite world and are not part of the "beyond sex" Deity - God is not sexual and therefore, is not a "he" or "she") is to open the door to that fellowship.

Since The Eternal One is all that exists, any who have developed character unlike God are in the presence of what is most uncomfortable. To offer an illustration, for which I apologize before giving it, suppose that you have developed an affinity for great classical music and you find yourself surrounded by a performance from which you cannot escape. Since that is your greatest delight and it completely permeates your experience, it would be a heavenly experience - beyond delight! But if classical music is a hated bane to you, yet you cannot escape it, since that is all that there is, it would be a tormenting hell - much worse than the old physical hell fire. If that is taking the fire out of hell, any who understand my concept would find that in reality I have increased the intensity of what the symbol of "fire" represents by an infinite degree!

## THE KINGDOM - WHO DESERVES IT, WHO IS GRATEFUL, AND WHEN CAN IT BE EXPECTED: pp. 139-140

Luke provided his readers with another parable which attempted to show the need for an awareness that no person in the kingdom receives what he/she deserves, All who come to God and who have done everything they could, have still only done what their obligations indicated and they have no claim on God. It is a short parable and more than likely is an effort to indicate that keeping all the laws of God and doing everything that has been commanded still shows the failure of legalistic religion.

In the story of the healing of the ten lepers the major issue is gratitude. All ten lepers were commanded to go and show themselves to the priest so that they could be restored to society. In response to that command, even before they were healed, they were on their way to the priest because of their faith in Jesus. Only one of the ten turned back to show his gratitude to Jesus and, as is not uncommon in Luke's material, he was a Samaritan, one outside of Judaism. It is interesting that they all must have responded to Jesus' command and all must have been healed because of that faith, but in this parable while all of them may have been grateful, the one who demonstrates that gratitude is the one from whom it is least expected and certainly an outsider..

With all the parables about the kingdom of God there must have been many who wondered about when the event would occur, especially since most of them were still thinking about a physical kingdom and deliverance from Roman domination. In response to a question by the Pharisees about when the Kingdom was coming, Jesus' reply was probably the closest he had ever come to pointing out that the kingdom was spiritual. It is easy to look back, knowing what we know (or think we know) and having all the theological development that has occurred, and wonder why they could not understand. Jesus answered their question by telling them that the kingdom could not be observed physically but was, as some translations put it, "within you." St. Paul indicated to that "flesh and blood cannot inherit the kingdom of God, nor does the perishable inherit the imperishable." (I Corinthians 15:50) That is not an easy issue to deal with for one must be aware that there are still, in the present time, those who interpret the kingdom as a future reality, almost physical, and that it will be on this earth, and they do so with sincerity. (Do not all of us, if we try to visualize our departed loved ones, envision them physically? That is the only way we can think, even though we may be convinced that it isn't correct!) Jesus repeated that the efforts to physically see the kingdom are futile, but the big issue is to be prepared for his suffering. He tried to warn them that there would be no signal that the end was coming, for everything would be going on in normal fashion, eating, drinking, marrying, buying, selling, and planting. Suddenly and unexpectedly the Son of Man would be revealed. (Much of this discussion needs to be reserved for dealing with the disciples' questions which are recorded in Matthew, for those questions in Matthew 24 are extremely difficult to separate, and the major one of them is about the destruction of Jerusalem.) Luke's own understanding of the kingdom and the future return, must have entered into his selection and placement of this material, which may be a partial doublet of that which is repeated later. It really makes no difference whether this discussion in Luke deals with the end of time or the war with the Romans in 66-70 A.D., the fact is that no preparatory warning is given. It is not hard to see that Jesus' closest followers were confused, nor is it hard to understand why, since even with our advantages we also cannot know some of these answers.

## TWO OF LUKE"S CONCLUDING SPECIAL PARABLES: 141-142

The parable of the widow and the unjust judge has already been referred to and is much like the story of the friend at midnight who finally responded due to persistence. The character of the judge is not the important part of this story. The teaching was that if the unjust judge finally issued justice because of her persistence and confidence in that judge, how much more will God grant justice to those who have faith in him!

The closing parable of this section deals with the Pharisee and the publican, both of whom prayed. As Luke introduces it, the problem has to do with those who trusted in their own righteousness and as a result of that the passed  negative judgment on others. This Pharisee was a haughty, self righteous man who boasted that he was not like other sinners, even like the tax collector. He recited that he performed all of his religious deeds, that he fasted regularly and gave a tenth of his income. The other (outcast) man was rife with repentance. He did not boast of his goodness; he only pled for forgiveness. This is one of the few parables in which Jesus gave the lesson without waiting for the story to digest. The essence of the parable taught that humility was an absolute essential before God. An obvious warning is that even among religious people it is easy to become a "Pharisee." All leaders face the problem of arrogance but religious leaders especially often face the problem of taking to heart complimentary statements from well meaning parishioners. It is good and necessary to have compliments, but if one takes them too seriously, he/she runs the risk of becoming arrogant.

# CHAPTER XVI
## THE JOURNEY TO JERUSALEM

## A SECOND TEACHING ON MARRIAGE AND DIVORCE: 143-144

As has already been seen, the issue of divorce must have been a difficult one for the people of the first century. The Rabbinical Schools were divided about the grounds for such action. In this narrative the Pharisees came to test him; to see which Rabbi he would agree with, Shammai or Hillel. Actually, Jesus responded by showing them that in a sinful world there had always been reasons why people violated the Intentional Will of God. Jesus replied to their question by asking them to refer to the great law-giver, Moses. What did he say? It has already been noted that Moses allowed divorce, but required a certificate stating the conditions of the divorce. Much of that must have been for the protection of women, because before Moses' time no reasons had to be spelled out. With a certificate, assuming that the woman had not been involved with a man who was not her husband, the wife could defend herself against charges of immorality. Jesus plainly stated that God's purpose was that a marriage was intended to be permanent and that the two were joined in the strongest union possible. But that was before sin, or as Jesus put it, "the hardness of your heart," entered into the picture. In spite of the fact that earlier there had been both polygamy and polyandry, Jesus taught that the original intent was that a marriage was to be a life-time commitment between one man and one woman. Even with that having been said, sin and abuse and a thousand other problems enter in to destroy marriages.

The "M" source incorporated the portion of the narrative in which the disciples heard this "hard saying," and they suggested that if one could not get out of a marriage it would be better that no one ever got involved. (Keep in mind that all of this discussion and any discussion among first century Jews would have been made from the male point of view.) When he responded to the attitude expressed by the disciples Jesus appears to have recognized that there are some who, by nature, are incapable of or uninterested in marriage. It is very hard to know to whom he referred. Perhaps he was thinking of some bachelors, even like Lazarus (?) who lived with his two sisters. It would be a stretch to argue that in this passage he was speaking about homosexuals (but he could have been). The term "eunuch" primarily dealt with those who had undergone castration and who served in harems and those are the ones who "have been made eunuchs by others." Yet a third group are those who have made the personal choice because of the kingdom. He gave no indication that any one of these conditions was superior to the others, but certainly in the time of first century Christian missionary activity a family would have produced frustrating difficulties. There is no view expressed that sexual unions are in any sense inferior to remaining single for there were noble followers such as Aquila and Priscilla and many other unnamed couples who served in significant roles in the early church. And we are all aware of the support that a good spouse (whether male or female) can provide. Neither should this passage be used for support of the idea of the ascetic-like concept that the ministry should not marry. Even though Paul indicated that in view of the "impending stress," in his opinion, it would be better not to have marriage and family responsibilities to compound the difficulties, there does not seem to be any scriptural support or bias that a celibate position was a superior one.

All three of the Synoptic Gospels include the point of Jesus blessing and commending the little children. It would almost appear that the disciples felt that the children and the expectations of their parents were a distraction to Jesus' work, but he disallowed that and even pointed out that childlike faith is necessary to entering the kingdom.

## THE RICH YOUNG MAN: pp. 145-147

There are numerous stories of rich people coming to Jesus and wanting to be a part of the kingdom. In each case the primary message was that riches could often be a hindrance to entering the kingdom. This does not appear to be a challenge to take a "pauper's" oath. The teaching may have been necessary because the prevailing idea among the Jews was that if one was rich, he/she must be blessed by God, a forerunner of "success-theology." In this case the young man wanted to know what he could do to earn eternal life. Although this might have been a perfect opportunity to deal with the fact that legalistic righteousness does not stand a chance before God, Jesus began by making the man aware of the challenges of the Law. Those specific laws he mentioned were the essence of the Ten Commandments. There was no argument when the young man stated that he had kept all of these - but he still lacked something. It was then that Jesus, as he had done before, showed that the riches were standing between the young man and surrender to the Lordship of Christ. Again, it is imperative to see that many different things can stand between a man and God, not just riches, but they do present a subtle problem! They (mammon) tend to creep into ones life and become the Pivotal Value. So the puzzled disciples hear Jesus' little parabolic statement that "it is easier for a camel to go through the eye of a needle than for a rich man to enter the kingdom of God." There have been those who have tried to soften that remark! It has been suggested that the Greek term for camel, *kamelos,* (the "e" representing the Greek eta) is only one letter different than the term for rope or cable, *kamilos* (where the eta is changed to an iota) so that Jesus' figure is not quite so exaggerated. But to anyone who has tried to thread a needle, trying to put a rope through the eye would be no easier than putting a camel through it. It is impossible! Others have tried to suggest that Jesus was talking about a "needle's eye" gate in the wall of Jerusalem and that a loaded camel would have to crawl through or be pushed on its knees. But very few believe either of these to have any validity.

*This also has been a problem. Cyril of Alexandria, a few later Greek MSS, and the Armenian version have kamilos for kamelos, i.e., a cable or hawser - as if a needle might be threaded with a ship's cable, even if a camel could not go through its eye! Perhaps the "cable" was thought to be a more appropriate hyperbole; but it was an unnecessary change. "An elephant through the eye of a needle" seems to have been another Jewish expression. A far later fancy which arose in the fifteenth century, is the supposed "needle's eye" gate, a small postern entrance beside the large city gate, used after nightfall, and to be entered, it is argued, by a loaded camel on its knees. Only so also, according to this view, can a rich man enter the kingdom of God. But such a gate was far too small for a camel, loaded or unloaded; and whoever saw a camel crawl on its four knees!* (Frederick E. Grant, *The Interpreter's Bible, Vol. VII* [Nashville: Abingdon-Cokesbury Press, 1951] 806,807)

This hyperbole is another one of Jesus' humorously exaggerated figures which point out an impossibility. If a wealthy man's possessions stand between him and God, it is impossible for him to enter until the devotion to possessions is reversed. There have been some who have taken this urging to give up all of ones wealth literally, but even the most ardent literalists of the present day do not take this passage literally. Apparently, the disciples thought (as did most Jews) that wealth was a blessing from God, and were astounded by the idea that if one blessed by God could not enter, who could? Peter, in a somewhat self elevating statement indicated that the disciples had left everything and followed. He asked, "What will we get out of it?" Jesus stated that they would inherit much more than what they had left. (Matthew 19:28-30)

# THE BARGAINING SPIRIT: pp. 147

It has already been stated that the stories of the gospels circulated in isolated units and that there was little if any certain chronological value in them. Matthew placed the parable of the Laborers in the Vineyard immediately after the discussion about the rich man and Peter's question, "What are we going to get out of it." (Matthew 19:27) He must have placed this story at this point because there is something in the context which clues one in on the teaching of the parable. It is another ridiculous story, if taken literally. The owner of the vineyard is in search of laborers and he went to the town center and found some, but not enough. So he returned at a later hour to hire some more. Assuming that a work day would have been from about six in the morning until six in the evening, one fourth of the day has already been spent. Three other times he returned to get laborers, at noon, at three o'clock, and at five, apparently telling each group he would pay them what was right. The punch line of the parable comes at the time for paying each laborer for his day's work. To the surprise of everyone the pay line is reversed and those who had worked only one hour were paid first - a full day's wage! Back down the line the news must have gone. The owner is extremely generous and if those workers only spent one hour, working in the cool of the day, surely we who worked three hours will get three days wages, we who worked six hours, during the heat of the day, will receive six denarii, and surely we who worked all day will receive twelve denarii. What a deal! But it didn't work that way, and everyone, greedy as most are and feeling justified, grumbled when they were paid exactly what they were promised, the usual day's wage. Obviously, the story was designed to teach some main point. The owner justifies what he did by saying that he paid what was agreed upon and that he had the right to do whatever he wished with his money. What would happen to the entire economic system if employers did that sort of thing? (Who hasn't often wished he/she had a job where one reported to work at eleven o'clock, got an hour off for lunch and did not have to return?) Often people have interpreted this story as teaching that God can do whatever He wishes in terms of his gifts to people and if He is generous to some, no one should complain. Certainly no one would dispute that God can do whatever He chooses, within the confines of His own character. But, in the light of the context in which Matthew placed this parable, that does not seem to be the teaching. Keep in mind what Peter had just said, "We have left everything and followed you. What will we then have?" (19:27). Most likely, the parable teaches a fundamental truth that there is no occasion or possibility of bargaining with God. Many times people try to bargain with God by saying , "If you will do this or that for me, then I will serve you." And then after receiving whatever they desired, whether they forget the promise or to fulfill their duty is of no consequence.. God does not work that way. He never bribes people to serve him and, as Jesus put it, "For he makes his sun to rise on the evil and the good, and sends rain on the righteous and the unrighteous." (Matthew 5:45) Humans have no claim on God with which to bargain, they can only trust His grace!

At several points on this trip to Jerusalem, Jesus again attempted to prepare the disciples for his death. Luke indicated that even at this point they did not understand what he was saying to them.

## THE SONS OF ZEBEDEE: pp. 148-149

It is not possible to know who was responsible for this request that was made to Jesus. Matthew recorded that the mother of James and John was the one who asked for the position of power while Mark indicated that it was the brothers themselves who asked. A mother's desire for her children might easily have prompted the request, but if so, it is evident that she did not understand the nature of the kingdom that Jesus talked about. She saw it as a physical kingdom with the highest positions of authority (the right hand and the left) being granted to her sons. Of course, the same error in thinking is present if the sons asked for the power. Both accounts indicate that the other ten were indignant. Could it be that they had been beaten to the punch? Jesus took this as an opportunity to teach a principle of greatness which he had shared before. True greatness in the kingdom is to forget about it and become a servant or slave. That is one of the things that Nietzsche pointed to when he indicated that Jesus' sense of values was completely opposite to those of the  world, and he was not giving Jesus a compliment. The world, since the beginning of recorded history has functioned on power, manipulation, control, greed, force, etc. All of those have repeatedly plunged humanity into war, slavery, economic hardship and other things. Jesus' discussion was diametrically opposed to that and it may be one reason why he was killed. One can never know how many times Jesus spoke to the disciples about being the Suffering Servant, but in this context it is evident that they still did not understand it, even when he said, "the Son of Man came not to be served but to serve and to give his life as a ransom for many." (Mark 10:45)

## THE JERICHO HAPPENINGS: pp. 149-150

On the way to Jerusalem and as they passed through Jericho all three Synoptics told the story of the healings of the blind. In Matthew there were two men described while in Mark and Luke there was only one. (Mark gave the name Bartimaeus) In all of the accounts of this healing there was no command such as he had given before, not to tell anyone, simply the note that this man (or men) followed Jesus.

Even though the exact chronology cannot be known, the narrative proceeds in Luke to the event with Zacchaeus. Zachaeus was described as a "chief tax collector" and that causes one to think that he was the superior over the other tax collectors in Jericho. The Roman system for collecting taxes left the gate wide open for graft, and there must have been plenty of it. The system allowed the tax collectors to be both appraisers and collectors. In any given territory the tax collector was charged with the responsibility for sending "x" amount to Rome. These were collectors of personal and private taxes and they could exact any mount they chose - the surplus was salary. Whether Zacchaeus collected his living from the other publicans or directly from the people taxed, it is no wonder that the common man hated both the Romans who occupied and the publicans who were all traitors to God and His people. So the narrative pictures a great crowd lining the street and making it impossible for a short man to see. Zacchaeus solved that problem by going ahead and shedding all his dignity - he climbed a tree. One can easily imagine the taunts and name calling which must have occurred, and Jesus would have heard that. When he came to the tree he commanded the little tax collector to come down and invited himself into Zacchaeus' home, even as the crowd grumbled.

The narrative does not allow knowledge of what was said by Jesus along the way, but something happened to Zacchaeus. Many have believed that Zacchaeus was a good man and an honest one because the proposal he made exacted a lot from him. First he indicated that he had lost whatever devotion he had to mammon, for he offered to give half of everything he had to the poor. (That would not have escaped the view of Luke.) Then he offered to repay anyone whom he had defrauded four times the amount out of which they had been cheated. It was because of that radical change of attitude that Jesus saw that salvation, a fantastic transformation, had come to Zaccheus and that he was a part of or was restored to the family of Abraham! .

## THE PARABLE OF THE POUNDS: pp. 149-150

As Jesus was approaching Jerusalem for this last time, he told a parable about responsibility of stewardship. There is a slight difference in the parables as they are told in Matthew and Luke and they were placed in different contexts, but the essence and the teaching are identical. Matthew told of a man who was going on a journey and he called together his slaves and gave to each of them a responsibility, to each one according to his ability. To one man he entrusted five talents, to another he entrusted two and to another one. In the Luke story an added dimension has a nobleman going into a distant country, apparently to the governor or whoever had the power of appointment, in order to get the right to rule. The citizens under that ruler hated him and also sent to the ruling power a request indicating that they did not want the man to rule over them. Luke indicated that all of this particular teaching occurred because he was near Jerusalem and the people were expecting the kingdom of God to come immediately. It was still obvious that they were thinking about a kingdom to deliver them from the rule of Rome. But the primary reason for the parable was to show the responsibility for whatever had been entrusted. In both accounts of the parable, the one who had been given much, in Matthew five talents and in Luke ten *mina* (which represented about three months wages), was able to double the master's money. Likewise the man who had been given a lesser amount also had a one hundred percent increase. But the man who had only one talent or *mina* had done nothing with it. He had decided to try to keep it safe and hid it. Both of the first men were commended, but the last one was severely condemned, apparently because he had wasted his opportunity. In the Matthew account the man was cast out and "there," meaning in that place or condition, there would be great sorrow. In the Lucan account the man has his money taken away from him and in both accounts the man/men who had used the investment wisely received even more while the negligent slave lost everything. Jesus was apparently teaching that wise use of ones opportunities made even an expanded significance possible. It would not be hard to see in this story an inclination to believe that those who are blessed with many talents usually seem to at least be doing something, while those who have little ability tend to neglect even the opportunities they have, perhaps because of inferior feelings. One cannot help but wonder what the outcome of the parable would have been should any of the men who invested and worked have, because of economic circumstances, lost their money.

Even though Jesus told the parable, he was not responsible for the ruler wreaking vengeance on those who had sent the embassy to ask for his removal, as Luke told it. That was probably just the way the rulers of the time reacted to opposition. People who live in a democratic society in the modern world would have trouble understanding that rather vicious command that they be slaughtered right there in his presence, although coups currently occur in parts of the world with such serious repercussions. One is reminded how Herod the Great even had some of his own family put to death and how he tried to make certain that the baby king that the Magi told him about would never live to become a threat. But this vengeance element is probably not an integral part of the teaching of the parable.

# CHAPTER XVII
## THE DAYS IN JERUSALEM

### THE ENTRY INTO JERUSALEM pp. 153-54

Much has been written about the day Christians call Palm Sunday. There is Synoptic agreement that it occurred just before the Feast of the Passover. It was a planned entry and Matthew again found a proof-text from Zechariah 9:9 to show that deliberation. The narrative indicated that Jesus had made provision to rent the animal that he rode on and most translations do not indicate that as plainly as they should. Jesus said, "If anyone says anything to you, just say this, 'Its (the term *autou* is in the genitive or possessive case) master has need of it.'" The term *kurios* may mean owner, or master or at times even "sir," but it probably had not at this time attained the meaning of "Lord" as it later did in New Testament usage. Both Mark and Luke indicate that there was one animal and many believe that the author of Matthew may have misunderstood the Hebrew poetic parallelism and thought there were two animals when in reality there was only one. Many met this peculiar procession and gave cries of "Hosanna" to the one who was coming as king. It is impossible to estimate how many were in the "very large crowd," but Matthew's statement (probably hyperbolic) that the whole city was in turmoil (21:10) is almost identical in meaning to his statement that at the news from the Magi concerning the birth of Jesus,

Herod was frightened and all Jerusalem with him. (2:3) Whether this entrance was as pronounced as later Christianity has made it seem, may be debated. Some have wondered what happened to this crowd of supporters between this day and the day of the trials, but either the crowd was not that large and supportive as has been assumed or they had lost interest because Jesus was not acting as the conquering hero they were looking for or they were cowed by the religious leaders and the political process. When some of the Pharisees tried to get Jesus to stop this demonstration, he indicated the impossibility of that with another figure of speech, "the stones would shout out." In one of the most direct and plain statements Jesus warned them that because they had not recognized what his message had been and had ignored it, the entire city would ultimately be crushed, all because they had not recognized the "visitation of God." This theme will be amplified and seen again in a later account taken from the Marcan material.

## THE CLEANSING OF THE TEMPLE pp. 154-155

There is some confusion between the versions of Matthew and Luke in regard to when the event of cleansing the Temple occurred and that of Mark. Mark stated that Jesus entered the Temple, looked around, and the went back to Bethany. To both Matthew and Luke, the cleansing took place before returning to Bethany. The event is a critical juncture in the last week of Jesus' life. Something incensed Jesus about what was taking place in the Temple area. For many years, people had come to the Holy City to offer their sacrifices and pay their Temple taxes. There are statements in the Leviticus and Numbers that the sacrificial animals were to be "without any blemish." That originally meant that any sacrifice had to be something of real value to the one making the offering. A person was not allowed to look over his flock and select a deformed animal or a sick one which would probably die soon anyway, for giving useless or left over things to God was and is an insult. Therefore, the priests set up an inspection system which carefully looked for flaws. Imagine that you were from Galilee and had set out with a lamb for the Paschal offering. It had not been an easy task to get the animal there in the first place, but when you presented it to the priests they found a spot where the wool or a small piece of an ear had been torn away, probably by a briar which the animal had brushed or perhaps was caught in. So the animal would not do for a sacrifice. What was one to do? Two options were open - either the farmer can take it all the way back to Galilee or sell it in the Jerusalem meat market. Everyone knows what happens to the price of anything when it is imperative that it be sold quickly. But if he sold it the farmer was left with no sacrificial animal, and the only place he could get one was from the pre-inspected flock that the priests managed. Soon Galileans and others stopped bringing their sheep on the long journey and simply bought one (or doves) in the Temple, and the price went up! That was an injustice, but how could one counter it? Also, the Temple tax was to be paid in half-shekels and there were none in circulation. The Priests had them all, but they could be exchanged for Roman currency, and the exchange rate also went up! It was that merchandising scenario which Jesus confronted. It must have been chaotic when he upset the money-changers' tables and drove out the sellers of the sheep and doves. He had attacked the priestly system.

E. F. Scott has stated, and probably very correctly so, that the cleansing of the Temple was the straw that broke the camel's back, for within a few days, Jesus was dead. (*The Crisis in the Life of Jesus* [New York: Charles Scribner's Sons, 1952] 101ff) The author of the Gospel of John placed this event at the beginning of his work in a chapter which attempted to show something about the difference Jesus made. He was not concerned with chronology but with ideas and it would take a huge stretch of the imagination to think that Jesus could have gotten away with such an act at the beginning of his ministry when, according to the Synoptics, it caused such a ruckus at the beginning of the last week. It is true that both sellers and buyers were indicted by Jesus' statement, "My house shall be called a house of prayer' (Isaiah 56:7); but you have made it a den of robbers," for everyone was involved in that commercialization. The whole worship process had been prostituted and the Temple worship had become a farce! Matthew stated that when the chief priests and scribes saw the amazing things that he did and the resulting praise from the common people, they became angry. Jesus did not stand a chance for a fair trial and whatever some may think about this all being the will of God, it surely would have been part of the Circumstantial Will. The die had been cast.

# THE CURSING OF THE FIG TREE pp. 155-157

Nearly every event during the last week of Jesus' life seems to have heightened the tension between himself and the religious leaders. It almost appears that Jesus believed that he had passed the point of no return for, if we accept the assessment of the Gospel of John, he told the disciples that his time had come. Most of what he did and said was deliberate and with great purpose, especially from this point on. The contexts in which Mark and Matthew place the cursing of the fig tree suggest that immediately after the experience of cleansing of the Temple he went to Bethany and on the following morning as they went back to Jerusalem he saw a fig tree in the distance with leaves on it. Mark reported that it was not the season for figs, so one must search for some explanation for what Jesus did beyond just causing a fig tree to wither. Luke did not use this story, perhaps because he had previously told a parable of the barren fig tree which taught exactly the same thing as Mark and Matthew teach here. That must mean that either the parable somehow became this story in the process of oral transmission (or visa-versa) or that Jesus did this action as an enacted (object lesson) parable. The position taken here is that it was a parable acted out to teach that the Jewish religious system had given every external appearance of being productive, but there had been no authentic fruit developed. Jesus was too much of a genius to have become angry because a tree did not have fruit on it in the off season and he would certainly have known that it was not the season for figs! Matthew reported (21:19,20) that the tree withered at once, but Mark implies that it was the next morning that the tree was discovered to have withered and Simon Peter called his attention to it. Then Jesus indicated what he had also taught earlier that with faith and prayer tremendous things which seem impossible can be done. Mark also includes the teaching on forgiveness which Matthew placed in the Sermon on the Mount and that teaching was that when one truly experiences forgiveness he/she becomes a forgiving person - forgiveness is a God-like character trait.

## CHALLENGES AND CHARGES pp. 157-164

## THE QUESTION OF AUTHORITY p. 157

When Jesus entered the Temple he was in the territory of the religious leaders, so on one occasion the chief priests, scribes, and elders prodded him to reveal the authority by which he did his works. He was not a member of any of the rabbinical schools, he was not a priest, he had not been granted authority (letters) such as Saul of Tarsus would later receive from the Sanhedrin. So what was his claim? Jesus saw that dilemma immediately and knew that no answer he could give would be satisfactory for them. So he offered to answer their question if they would answer his and he turned the dilemma back on them. Where did the authority that John the Baptist worked under come from? They had no answer. Since they knew that the people revered John as a prophet, if they said he received his authority from men they would face a riot and even feared being stoned. If they answered that the authority came from heaven, they knew that his immediate response would be, "Why did you not believe him?" So they did not give an answer and neither did Jesus give them one.

## CONFRONTATION PARABLES: pp. 158-164

But the question prompted several parables. From the "M" source came the parable of the two sons. When the father had asked them to go work in the vineyard one said at first that he would not go, but he later changed his mind and went. The other replied that he would go, but he never did. If the context which Matthew offers is followed, when the parable was finished it was the priests who were required to answer concerning which one actually did the bidding of the father, and the answer was so obvious that no one could escape it. Often Jesus allowed the parables to settle in the minds of his hearers and later ripen so that an internal conclusion was drawn. But in this case he applied the parable indicating that the ones the religious leaders considered outside the interest of God were the ones who would share in the kingdom. Because the religious leaders had heard John's righteous challenge but did not believe it they made themselves the outcast ones.

The second parable of this series comes from the common Marcan material. It too, is directed toward the religious leaders and they knew it! The master/owner had developed a  vineyard,  had fenced the vineyard in, made a wine press, and even built a protecting tower and then leased it to tenants.  Even in early history tenant farming required the payment of a portion of the harvest to the owner, but in this case these tenants refused to pay.  Various slaves were sent to collect the rent, but they were badly mistreated and returned to the master with nothing.  Finally, almost in desperation he sent his son, but he did not get any respect either and they decided that this was their chance, so they killed him and tried to take possession of the vineyard.  Jesus then posed the question, "What will the owner do to those tenants?" Again following the idea that Matthew seems to have believed that the Hebrews, because of their lack of "fruit," had forfeited their opportunity, they responded to the question and suggested that the wicked tenants would be destroyed.  In Mark and Luke the conclusion seems to be a part of the parable, but even if it was, the violence is not that of Jesus but the reaction of the father whose son had been slain.  Jesus changed figures and proceeded to refer to Psalm 118:22-23 to indicate that a stone which the builders had decided would not serve and had rejected had become the cornerstone.  In the first century a cornerstone was not a decorative stone as it is in the modern world, but it was the stone which governed the accuracy of the corner of the building,  It therefore was tremendously important.  This parable also must refer to the fact that God had not been getting the fruit that he expected and deserved. What they were experiencing and were now rejecting was to become the most important item they would confront.  In all three gospels the chief priests, scribes, and Pharisees knew that the parable had applied to them and the only reason that Jesus was not arrested was their fear of the people, fear which had already been exposed in the question about John's authority.

At this point in Matthew's chronology Jesus told the parable of the wedding banquet. (It is easy to understand why some suggest that these parables should be seen as allegories.) Proper invitations had been sent and now that the feast was prepared those invited were expected to attend.  First century etiquette appears to have followed the procedure of sending the notice early and then when the feast was ready, a second notice indicated that it was time to come to the feast. There would have been little conflict regarding attendance in the first century because social calendars were not as crowded as modern ones. But in the case of this parable, and a similar one in Luke where feeble excuses were offered, those invited refused to come. The king was insulted and some of his messengers had even been killed, so in his rage those responsible were destroyed and the slaves were told to gather anyone they could find to come in to the feast, and the wedding hall was filled.

The story of the guest without a wedding garment is probably another parable that Matthew adds at this point.

> *Clearly the Wedding Garment is an independent parable. Matthew placed the parable after the Marriage Feast to avoid a misunderstanding of the promiscuous invitation in vs. 9. This verse seemed to suggest that the conduct of the called was unimportant, that the church took into its fold "both bad and good" (vs.10). In the context of the verse , the gospel of the free grace of God might be interpreted to relieve its members of moral responsibility. The Wedding Garment attached to the Marriage Feast served as a corrective. It stressed the need for righteousness (or repentance). (Connick, 232)*

It is debatable whether in the first century the host might have provided wedding garments, but one of those who came in did not wear one, So because he was not properly prepared he was cast out, as Matthew put it into "outer darkness." The concluding statement "For many are called, but few are chosen" must refer to those who do not properly respond, either by refusing the invitation or by not donning the required garment.

## CLIMAXING DILEMMAS pp. 161-164

When some attempts to trap Jesus failed others tried a different tactic. The Pharisees posed another dilemma, which they hoped he could not escape. In a statement, probably of feigned respect, they asked, "We know that you are sincere, and teach the way of God in accordance with truth, and show deference to no one; for you do not regard partiality. Is it proper to pay taxes to Rome or not?" Surely there was no way to avoid answering that one! Everyone knew that the Jews hated paying taxes to a foreign power, so he could not answer "Yes." But on the other hand they since they were out to get him, a "No" answer would brand him as an insurrectionist. They had him this time! But his genius prevailed again and as he used the coin to make his answer, "Render to Caesar the things that are Caesar's and to God the things that are God's" he plainly taught something to the effect that "You have responsibilities both to God and to the governing powers," and the Pharisees gave up.

When they saw that he had rebuffed the Pharisees, the Sadducees immediately proposed another dilemma which had probably always stopped the debate about the issue of resurrection. Keep in mind that the Pharisees believed in a literal, physical, bodily resurrection (almost resuscitation) and to the Sadducees that was so absurd that they often were labeled as not believing in an after life. Remembering the old Levirate Marriage Law, they proposed the question of seven brothers who, since there must have been no offspring, each had in turn married the same woman. They all died and finally, so did the woman. The problem was, "Whose wife will she be in the resurrection?" Jesus gave a new interpretation to what the eternal realm would be like, i.e., marriage, and presumably sex, are a part of the material world and age, but those things do not pertain in the spirit realm. He also indicated by quoting a statement from the Old Testament (Exodus 3:6) that God IS the God of the living. Some groups, even some other religions such as Islam, currently believe that eternity will be physical and many in the modern age have great difficulty with the concept of a spirit age that has continuity with this age, but is also radically different. If we accept Jesus' thought, the temporal relationships do not carry over and physical things such as marriage and sex are limited to this biological life. Since everything we know (or think we know) is tied to the present material age, and we have no way to describe the eternal spirit world, it is not surprising that even in this modern age people still think of eternity in materialistic terms. (cf. We still repeat The Apostles' Creed) No wonder that those who heard him were amazed!.

In this series of confrontations with the religious leaders, one who is described as a member of the Pharisee group who seemed delighted that Jesus had rebuffed the Sadducees on the resurrection question, asked him about the greatest commandment of the law. This story may be another case of a story being used in different contexts by different writers, for it is very similar to an earlier one in Luke (10:25-28). However, Luke used that one to introduce the parable of the Good Samaritan while this story may be the result of a very sincere inquiry. The request asked about what was the greatest commandment and Jesus' answer referred to the lead paragraph of the Jewish *Shema*. (Deuteronomy 6:3 and Leviticus 19:18) In the account given in Mark, Jesus seemed to have felt that the man was sincere and that he was close to understanding and accepting the challenge of the kingdom.

Later, Jesus was in the Temple teaching and he asked the Pharisees how the relationship between the Messiah and King David could be explained. He used Psalm 110, which was seen as a Messianic Psalm, to pose the problem of how the Messiah could be David's son and yet David called him "Lord." Since no one could give an answer (and the other attempts to trap him had failed) the interrogation seems to have stopped, but it did not stop Jesus from pointing out the discrepancies (or hypocrisies) between the teachings of the scribes and Pharisees and their actions. In Matthew's account he then pronounced seven "woes" on those leaders. Most of the things he dealt with have been discussed earlier, and this may be another case of a different account of the same confrontation, but it may be more appropriate in this context of the last week of his earthly life since the woes are more pointed and occurred during the harshest conflicts between Jesus and these leaders. It may be difficult to determine when and where these accusations occurred, but as in the previous account (Luke 11:45 and 53) anger was inevitable. The first woe had to do not only with their rejection of Jesus' message about the kingdom, but they prevented others from responding. The second woe pictured the Pharisees intensive efforts to make proselytes to their religion, but the implication was that those "converts" were left twice as bad off than they had been before. The third woe attacked their blindness in terms of swearing oaths. Making the distinction that an oath sworn by the sanctuary was not binding but one sworn by the gold of the sanctuary was, would be hypocritical and was probably what Jesus was referring to in the Sermon on the Mount when he indicated that oaths should be unnecessary because kingdom character demands honesty and one did not need oaths to bind him to honesty. The fourth woe blasted them for doing the minute legal things, "tithing mint dill and cumin," all externals, but they did not consider the more important matters such as justice, mercy, and faith. The fifth woe was concerned with their externalism. Apparently, Jesus saw a falseness in the pious front the religious leaders put on while inwardly they were corrupt. It reminds one of Kierkegaard's claim that the burgers of his day came to the church and put on their robes of righteousness (which were symbolically hanging in the vestibule) and sat piously in the pews. Then when the service was over they took off their robes of righteousness, left them hanging on the pegs and went about their business as usual. The sixth of these woes followed the same general intent of the narrative in Luke (11:39) when he compared them to graves that were full of decay while they tried to keep the outside looking clean. It was that appearance versus reality that he was concerned about. The seventh dealt with the inconsistency of building and decorating monuments to the prophets, yet they claim that they would not have participated in the killing of the prophets. (He seems to have seen them as guilty as their ancestors.) Whether Jesus was saying that they were currently rejecting God's prophet themselves or just that they were identified with the acts of their ancestors is difficult to ascertain. There were probably good scribes and good Pharisees, but the group as a whole stood condemned in the eyes of Jesus. He wept over the Holy City because its citizens had stoned and killed God's messengers and he saw destruction coming as a certainty because of that rejection.

## THE WIDOW'S GIFT: p. 169

Matthew did not include the story of the poor widow. Some have suggested that he omitted it because it did not pertain to the theme of judgment. Both Mark and Luke preserved it for posterity. The narrative dealt with the conception that the significance of ones gift must be measured, not in the amount given, but what it meant in terms of sacrifice. The widow had given sacrificially, offering two small coins which were probably worth about one or two cents, while others may have offered larger sums but must have had much left over. There was and is always the temptation to praise large gifts and publicize them.

Jesus knew that every gift represented an internal attitude no matter what the value of the gift might be. The acceptability from God's perspective has to do with that attitude because every offering is a representation of the love one has for God. By way of illustration, suppose that a relatively poor man had been saving every penny he could to buy a birthday gift for his wife. As the day approached, he just happened to see in a local store, on sale for today only, a rod and reel that he had wanted for years, but was unable to buy. Now he had a few dollars, say fifty of them which he had scraped to save. The temptation was too much! He bought the rod and reel for $39.50 and then tried to find something that he could buy with the remainder. What does that say about his love and priorities? I am quite certain that any devoted wife would be happy with the $10.50 gift, if that was all he could muster, but he loved himself and his desires more than he loved her. Wonder if God ever feels that way about our great "sacrifices?" This is again reflective of the Sermon on the Mount in which giving to be recognized by men is contrasted with giving from the correct motive.

# CHAPTER XVIII
## WARNINGS OF TRAGEDY

### DESTRUCTION OF THE TEMPLE  169-175

As the disciples pointed out the huge stones of the Temple building (Archeologists have suggested that they may have measured 12 feet by 12 feet by 24 feet), Jesus warned them that the Temple would soon be destroyed and the stones would be thrown down. That led them to ask him some questions in private. In Matthew's account there are three questions. 1) When will this be? (Referring to the destruction of the Temple.) 2) What will be the sign of Jesus' coming? 3) And what will be the sign of the end of the age? Exactly what was meant by the question, "What will be the sign of your coming?" is difficult to discern, especially since it is so different from the question in Mark and Luke. In those accounts by Mark and Luke there was only one question and that was: "When will this occur and what will be the sign that these things are about to occur?" So Mark 13 and Luke 21 are concerned primarily with the destruction of the great Temple, but they also brought other issues into their works.

## SIGNS OF THE END OF THE AGE p. 170

Even though Mark and Luke only had one question, the apocalyptic section deals with the fact that the end is not immediate. Jesus believed that there would be many who would lay claim to the title of Messiah and, depending on how one interprets the idea of claiming to be a deliverer, that belief was borne out, probably by some of the Zealots who may have led the revolt against Rome in 66-70 C.E. and later by the man known as Bar Cocheba who led a rebellion between 132-135. Jesus knew that many would be led astray by those pretenders and so he warned the disciples. He indicated that the world affairs would go on as usual, wars and rumors of wars, but that was just the beginning. He even warned them that they would be tortured and that they would be hated because of him. None of that would stop the news of the kingdom being spread throughout the world. That obviously meant some time would elapse before the end of the age, but he never stated anything that would indicate when the end would come. At some points it is very difficult to determine exactly which of the three questions Matthew has Jesus answering. Verses 15-22 seem to be talking about the destruction of the Temple for he referred to the desecration by using that which had been said in Daniel. Most probably the Daniel passage originally referred to the acts of Antiochus Epiphanes when he offered sacrifices to the Greek gods (even of swine) on Jehovah's altar. The Jews have never forgotten that, even to the present day. The holy days of Hanuka are observed near the time of the Christian Christmas season over an eight day period and commemorate the rededication of the Temple in Jerusalem in 165 B.C.E. (Robert S. Ellwood, *Many Peoples, Many Faiths 4th ed.* [Englewood Cliffs, New Jersey: Prentice Hall, 1992] 260) There are two intriguing statements in both Mark and Matthew which say "let the reader understand" which most likely mean that the event of the siege of Jerusalem and the destruction of the Temple had already occurred when those words were written and the other, after talking about the difficulties of that period stated, "And if those days had not been cut short no one would be saved." Since Jesus indicated that there would be no signs regarding the end and that he had no knowledge about it, one cannot help but wonder if verses 32-34 (the lesson of the Fig Tree) do not belong to the discussion of the destruction of the

Temple, especially since he indicated that what he had talked about would occur before that generation passed away.

That same theme of false Messiahs is repeated with the warning not to go after those false ones. because whatever he was talking about would be swift and sudden. Then he began some of the apocalyptic language which should never be taken literally. All apocalyptic literature was symbolic and used cosmic upheavals to represent sudden fearful occurrences. Usually the people who wrote this literature despaired of what was happening on the earth and believed that things would go from bad to worse until God finally intervened. They believed that God's intervention would probably be in the near future and would be accomplished by some heavenly or supernatural figure. Most often apocalyptic was pseudonymous and usually took the name of some hero of the past. The main characteristic of this type of literature was its weird symbolism, mythological beasts and the like because it was usually underground resistance literature. It also believed heavily in life after death as against the Hebrew belief in a shadowy existence in *Sheol*.

Of course, some of that is not true in this section of the gospels but cosmic upheavals were pictured. It is possible that in some of these passages Jesus may have been talking about the end of history, but there are no signs. Jesus even point-blank told them no one knew when the end time would come, not angels or he himself, but only God. (Matthew 24:36, Mark 13:32) The things one might be tempted to call signs are ordinary events. He suggested that eating, drinking, marrying, working in the fields would be going on in normal fashion and, if the coming of the Son of Man meant the end of history, it will come unexpectedly. The graphic separations which were described should not be played upon for emotional evangelism. The major emphasis which he gave to them in all three gospels was that they should always be prepared. In Matthew's account that led to several parables which dealt with preparedness. .

## THE WATCHFUL HOUSE OWNER: p. 176

Luke had given this parable in another context, but the only conclusion about its meaning is that just as no one knows when a thief is coming, so no one has the slightest idea about the end. There have always been those who have tried to decipher the "signs of the times" and they have never been correct. Sometimes, because there has been a long period between what Jesus said and the future end, some have thought it might never occur, but every indication, both scientifically and religiously points to a necessary end at some point. Apocalyptic thought has always come to the fore in times of stress and danger. That was part of the reason for its development in the first place. To take this material and particularly the Apocalypse as giving a pattern for the coming of the end seems to be foreign to the teaching of Jesus and of the nature of apocalyptic literature. To be sure, there is to be an end and a separation, There appears to be a beautiful blissful security in God. It is somewhat tragic that sensationalism has been adopted by many who claim to have the answers about the end, especially in regard to the Book of Revelation, but the Apocalypse was written to first century Christians who were undergoing horrible torture and even death. The primary question of that book is not to determine the time or signs of the end, but to answer the questions, (a) Who is ultimately Lord, Christ or Caesar? and (b) Is it worth it to be faithful? Everyone needs to keep in mind that Jesus gave no signs of the end and he, himself, did not know when it would occur - how dare any of us claim that we know?.

## PARABLES OF PREPAREDNESS: p. 177

The story of the Faithful and Wise Slave and that of the Ten Bridesmaids fit this context perfectly. These ideas have already been looked at but obviously, when slaves are put in charge of the master's business and he absents himself for a time, good slaves will treat the other slaves well but a wicked slave will waste his opportunities and treat the slaves under him in a bad fashion. His warning about preparedness also includes that the fact that the time of the return of the master is absolutely unknown, completely in keeping with what had been said in previous warnings.

The story of the Ten Bridesmaids drew on the customs of the time regarding weddings. It is difficult to be certain about those customs, but it would appear that all of the arrangements (the betrothal, the giving of the dowry, a waiting period - normally a year, and the preparations for the wedding feast) had been made. The bridegroom usually went to the home of the bride in procession and escorted her back to his home for the feast and the finalizing of the marriage. The feast would have begun when the procession came back to the home of the bridegroom and only those invited and present when the doors were closed were allowed in. There does not seem to have been any ceremony conducted by a rabbi. The story depicts five maids who had foresight and were prepared and five who were not prepared. The little lamps are vividly pictured as flickering and in the process of going out, so the wise ones were able to replenish the oil supply with the extra they had. Those who had not had foresight tried to beg some oil, but they were not given any. That may seem heartless, but there was no way of knowing how long the procession would be in coming and there might be a need for a second or third replenishing. So they replied to the unprepared ones that they needed to go and buy some oil, for no one knew when the bridegroom would come back. The story indicates that while they were gone to search for oil, the procession came, entered the home, and shut the doors. And when the maidens returned from purchasing the oil, it was too late! There is no other meaning than that one should always be prepared, for the hour is not known.

## A PARABLE OF CHARACTER: pp. 179-180

As was the case with the parable of preparedness dealing with the ten maidens, so in this parable, Matthew is the only one who preserves the story. In dealing with this parable one must sense that in the New Testament there are two strains of thought dealing with what happens in the after life. The first one, which is closely tied with Jesus' apocalyptic thought suggests a Day of Judgment at which all persons of all time will stand in line to be judged. That was a typical thought that prevailed from the time the Jews began to consider the possibility of life after death. It was connected also with the judgment of Israel and the Day of the Lord became a phrase which applied to that time. In this parable and in some of Saint Paul's teaching it would appear that there was the thought of some future time when there would be a bodily resurrection and a judgment (1st Corinthians 15:33ff and 1st Thessalonians 4:13-5:11) but in other places it would appear that Jesus believed there would be an immediate entrance into Paradise (Luke 23:43) and some of what Saint Paul said (2nd Corinthians 5:6-10) seems to indicate that immediately upon death a believer goes to be with the Lord and yet there is still that concept of standing before him in judgment. It is a perplexing thought but most current Christianity does not believe in a suspended state between the time one dies and the end, but rather, the Day of Judgment is a term referring to what occurs throughout history as each person dies. For most people the latter is the most preferable of the two ideas and the only thing that caused a problem with that interpretation lay in the notion that the influence of ones life could never run its full course until the end of time and so judgment could not be complete until then! That can be answered by suggesting that it is actually not ones influence which is involved in the judgment (or even deeds) but his/her character and that seems to be what this parable is about. No one can ever claim or pretend to know much about the eternal situation - that is beyond us. But eternity is not physical for, as Paul, says we are to be given a spiritual body. (1st Corinthians 15: 35-49) Who could dare guess what that is?

There are many people who, because they can think no other way, believe that the spiritual body is like the physical one - but at what stage (in the prime of life or what)? So it is necessary to ask, what carries over into eternity? The interpretation of this parable given here is that ones character, the real essence of what one is represents a part of ones eternal spirit, and the Christlikeness or lack of it is developed through communion and identity with Christ during this life. In that line of thinking, the salvation by grace through faith concept is strongly affirmed but the level of Christlikeness determines the capacity of fellowship in which one can participate. One can share with God in exact proportion to the likeness to Christ he/she has developed by growing in grace during ones life in Christ. This parable which discusses Judgment indicates that a moral separation will occur, either progressively as each believer dies or at the end of the age. Those who were accepted by the judge were commended for having offered themselves in service. He suggested that they had fed him, they had slaked his thirst, they had clothed him, they had visited him when he was sick, they had even visited in the prison. When that judgment was pronounced those people did not even know that they had done such things and asked about that. The surprise of the parable is that they did not know and that is probably its key. (Hold that issue for a few moments and read about the rejected group.)

The same things were said negatively about those who were rejected, for they had done none of the things the judge talked about. They imply that they believed they had done all those things, almost saying, "Oh, but we did!" What is the difference in the two groups? The real issue is that of character, for one group had done the things they had done in service to others simply because that was what they were inside, that was their character trait and they had done service without counting up the credit for it. Apparently the others had "kept score." They knew they had done some good things and could not see where they had failed to serve the judge. (That is salvation by works!) At the conclusion of the parable Jesus interposed the idea that when one served one of the Master's "little ones" they served him! Many have simply taken this to be a social action parable and it certainly has that in it, but that is not its primary significance. If the conceptions held in this work are correct, every act which is done in the spirit of Jesus is an act of worship.

As was indicated in the discussion relating to the spiritually real, heaven and hell, no one can claim to understand much about eternity. But the things that seem to carry over are the things relating to character likeness to Christ. A couple of generations ago Charles Sheldon wrote a novel, *In His Steps,* in which all of the characters before every decision of their lives were supposed to ask themselves the question, "What would Jesus do?" That can be a noble thought, but trying to imitate Christ is not character. Character traits must be developed gradually, over a period of time, so that we serve like Jesus because we have become servants like he is/was, we forgive like Jesus because we have become forgivers, we learn to be compassionate and caring because we have become like him, we become generous stewards because we have sensed that he was that kind of steward, not because one tries to do good works and copy him. And so it is with all of the character traits of Jesus that we can find in the story, as we have it. That seems to mean that Christianity is a process of "becoming" rather than just a conversion. It is vital to understand, and often the church has not sensed, that Christianity is not a religion of doing things, but of becoming something, namely Christlike (character development in Christlikeness)!

# CHAPTER XIX
## THE PASSION STORY

### THE CONSPIRACY  p. 181

For quite a long time the religious leaders had wanted to arrest Jesus but according to the narrative they had been afraid of a revolt. Because Jesus was aware of that and of the fact that things had apparently come to a head, he warned the disciples about the impending crisis. Matthew indicated that the planning for the arrest took place at the palace of the High Priest, Caiaphas. All three gospels indicate that there was a decision to try to take Jesus by stealth and kill him. With the crowd that had gathered for the Passover it was difficult to find a way to do that, but their plans were laid.

### THE ANNOINTING AT BETHANY:  pp. 181-182

Mark and Matthew tell the story of an unidentified woman who anointed Jesus' head with some very costly ointment at a dinner in Simon the leper's home. Previously Luke had given an account of another anointing had placed it at the home of Simon the Pharisee. Perhaps these are two different events, for they certainly have a different significance for Jesus. Matthew's account indicated that the disciples were incensed that such a waste should take place, for the ointment must have been valued at about a year's wages. Jesus, however, interpreted the action in a way that they had not anticipated, for if they so chose they would have ample time to care for the poor. His death and burial, however, were looming before them in the immediate future. Because they seem almost oblivious to the coming events, one cannot help but wonder if they had any understanding of what he was saying, even at this late hour. Jesus probably spent the latter part of Tuesday, all of Wednesday and until Thursday night with the disciples. How much he was in Jerusalem it is not possible to say.

At some point in this series of events Judas had made contact with the priests to hand him over to them. The thirty pieces of silver was a small amount and the account in Matthew may reflect the hire of a shepherd in Zechariah 11:13. Since it was not a large amount of money, something else must have motivated Judas. In Luke's account there is the statement that Satan entered into Judas, and certainly Judas has always borne a great stain from the betrayal. (Rarely does anyone name a son Judas.) Other than the claim that all of this was done according to the will of God, the most plausible theory, for which there is no real evidence, was that Judas was disturbed by the fact that Jesus did not go on to announce his political kingdom and begin what they had all been looking for. That could possibly account for the remorse that overcame him when he saw what the outcome had become and he could not live with himself any longer, so he hanged himself. Incidentally, in the listings of the apostles Judas is always placed next to Simon Zelotes (the Zealot). Maybe Judas was a Zealot also. There is no way to get inside Judas' head and know why he committed this deed, but maybe he never expected such a tragic outcome. There have been those who have suggested that he may have thought he could force Jesus to step forward and make his claim to the kingdom, but we can never know. The feeling of the early church, especially as it can be seen in the Gospel of John, was that Judas had been a bad egg from the very beginning, but one must remember that he seems to have been the treasurer of the band (he controlled the purse) and that would not have happened if he had been seen as satanic even before the betrayal. It seems more likely that in retrospect they viewed Judas in an entirely different light after the betrayal, since everything that was written about it came after the total event; that is a very human characteristic! If their misunderstanding of the nature of the kingdom was as prominent as it appears to have been, even after the resurrection (Acts 1:6), most anything might have run through their minds. But it was a mistaken and dastardly deed! Most Christians probably believe that Judas was a "damned" person and that he will have no place in the heavenly realm. But if his was not an act of vicious hatred and purely evil, who can say what his eternal situation may be. Many people, including Jesus' own family, encouraged him to take the position of an earthly king and just maybe that was what Judas was trying to do.

## PREPARATIONS FOR THE PASSOVER  pp. 182-183

On the first day of Unleavened Bread when the Passover lamb was sacrificed the disciples asked Jesus about preparations for the Passover. Perhaps it was a planned signal but the disciples are told to go into the city and find a man carrying a jar of water; it might have been unusual for a man to be carrying the water home. They were to follow him and find the place for which Jesus had arranged.    Following the Synoptic account, that would have been on what modern Christians call Maundy Thursday, and they were shown to the large upstairs room where they prepared the Passover meal. Jesus and the twelve disciples were eating the meal when he told them that one of them would betray him. That caused great consternation among them and each seemed to wonder if he would be the culprit. Again, if Judas was believed to be satanic from the beginning, they would probably immediately have accused him. Matthew indicated that Jesus said the one who had already dipped into the dish with him would be the one. Judas responded, "Surely not I" and Jesus, "You have said so." That did not seem to indicate to the group who the person would be for they were still puzzled about it. Jesus indicated the severity of what was about to be done, by suggesting that the one who betrayed him would be better off to have never existed.

## THE INSTITUTION OF THE Lord's Supper  pp. 184-185

It was at this juncture, while they were reclining at the table, that the Lord's Supper, later to be know as Communion and the Eucharist (meaning "thanksgiving")  was instituted. The elements used in the supper were common elements from the Passover meal. The meaning of what Jesus did must not have been evident to them at that time, but he took the loaf of bread and said, "Take, eat, this is my body." (In none of the accounts do any of the early manuscripts have the word "broken.") That declaration along with that made about the cup being his "blood of the covenant" must have been puzzling to them especially since he said "I will never again drink of this fruit of the vine until that day when I drink it new with you in my Father's Kingdom." Those must have been tense, trying, and puzzling moments in the lives of those followers, leaving them pondering what it all meant. The symbolism would not be understood by them until much later.

As every student of Christianity knows, there have been three major interpretations in regard to what Jesus said and meant. The position of the Roman Catholic Church, usually called "Trans-substantiation," has been that when the elements of the Eucharist are blessed they mystically become the body and blood of Jesus. A somewhat "in between" interpretation, which is usually attributed to Luther, is termed "Con-substantiation" and suggests that the elements become spiritually the body of Christ, not literally. And the third position has been that these are symbols of his body and blood and vitally significant. (The reader is reminded again of the seriousness and the meaning of the term "symbol.") Which ever one chooses to follow, this was a sobering event and it became intensely meaningful to the early church. Saint Paul warned about the seriousness of participating in this ritual in a glib manner, for it became the one ritual where the unity of Christ with his body was represented in his church and it was a sobering reminder of the event of his death. One must keep in mind that since all genuine worship is inward and spiritual and that rituals and symbols are things which point beyond themselves to a greater reality.. The value of the Eucharist lies in the inward appropriation of its meaning by the individual worshipper. To go through the motions of the event with divisiveness in the community or with unconcern in the hearts of the participants was (and is) a farce and thus sinful.

## IN GETHSAMANE pp. 187-189

The arrangement of the narrative is a little confusing because Luke places the prediction of Peter's denial before they left the room, while the other two gospels suggest that it occurred after they left the room. It should be understood that Jesus not only said that Peter would deny Jesus, but that all of them would desert him. They were facing a night that was more trying than they knew. It was when Jesus said that they all would desert him that Peter voiced the willingness to die with Jesus and that he would never be a deserter, and they all made the same claim.. Peter probably was very serious for, when the pressures are not heavy humans often pledge a commitment and then when the trials come, they are unable to carry through; no one ever knows his/her strength before testing comes. We would like to believe, like Peter, that we would be willing to die for Jesus, and I hope we would, but often self preservation and human weakness make it very difficult to make that sacrifice.

With adrenalin pumping, as Jesus had experienced it, he divided the group and took three with him. (There have recently been some remarkable discoveries about the grotto they may have been in and the state of the Mount of Olives area.) Jesus was in a very stressful situation because he was convinced that the crisis was immediately upon him. More than likely he was aware of the plans of the religious leaders to take him and kill him secretly, but one cannot read the story of the scene without feeling the pressure that was on him. With a very vivid symbol, the gospel of Luke reported, "In his anguish he prayed more earnestly, and his sweat became like great drops of blood falling on the ground," another vivid symbol. (22:44) (No one should ever diminish the agony of Jesus by suggesting that he knew he would be resurrected or anything else that tends to make him less human.) He moved deep into the garden three times and each time as he returned he found them sleeping. They did not feel the intensity of the crisis that Jesus did. Moderns should not fault them for sleeping! Not only did they not have the same intensity as Jesus, they lived in a culture where people did not keep late night hours, and it is difficult to know what the hour was when the large crowd, probably the Temple police, came to arrest him. The Fourth Gospel tells us that it was Peter who drew his sword, apparently willing to die as he had said, and struck a servant of the high priest, cutting off his ear. Jesus refused the effort to resist and went with them peaceably. Strangely, the followers of Jesus were not arrested. There is an intriguing verse in Mark which leaves so much unsaid that any effort to interpret it is little more than a guess. It says, "A certain young man was following him wearing nothing but a linen cloth. They caught hold of him, but he left the linen cloth and ran off naked." (14:51-52) There are two things in tradition which may help in a conjecture about this. Tradition stated that the upper room where the supper was held was in the home of Mark's mother. If that is correct and young Mark could have been preparing for bed and the Temple police came to the house first with hopes of finding Jesus there, he must have wanted to warn the little disciple band. Assuming that he had just taken his cloths off and had not yet been able to put on any night clothes (not even considering that he might have slept nude), he could have grabbed a sheet (no time to dress), wrapped it around him, and run as rapidly as he could to the garden. Gethsemane must have been a favorite spot for Jesus and the disciples, known to many. If that had been the case, the young man would have been covered only by the linen sheet. Couple that with the concept that Mark was nicknamed "stub fingers," which might have come about, not because his fingers were naturally short, as some have suggested, but that as he fled someone took a swipe at him, clipped off some fingers, and grabbed the sheet. We cannot know, but one must ask why this peculiar piece of narrative, which really has nothing to do with the arrest, is in the gospel? So why is it in Mark and Mark only? If it had been you streaking through the back streets of Jerusalem, trying to get home un-noticed, wouldn't that have been one of the things you would have never been able to forget about that night? (Of course, all of that assumes that John Mark was the author of the gospel.)

## THE TRIALS OF JESUS pp. 190-197

Even though most scholars believe that the Passion Narrative may have been part of the earliest written material, it is still difficult to bring order out of the stories of the trials. It is necessary also to consider the account in the Fourth Gospel and attempt to make some sense of harmony out of these reports. That gospel said that Jesus was first taken to Annas, the father-in-law of the high priest. Annas had formerly been the high priest but had been banished from the office by the Roman authorities so he had no legal standing. Many have felt that he was in charge of the bazaars in the Temple area, and if so, his mind set would have already been pre-disposed because of the action Jesus took in the Temple, cleansing it.. All of this took place during the night and was illegal (Matthew 27:1-2 and Mark 15:1) no matter whether we are talking about being before Annas or Caiaphas. How much of the questioning was before Annas, or whether he did the questioning we cannot tell, but according to the gospel of John it would appear that this first inquisition was before Annas and then Jesus was sent, bound, to Caiaphas. The Synoptic account seems to indicate that they tried Jesus before Caiaphas on the evidence of two who testified that he had said he was able to destroy the Temple and build it again in three days. But that was not evidence enough to convict him of anything more than arrogance. Caiaphas pushed the investigation with the question about Messiahship and three different accounts are given. Matthew wrote that Jesus answered, "You have said so." That really did not answer the question. Mark wrote that Jesus said, "I am." and Luke indicated that Jesus said, "If I tell you, you will not believe." There is some confusion about his answer but when he went on to indicate that the Son of Man would be coming from the heavens and had the authority of God (seated at the right hand) they concluded that he had blasphemed. But even so, there was nothing that could be done except banish him from the synagogue and Temple. The group had already determined that he should be put to death, but they had no authority to bring about that execution. After morning arrived they held a meeting with the entire Sanhedrin (the whole council), apparently to try to make the action legal, and they took Jesus and handed him over to Pilate. The conclusion of those hearings was that he was guilty of blasphemy. That was a religious charge and not one that Pilate would have been concerned about. There had been three "ecclesiastical" trials; one was at night and before an illegitimate authority, Annas. Since the high priest at the time of Jesus' trials was Caiaphas, the son-in-law of Annas, Annas had no official standing, but he still carried great influence. Another trial was subsequently held before the current and proper high priest, Caiaphas, and perhaps part of the Sanhedrin. It was also held before dawn and therefore was also illegal. A last part of these ecclesiastical trials was held, according to Mark, by the whole Sanhedrin (council) and was done after dawn to legalize what had been decided earlier. The illegality of those hearings has been summarized in the following quote:

But let us first summarize the points at which the proceedings thus far had offended against the elementary rules of law and justice. In what respects was the Sanhedrin's judgment illegal?

a) It was illegal in that the court which was to decide Jesus' case was also an accomplice in his betrayal. Members of the Sanhedrin were inextricably implicated in the secret plots that had culminated in Judas' deed of treachery. Yet these same men were now to act as a jury.

b) The trial did not begin, as Jewish law demanded, with a statement of a definite charge against the accused. . . . When the witnesses disagreed and no charge was forthcoming, it was the court's duty to abandon the case.

c) Moreover, the judge trying the case was also a leader for the prosecution. . . .

d) Further, there were no witnesses for the defense. None was summoned. . . .

e) But the crowning illegality of the trial was the haste with which it was completed. In the dead of night the case was hurried through. The holding of a brief, formal meeting at sunrise to ratify the night's work and to give a faint show of legality to what had been done did not alter the fact that the Sanhedrin's midnight investigation was a flagrant breach of its own laws. But that was not the worst. There was a law that in capital charges sentence of death could be pronounced only on the day after the trial; twenty four hours had to elapse. (James S. Stewart, *The Life and Teachings of Jesus* [New York-Nashville: Abingdon Press] 159,160)

While all of this had been going on, Peter had been taken into the courtyard of the high priest by one of the disciples who was known to the high priest and while there he was asked by the woman who guarded the gate, "You are not also one of this man's disciples, are you?" According to the Fourth Gospel Peter replied, "I am not." Luke indicated that he said, "Woman, I do not know him." A little later while Peter was warming himself by the fire someone else, Luke said it was the servant girl again, accused him of being one of them, and Peter denied it with an oath. A third time some of them accused him saying that his accent was that of a Galilean. That time the narrative said that Peter began to curse (there is no reason to suggest that Peter pronounced a curse against himself, he probably resorted to his "fisherman's" language) and swore another oath indicating that he did not know the man. (This bolsters the teaching of Jesus in the Sermon on the Mount that oaths do not in any sense create or enhance the truth.) At that moment a cock crowed and Peter remembered what Jesus had said and broke down and wept bitterly.

So, since the charge on which Jesus was condemned was that of blasphemy, and no Roman governor would consider that as deserving of death, Luke indicated that when they brought Jesus to Pilate they charged him with claiming to be a king. (23:2) Most lay persons know but little about the fine points of the law, but if a person is convicted on a charge and then taken to a higher court he should be prosecuted on that same charge. But since the charge of blasphemy would probably have been thrown out, they changed to a political charge of treason, "He claimed to be a king." At this point Matthew recorded the death of Judas. It was a sad story of a man who tried to repent and undo what had been done, if Matthew is correct about the timing, even before the hearing before Pilate. He attempted to give back the money and when that failed he threw it down in the Temple and went out and hanged himself. The priests indicated that they could not pollute the treasury by putting the money in it, so they took it and bought a plot to bury foreigners in. Matthew found another parallel proof text in Jeremiah (32:6-15) and likened this event to that passage.

At this point they had Jesus before the Romans. If they could get a verdict, they could succeed in removing him from the scene. The best information seems to suggest that this time the Sanhedrin did not have the authority to carry out the death sentence, but that had to be done by the Romans. Pilate questioned Jesus and indicated to the religious leaders that he could find no way to support the accusations against Jesus. They tried to influence Pilate by suggesting that a riot would probably occur because of Jesus' teaching. With such a confusing dilemma before him, Pilate discovered that Jesus was from Galilee so that meant that he needed to be under the jurisdiction of Herod Antipas. At least that would get the "monkey off Pilate's back." Herod was in Jerusalem, probably because of the Passover, so Pilate sent Jesus to Antipas. Herod had wanted to talk with Jesus for some time, especially since he had once said he thought Jesus was John the Baptist who had come back to life. With all the vehement accusations against Jesus, Herod had to do something, so he allowed the soldiers to mock him, placed an elegant robe on him and sent him back to Pilate. Pilate may have done this either as a courtesy to Herod, since Jesus was a Galilean or because he wanted Herod to be responsible for the hearing. There are several indications that Pilate was a hard governor, almost heartless, and that he had little capacity for mercy. Certainly his major concern was with keeping order. Luke suggested that there had been some animosity between the two prior to this (23:12) but that after this event they became friends. Pilate indicated to the chief priests that neither he nor Herod had found any way to sustain the charges which they had levied against Jesus and he offered to administer a lesser punishment of flogging and then to release Jesus. If one follows the gospel of Mark, those who came to Pilate to ask for the release of a prisoner may not have known about the trial of Jesus and may have simply asked for the policy of releasing a prisoner to be followed. No one has found any evidence of releasing a prisoner being more than just something Pilate may have done, and Beck states that this is the only information we have about such a custom. (315) At any rate, it was the religious leaders who stirred up the crowd and got them to ask for the murderer and insurrectionist, Barabbas, to be released. Several times Pilate tried to avoid sending Jesus to execution; his wife had warned him and he seems to have been very hesitant himself.

A stronger man might have done justice, but Pilate succumbed to the pressure and symbolically, tried to wash his hands of the responsibility. Then he handed Jesus over to be crucified which had to be done by Roman authority.

In the narrative there is a short statement about the way the Roman soldiers abused Jesus and mocked him. They put a "royal" robe on him and then mockingly cried out "Hail, King of the Jews." He was struck with reeds, spat upon and insulted with demands that he prophesy about who struck him while he was blindfolded. Then as the procession started toward the site for the crucifixion they stripped off the robe and replaced it with his own clothes. Just how much scourging he suffered or whether he lost great amounts of blood cannot be accurately known for surprisingly, the gospel writers give a rather subdued description of what took place. Non scriptural writers have expanded on what we actually know about his torment that night and they emphasized great agony which is not included in the Gospel narrative.

Usually the condemned was required to carry the main beam of the cross and as they went along a man from Cyrene, named Simon, was compelled to help Jesus. We know little about that man, whether he was a follower of Jesus or just "passer-by" who got drafted. ( Mark named Simon's sons, as if they should have been known to his readers, with no added explanation.) Luke included in the crowd that followed along some women who were wailing for him, No one can do more than guess whether those women were followers or just some who were sympathetic to any person bearing such agony.

Crucifixion was a horrible way to die! Many have gone to great lengths to dramatize the suffering of Jesus, and there is no doubt that the suffering was tragic. It was a common method of execution among the Carthaginians and perhaps the Romans adopted it from them. With the number of crucifixions which occurred it is a little strange that almost no real evidence is available to describe it. One nail passing through a heel bone and bent seems to be about all that archeologists have been able to discover. Roman citizens were exempt from it and only slaves and criminals suffered its embarrassment, agony and humiliation. There is no easy way to bring about execution, but some methods were, and are, more "civil" than others. For instance, modern methods of execution by the use of injection or even electrocution may be seen as rather humane, but no one can ever know exactly what anticipation and suffering the condemned endures. The guillotine or any other kind of beheading was much faster and carried instant death and, apparently, there was little pain with it. Even hanging was (and is) a relatively quick death. The practice of some American Indians of staking the prisoner down and tying him, spread eagle fashion, with wet leather thongs and letting those shrink gradually as they dried, and allowing him to die of thirst or tying the victim between two horses and driving them off in different directions, thus tearing the victim apart were filled with horror. It may be argued that burning one alive is also filled with untold agony, but all of those were faster than crucifixion There are records of victims of crucifixion suffering the agonies of excruciating thirst, pain, and shock for as long as seven days before finally dying.

Mark gave the hour for the beginning of the crucifixion as nine o'clock. The procession began at the palace of Pilate but the path is almost impossible to trace. The one which is generally shown to tourists, along with the Stations of the Cross, called the Via Doloroso, had its origin in the thirteenth century. The actual place of the crucifixion has been debated by many archaeologists, however, we can be relatively certain that it was outside the city wall (Hebrews 13:12) and what is sometimes called Gordon's Calvary, may be the site.

Often people maintain that they cannot forgive, but when one reads the account of what Jesus endured and that even after that he prayed for the forgiveness, probably both for the soldiers, for the masses of the people, and perhaps even for the religious leaders, his manifestation of the forgiving nature and character of God is overwhelming. Two criminals were executed with Jesus and the two men responded in completely different ways. Luke was the evangelist who saved for us the repentant response one of the thieves made. (It offers support to the concept that immediately after death one enters into eternal bliss.)

It is easy to dramatize, perhaps overmuch, the pain that Jesus went through and spend time focusing on the physical aspects of it the crucifixion rather than to attempt to discover what God was doing throughout the whole process. An inscription was normally placed over the head of the victim which explained the reason for the execution and this one was a political charge which read, "The King of the Jews." The Fourth Gospel tells of a protest from the priests who wanted the placard changed to read, "This man said, 'I am the King of the Jews.'" It was ignored! They took Jesus' clothes, including a woven robe, (John 19:23-24) and the soldiers divided them among themselves. Some kind of darkness came over the land from noon until three o'clock. At that point Jesus cried out the peculiar saying *"Eloi, Eloi, lema, sabachthani"* which has been translated "My God, My God, why have you forsaken me?" There has been a suggestion that he might have been asking, "My

God, My God, why does it have to be left this way?" Certainly Jesus was never more in harmony with the Circumstantial Will of God than when he died, therefore he was not forsaken!. The mental anguish of knowing that God's message and work he had done had been rejected must have been much more difficult to bear than the physical pain.

Many of the events reported as accompanying the crucifixion are clouded in mystery. Mark and Matthew report that the great veil in the Temple was split when Jesus died. It is very difficult to know whether that statement was about a literal event or was figurative. (More will be said about that later in the discussion of what all this meant.) Matthew also told of an earthquake and of tombs being opened. (He also is the only one who records that there were some dead who were raised and entered the city.) The Fourth Gospel also reported that Jesus charged "the disciple whom he loved" with caring for his mother. Others looked on all these events from a distance. The gospels reported that Jesus died around three o'clock and that would be remarkably fast for a crucifixion. The Fourth Gospel stated that at the request of the religious leaders who did not want the bodies of the three men hanging on crosses during the Sabbath, the leg bones of the men were to be broken. It has already been indicated that people who were crucified died from thirst, shock and finally from a combination of strangulation and suffocation. On the upright bar of the cross there was a small board or ledge, which was provided so that the crucified could push up and relieve the pressure, especially that connected with breathing. If the leg bones were broken the death would have been hastened and that is what the request was all about. But when they came to Jesus he was already dead and when a soldier pierced his side blood and water (probably collected in his abdomen from the shock) came out and that also corroborated the fact that he was dead, so his legs were not broken.

At that point the gospels introduced the character of Joseph of Arimathea who was a member of the Sanhedrin and had not agreed with what they did. He asked for the privilege of burying the body of Jesus and Pilate, who was astonished that he was already dead, granted that request. Joseph had the body wrapped in a linen cloth and placed in the tomb, but it was too late for a proper burial with spices and ointments placed in the folds of the cloth in which his body had been wrapped; that waited until after the Sabbath. Matthew reported the request that the tomb be sealed and guarded. That request appears to have been made to Pilate; the guards were Roman soldiers. The tomb was secure!

# CHAPTER XX
## THE RESURRECTION AND ASCENSION

### THE EMPTY TOMB  pp. 204-206

Since the narratives relating to the resurrection seem to be disconnected pieces, they have always been difficult to place in any order. The discovery of the empty tomb appears to have been by Mary Magdalene, Mary the mother of James, and Salome who went there early on the morning after the Sabbath with spices so that they might anoint his body. There is an air of disbelief and amazement even as they found the stone rolled back from the opening of the tomb and a young man (Mark 16:5) sitting there. The women did not know what to make of what they saw and were terrified and according to Mark they did not tell anyone, but fled. (Matthew called the young man an angel and Luke told of two men in dazzling clothes.) The guards were apparently petrified! Matthew reported the story of the bribing of the soldiers by the priests, and he indicated that the story that the disciples had stolen the body was still being told when the gospel was written. The women were instructed to go and tell the disciples and Peter that Jesus was going to Galilee as he had told them. It is not at all surprising that they were confused and Mark indicated that they were afraid to tell anyone, but Luke and Matthew reported that the women told the disciples and that they were not believed, for to them the report sounded like a hysterical fantasy. The Fourth Gospel indicated that Peter and "the other disciple" ran to the tomb to investigate and found the tomb empty except for the grave clothes.

## THE ROAD TO EMMAUS:  pp.207-208

Luke's story of the two men on the road to Emmaus who met Jesus, is filled with disappointment, despair, and even fear regarding everything tragic that had happened when all hope had been lost.  It is only at the point when Jesus revealed to them who he was as the bread was broken that they half-way began to understand.  The fact that they did not recognize him has puzzled many, but the whole series of bodily appearances is filled with disbelief and amazement on the part of the followers,  but how else could it have been?  One of the most powerful proofs regarding the resurrection is the transformation which took place in the lives of his followers.  No one could fabricate the psychological change from fear and disillusionment about the tragic end of their hopes regarding the kingdom to the attitude they demonstrate after the period of the appearances.  Something totally outside of the realm of human understanding had to have taken place.  One of my old professors from two generations ago stated that during the resurrection appearances Jesus had a body for the disciples' sakes.   Since he sometimes was not recognizable and even sometimes appeared suddenly in closed rooms, we are left with feelings of awe also. No one can grasp what the ultimate spiritual body is like or even know if Jesus appeared in a spiritual body.

## THE APPEARANCES TO THE DISCIPLES: John 20: 19-29

The Fourth Gospel recorded one appearance to Mary, probably Magdalene, when she was still puzzled and thought that the body had been moved.  At that point, when she recognized him, the King James Version translated the verb as "Do not touch me," but the proper translation means "Do not continue hanging on to me." He had not left them (and would not for about forty days) and she needed to report immediately to the disciples what she had experienced.

The Fourth Gospel also recorded the first appearance to the group of the apostles on the evening of that first dramatic week-end. Jesus showed them a continuity  between what they were seeing and the experience of the crucifixion. They were filled with ecstasy, but Thomas was not with them. He has often been castigated and called "doubting Thomas," but that seems highly unfair. Remember that the other disciples could not believe the report of the women - had we been there at that time would any of us have believed that impossible tale? When he was present the next week, apparently Thomas did not require placing his hands in the wounds which he had said he needed to do in order to be convinced, but he worshipped his "Lord and God." (John 20:27)

John recorded another appearance by the Sea of Tiberias in Galilee. It is not possible to know exactly what Peter meant by "I am going fishing." Had he not yet been convinced and was he going back to his old manner of life? When, at Jesus suggestion from the shore, they hauled in a huge catch of fish, Peter understood who he was and eagerly jumped in to get to the shore and be with him. It was during this time of being with them that Jesus asked Peter, "Do you love me more than these?" It is not possible to know what Jesus may have meant by that question. He may have meant do you love me more than these others do? Or he may have meant do you love me more than you love these things (boats and nets)? Or even do you love me more than you love these others? Whatever he meant, he used the word *agape'* indicating that unselfish, unqualified, God like kind of love. Each time when Peter answered he replied with the Greek term *phileo* which is that friendship kind of love. A second time he asked the same question with the same wording and Peter replied just as he had done before. When Jesus asked the question the third time he came down to Peter's word for love, by which he seems to have meant - do you really even love me with the friendship kind of love? It makes no sense to suggest that Peter felt hurt just because Jesus asked him the same question three times, but if he suddenly understood the radical difference in the kind of love Jesus had asked about and what he had answered, no wonder he was grieved. Peter learned lessons the hard way, but he did learn! Then Jesus indicated what many who have lived to old age have learned, there comes a time when youthful strength forsakes everyone who lives long enough, and in the loss of independence they must depend on others, and Peter would die. Impetuous and inquisitive Peter asked about what would happen to "the one whom Jesus loved." Some have tried to suggest Jesus said that that disciple would never die, but that is not what he said. In effect his answer simply was something like, "That is none of your business. All you need to do is follow me. What happens to him is of no consequence you." (John 21:1-23)

It is interesting that the authentic verses of the gospel of Mark offered only one short story regarding the resurrection. That might support the idea that the original ending of Mark was lost and that the spurious ending was supplied to complete the story.

There have always been those who have found it difficult to believe that such a thing as the resurrection could have occurred and there is obviously no way to prove it. But there are not only testimonies from eyewitnesses, there is an emotional-psychological element which enters into the story. The resurrection is the hinge point of Christianity. Without it the movement would probably have fizzled or else become just another Jewish sect. That which happened in the lives of those who saw him cannot be explained by some kind of hoax. Those followers had lost everything! Not only did their deep love for Jesus suffer, but their misguided dreams about the restoration of the kingdom were crushed. No one can tell me they could pull off that bit of emotional, psychological faking? It is not possible that the personal transformation that they exhibited could occur without some radical, totally unexpected and unbelievable event that completely changed their emotional state. To think that the small band could all agree to change status and fake the joy and bravery that they showed in just a few days - that is idiocy - emotions cannot be commanded! No one can explain or prove what happened, but something fantastic did and it changed them all!

## THE ASCENSION  pp. 207 and 209

Matthew did not give the account of the ascension, but he did give a "commissioning" account. At some unnamed mountain he gave to them what is commonly known as "The Great Commission." It said, "As you are going  make disciples of all nations." The only Imperative in that passage is "make disciples." The rest of the charge indicated that as they lived their day to day lives they were to baptize followers and teach them what Jesus had taught. That was not just an instruction for "professional missionaries," but it is for all followers as they live their daily lives. Then according to the gospel of Luke and amplified in the first chapter of Acts, he "withdrew from them and was carried up into heaven." It is certain that what happened was that he was being completely removed from the material world into the spiritual realm. For the purposes of the Gospels the mechanics of that change were apparently not important and may be inexplicable!.

# CHAPTER XXI
## WHAT DID IT ALL MEAN?

Throughout the history of Christian thought many have attempted to explain the concept of the Atonement. Any attempt to summarize all of them and show their inadequacies would expand this work beyond its purpose.. However, it is necessary to mention a few of those theories and show the possibilities for a different approach. Perhaps the most needed statement is that in all probability no one can fathom the depths of the love of God in bringing about reconciliation and the meaning of the Atonement. However, that does not mean that we should not make an effort to understand what God did in Jesus, the Christ.

Since the time of the of the early church fathers there has been a theory, based on taking the term "ransom" literally in the statement of Jesus, "For the Son of Man came not to be served but to serve, and to give his life as a ransom for many." (Mark 10: 45) That sentence came out of a context in which Jesus was attempting to get the twelve to understand that greatness in the kingdom is not like the understanding of greatness in the world. It was not a simple statement about the Atonement. However, the interpretation of those who were taking the scriptural material literally was that since mankind was in bondage to sin, some sort of ransom had to be paid to release them. A ransom, taken literally, has both one who pays and one to whom the ransom is paid, so that led to an idea that God paid to Satan a perfect and sinless offering in the person of Christ. It is difficult to see in the first place how God could be in any sense inferior to Satan and thus be required to bargain. It also should mean that since the penalty for sin was eternal separation from God, the ransom should itself also be eternally separated. But as the writer of Hebrews pointed out, Jesus was raised from the dead and is seated "at the right hand of God." That would have to mean that in some sense God was some kind of "Indian giver" and that once the release of mankind was secured, God snatched Jesus back. Such thinking violates the nature and character of God and destroys His integrity.

The Penal Satisfaction theory, set forth by Anselm, sees the honor of God as being violated by sin. In order for that honor to be defended and since mankind cannot pay the infinite penalty of punishment, it was necessary for God to provide a defense of His honor by offering Jesus as a pure and infinite sacrifice. According to that theory, since Jesus was sinless he could be the representative of mankind and pay the debt. So Anselm suggested that, by dying an unnecessary and voluntary sacrificial death, Jesus earned an excess of merit (on the Roman Catholic theory) which could be applied to the credit of sinners, thus restoring God's honor.

There have been others who, taking the concept that Jesus did something for mankind that they could not do for themselves, used the substitution idea of a sinless one who died for the sins of the guilty, making redemption possible, assuming that mankind received the sacrifice. It is still difficult to see how one man dying for another does anything more than make the one left alive indebted to the one who gave his life.

Still others use the death of Jesus as some kind of moral influence and believe that his death was an example of that great influence, dying as a martyr. His example of loyalty to truth, even to the point of death, should inspire men to heroic moral struggle and victory. According to this theory, God needs no reconciliation in order to pardon. It is usually true that every theory has some element of truth in it and this one is no exception. Jesus was certainly a martyr to truth, loyalty, and obedience, but he was far more. (Edgar Young Mullins, *The Christian Religion in its Doctrinal Expression,* [Philadelphia: The Judson Press, 1946] 306-309)

It seems to me that there is something drastically wrong with most of those ideas. The very idea of God postulates a being above and beyond whom there is no other. Yet as we look at the idea of a ransom paid, that means that God was forced to recognize inferiority to or at least the equality with the one to whom the ransom was paid. Whatever your concept of Satan may be, whether he is a literal being or a designation of the total force of the influence of evil (wrong choices), to give satanic concepts equal status with God in any transaction and for even a short time is to do damage to the concept of God as Supreme. The same is true with the idea that somehow God's honor must be vindicated. Why should a principle of honor be something that God had to submit to and unless God has ego personality problems, why should honor matter. The entire body of scripture, especially the revelation in Jesus, indicates that God is forgiving in nature, so why should his honor be blackened because mankind rejected Him? The substitution idea is even worse. How does killing an innocent man substitute for me? To be sure, Jesus did something for me that I could not do for myself (which will be dealt with later), but the theory does not seem to explain that. Perhaps the moral influence theory avoids making God less than what He is, but it appears that it leads to little more than "hero" worship. It is true that according to the scriptures God has limited Himself in terms of his power. For when he created beings with the power of choice it was possible that they would choose other than what he wanted. The New Testament itself says that. "God is not willing that any should perish, but that all should come to repentance." But they do choose to perish! That self limitation may also apply to the concept of God's omniscience. Unless there is some other kind of knowledge which humanity cannot know and which can know all the outcomes without making them come true, God may have imposed a self-limitation on His knowledge. Whatever one may think of that, no satanic being or device can in any sense be superior to God - that would be a tragic error!

In the following attempt to help explain the work of Jesus there is no effort to argue that this is any kind of final statement. It is just an effort to show an understanding of where this journey in studying the materials relating to the ministry and teaching of Jesus has led regarding the tremendous, unified action of God in Christ.

Begin with the Genesis narrative, for that is where the story starts. No matter how one wishes to interpret the first eleven chapters of Genesis, some facts stand out. First, there is no account of what methods God used to bring his Creation to the point at which we engage it. At some point and in some way He brought about a being or beings who were capable of choice and that choice is a part of the process of worship. One can debate endlessly about why God created mankind in the first place. The position taken here is that God is a social being who desired fellowship and in order to have that there had to be freedom of will. There can be no worship or fellowship if there is not volition! So in the story, man-kind and female-kind are found in the idyllic garden of Eden. In that condition there was perfect harmony and obedience; God was God and the creature was the creature. In typical desert style the narrative states that God came in the "cool of the evening" and shared Himself with his creatures. That must have implied willing, voluntary response on the part of the humans involved for the the only place God can be shut out is in the mind of a being of free will. It was a beautiful, tranquil picture of joy, love, and peace and no one was violated, but God was still God! Then something happened! The figure of speech which posed the limits on humans who were already finite, was that of the fruit of a tree that should not be eaten. It was probably not a literal tree, certainly not an apple tree, but a figure representing a much larger principle, the possibility of choices between good and evil. The entire issue was whether the humans would recognize and allow God to be truly GOD! This discussion is not dealing with particular things humans call sin, BUT with the essence of distrust and disobedience in regard to God! Their decision was tragic for they decided to allow God to be GOD no longer; they acted as they chose. That disobedience was willful and it destroyed the whole concept of fellowship. So it was no longer possible to share in the beautiful fellowship and they became afraid of God and when God "came" the next time they tried in vain to hide. The banishment from the garden is a symbol which represents death as it expresses spiritual separation from God. (It seems futile to this author to argue that had the sin, which is disobedience, not entered into the creation there would have been no physical death. The whole process of biological life is a process of burning up and recreating the body and finally dying. There is no argument here that God could not have created a different kind of existence, but the biological structure we have now does not necessarily seem to be the consequence of disobedience.)

Suddenly, the whole atmosphere was changed and mankind found itself at enmity with God - not God at enmity with mankind! Even though there are pages and pages of historical material and growing spiritual insight, the remainder of the Biblical narrative is the answer to the question, "How can the patient, loving and caring God bring about reconciliation?" By way of illustration, my father was a very kind man and I knew without doubt that he loved me and cared for me intensely. But he was also a stern disciplinarian. I always wanted to be around him, helping as a boy would do with whatever he thought I could handle. One day, when I was about eleven years old I did something that I knew he would not approve of and if he found out things would be rather difficult. (What I did remains my secret.) When we went to the table I carried a healthy appetite of a growing boy. I always sat at one end of the table while Dad sat at the other; my brother on one side and my mother on the other. That night after we had the blessing I looked up and my eyes met his. I believe that was the meanest looking man I had ever seen. Fear gripped my heart and I said to myself, "How did he find out?" I suddenly lost my appetite and covering up as best I could I waited until I thought it reasonable and then I asked to be excused and went into the living room. When Dad finished his meal he came into the living room, picked up the newspaper, and sat down. I got up and left! I did not want to be close to him for it was miserable. Some sort of barrier had come between us. That kept up for some time and finally I decided that there wasn't any way I could live with that atmosphere, so I went to him and told him what I had done. (He didn't even know it.) After he had administered what he called corrective punishment, the fellowship was restored, but I never forgot that breach. It's like that with God except God knows!

So now, man was estranged from his very source of being and he began to wallow in more disobedience, substituting pleasure, self satisfaction, greed, arrogance, etc. in order to keep from facing ultimate reality. That is the condition God knew we were in and like a loving father or a caring shepherd he sent messenger after messenger, but often to no avail. Something more had to be done. There were many reasons for the Incarnation, but as long as God stayed off somewhere yonder, not geographically, but in the spirit realm, man would never know Him  and would continue to create all kinds of substitutions, including idols.  So at the proper time, and what human could ever say what that time was, He entered the world.  How that could occur will always be a mystery, but the fundamental truth is, "In Christ God was reconciling the world unto Himself." (II Corinthians 5:19 NRSV)  But why the horrible cross?

Diagrams are never flawless and there is no way to diagram the infinite God.  But this may help to visualize a little:

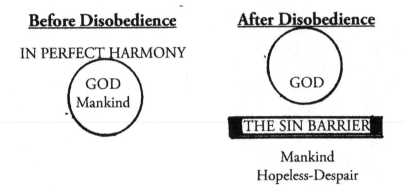

**Before Disobedience**

IN PERFECT HARMONY

GOD
Mankind

**After Disobedience**

GOD

THE SIN BARRIER

Mankind
Hopeless-Despair

From the days of the first Temple the great veil (it has been estimated as being as thick as from the heel of a man's hand to the tip of his thumb) which hung between the Holy of Holies and the Holy Place had symbolically prevented men from coming into the presence of God. The Jews believed that and the only person who should ever go behind that veil was the high priest and he was permitted to go only once a year on the Day of Atonement! That veil represented the barrier which has already been described.  For many people, God was a fearful being, far removed from them.  Something had to be done to demonstrate God's nature as love.  In the account by Matthew it was stated that when Jesus died the veil in the Temple was split.  Whether that was a figure of speech or a literal event will probably never be known but its meaning is spiritual and  should never be in question.  The writer of the Book of Hebrews stated that we have access to God to enter the sanctuary "by the new and living way that he opened for us through the veil (that is, through his flesh)." (Hebrews 10: 20)   How far would Jesus go to give evidence of the love of God?  It is pretty obvious that his entire life was lived perfectly in opposition to the sinful nature and acts of men. Those attitudes and acts are diametrically opposed to what God is and every act of Jesus, especially those which met with opposition, showed that. The answer was and is that he would continue to go far enough to break through the barrier of sin that separated man from God, even if it cost him his life.  So on the crucifixion day the battle became lethal.

Three courses were open.  Mankind could recognize who he was and turn and accept his message and his challenge, thus avoiding the ultimate conflict with sin.  It is apparent from the gospel narratives that such an acceptance had been made impossible by the attitude of the Jewish religious leaders.  A conviction to change their minds would have been more than a miracle.  The disobedient, sinful attitudes of mankind, not just the religious leaders, ran diametrically opposed to the love of God, so the impending clash became more than a possibility.

A second course would have involved a change in the attitude and direction of Jesus.  His entire life had been lived as a revelation of the love and care of God.  We are told that "God is love" and that is the picture throughout the entire life of Jesus.  We are not told of many of the temptations of Jesus, but we <u>are</u> told that "We do not have a high priest who is unable to sympathize with our weaknesses, but we have one who in every respect has been tested (tempted) as we are, yet without sin." (Hebrews 4:15)  The narratives include only a few of those temptations.  Many of them revolved around the question whether he would be faithful to his understanding of his mission.  He must have been tempted to take short cuts and follow the way of power, control, force, and many other evil ways of ruling instead of revealing the love character of God.  The same temptation as that  back in the Genesis narrative must have presented itself to him.  It would have gone something like this,

"The way you have begun is not working and you will never gain the kingship by following what you think is God's way of the Suffering Servant.  You know better than anyone what you must do.  Change your tactics."  More than anything else his goal had been to get men to follow him.  Why not try another way?

There would have been temptations to accept the accolades of men and do great works to gain fame. What man would not want that? There must have been many women followers who would gladly have given themselves to him. He could have become rich. There must have been some other ways for even some of his disciples and his family appear to have thought he was making the wrong decisions and seemed to want him to try another way. Of course, one can argue that if he had changed he would have forfeited the blessings of God and could not have succeeded, but Alexander the Great succeeded for a time, Cyrus had been a great leader, later in history there would be others. He could have reneged on his commitment to God (that is what the entire temptation story sequence is about). But if he changed and followed the ways of men, he would have never been able to demonstrate just how far he would go to manifest the love of God and certainly would not have become the savior we know nor could the hearts of men have been transformed! So he refused to stop showing how God loves and how God's righteousness differed from that of men. He chose not to change. So the course was set.

Or he could be true to God's call and die! His purpose was to break through the barrier between men and God, as one who should not have to die, and offer an avenue back into fellowship. We need to repeat: He chose to go all the way to provide that access, for his whole purpose was to break through the barrier and rescue mankind from itself. If our narratives are to be trusted, Jesus was "tempted in all points just as we are, yet without sin." That means that as the unique one from God, he did not deserve to die - all of us do! So in that sense he became a perfect and willing sacrifice, which no other man (no matter how good) could ever be, in order to go the ultimate to demonstrate that redeeming love of God that shrinks from nothing to reveal itself. In that sense the cross was inevitable, for he would not deviate from his mission as the Suffering Servant, no matter how difficult, and men would not change from their dogmatic, self appointed ways. And we know what he did! It was a deliberate act to break through the barrier and show mankind what sin was and what it would do. It was a deliberate act to reveal how far God in Christ would go to unfold his love. It was a deliberate act to reach down and redeem any of his lost sheep who would respond. There was no magic in it at all! He went all the way, as far as anyone could go - even to the miserable death on the cross.  Man and sin had beaten him!  Another set of diagrams may help.

**Option One**

Repentant Mankind
Responds and
Returns to God.
DIDN'T HAPPEN!

**Option Two**

Jesus opts for
Mankind's way -
Rejects God's
Suffering Servant!
DIDN'T HAPPEN

**Option Three**

Jesus remains
Faithful and faced
Man's anger

**GOD'S SOLUTION**

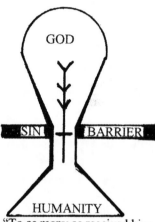

"GOD SO LOVED"

"To as many as received him
to them he gave the authority
T o become sons of God"

# EPILOGUE

But WAIT! The story was not over. God was not through and so Jesus was resurrected for our sake. God could have taken him to the spiritual realm without a resurrection, but we would have never known that God's love had successfully been revealed in its infinite-ness. How can that possibly redeem us? Only if individual men die to the sovereignty over their lives, die to self and surrender to the grace and Lordship of the Master. It takes a decisive act of will for a person to experience what God in Christ can do for him, an act that is diametrically opposed to the act of Adam! It must necessarily be an act of faith commitment. It is not an experience where man can claim he has done something good to deserve his reconciliation. (All religions that function on the level of man's good works, keeping laws, or anything else simply provide a new way for each man to proudly play God for himself.) Jesus' way is a way of humiliation, surrender, and acceptance. There can be no restoration without a repentant and submissive spirit to his love. So one must enter through the "new and living way", the rent in the veil which is his flesh. It is in that faith-commitment to His lordship over each individual life that one finds new life, not because it is earned, but because it has been provided by AMAZING INFINITE LOVE.

Actually, whether you, a reader, agrees with how I got here matters not. I would simply like for a reader to know about my convictions to use scholarship and to study this final statement, for I know that this is the meaning of Jesus' sacrifice and the completion of my journey. From that point on, the process is to progressively allow the Holy Spirit to lead in developing Christlike character!

# Bibliography

Aland, Black, Martini, Metzger, and Wikgren, <u>The Greek New Testament</u> 3<sup>rd</sup> edition, (Stuttgart: Biblia Druck, United Bible Societies, 1983)

Baille, John, <u>The Idea of Revelation in Recent Thought,</u> (New York: Columbia University Press, 1956)

Barclay, William, <u>The Mind of Jesus</u> (New York: Harper and Brothers, 1961)

Beck, D. M., <u>Through the Gospels to Jesus</u> (Hew York: Harper and Brothers, 1954)

Bonhoeffer, Deitrich, <u>The Cost of Discipleship</u> (New York: Macmillan Publishing Company, Inc., 1963)

Briggs, Robert Cooke, <u>Interpreting the Gospels</u> (Nashville: Abingdon Press, 1969)

Broadus, John A., <u>An American Commentary on the New Testament, vol. 1</u> (Philadelphia: The American Baptist Publication Society, 1886)

Brunner, Emil, <u>Revelation and Reason</u>, trans. Olive Wyon (London:

Student Movement Press, Ltd., 1947)

Charles, R. H., <u>The Apocrypha and Pseudepigrapha, vol II</u> (Oxford: Clarendon Press, 1913)

Connick, C. Milo, <u>Jesus, the Man, the Mission, and the Message</u> (Englewood Cliffs: Prentice Hall, Inc., 1974)

Danby Herbert, <u>The Mishnah</u> (London: Oxford University Press, 1954)

Dodd, C. H., <u>The Parables of the Kingdom</u> (London: Nisbet and Company, LTD., 1948)

Durant, Will, <u>The Story of Civilization: Part III, Caesar and Christ</u> (New York: Simon and Schuster, 1944)

Edersheim, Alfred, <u>The Life and Times of Jesus the Messiah</u> (New York: Longmans, Grant and Company, 1910)

Ellwood, Robert S., <u>Many Peoples, Many Faiths,</u> 5th ed. (Engelwood Cliffs, New Jersey: Prentice Hall, 1992)

Eusebius, <u>Ecclesiastical History, vol III</u> (New York: Macmillan Company, 1927)

Grant, Frederick E., <u>The Interpreter's Bible, vol. VII</u> (Nashville: Abingdon-Cokesbury Press, 1951)

Glueck, Nelson, <u>The River Jordan</u> (Philadelphia: The Westminster Press, 1946)

Hunter, A. M., <u>The Gospel According to Saint Mark</u> (London: SCM Press LTD, 1955)

James, M. R., <u>The New Testament Apocrypha</u> ( Berkeley, CA: Apocryphile Press, 2004)

Jeremias, Joachim, <u>The Parables of Jesus</u>, rev. ed. (New York: Charles Scribner's Sons, 1963)

Johnson, Sherman E., <u>The Interpreter's Bible, vol. 7</u> (Nashville: Abingdon, 1952)

Jones, W. T., <u>Kant and the Nineteenth Century, A History of Western Philosophy</u>, 2<sup>nd</sup> ed. (New York: Harcourt, Brace, Jovanovich, Inc., 1975)

Josephus, <u>The Antiquities of the Jews, Bk. XVIII, v, 4</u>, trans. William Whitson (Philadelphia: Henry Coates and Co.)

Klausner, Joseph, <u>Jesus of Nazareth, His Life, Times, and Teaching</u> (London: George Allen and Unwin, Ltd., 1947)

Laymon, Charles, <u>The Life and Teachings of Jesus</u> (New York, Nashville: Abingdon Press, 1952)

Mack, Burton L., <u>The Lost Gospel, The Book of "Q" and Christian Origins</u> (San Francisco: 1993)

Manson, T. W., <u>A Companion to the Bible</u> (Edinburgh: T. and T. Clark, 1950)

Metzger, Bruce, <u>The Text of the New Testament</u> 3<sup>rd</sup> ed. (New York, Oxford: Oxford University Press, 1992)

Monk, Hofheinz, Lawrence, Stamey, Affleck, Yamamori, <u>Exploring Religious Meaning</u> 7<sup>th</sup> ed. (Upper Saddle River, New Jersey: Prentice Hall, 1998)

Mould, Elmer K., <u>Essentials of Bible History</u>, 3<sup>rd</sup> ed. (New York: The Ronald Press Company, 1966)

Mullins, Edgar Y., <u>The Christian Religion in its Doctrinal Expression</u> (Philadelphia: The Judson Press, 1946)

Nun, Mendel, "Cast Your Net Upon the Waters" (The Biblical Archeology Review, vol. 19, November, 1996)

Oesterley, W. O. E., <u>A History of Israel, vol. II</u> (London: Oxford University Press, 1951)

Plummer, Alfred, <u>An Exegetical Commentary of the Gospel According to Matthew</u> (Grand Rapids: Wm. B. Eerdmans Publishing Company, 1956)

Ramsey, William, The Bearing of Recent Discoveries on the Trustworthiness of the New Testament, (London, New York, Toronto: Hodder and Stoughton, 1915)

Redlich, Basil, Form Criticism, (London: Duckworth Press, 1948)

Sayce, A. H., The Religions of the Ancient East, (Edinburgh: T. and T. Clark, 1902)

Schurer, Emil, A History of the Jewish People in the Time of Jesus Christ, 2nd div. Vol. 1 (New York: Charles Scribner's Sons)

Scott, E. F., The Crisis in the Life of Jesus (New York: Scribner's Sons, 1952)

Shepherd, J. W., The Christ of the Gospels (Grand Rapids: Eerdman's Publishing Company, 1954)

Souter, Alexander, The Text and Canon of the New Testament, 5th Impression (London: Duckworth Press, 1943)

Stewart, James, The Life and Teachings of Jesus (New York-Nashville: Abingdon Press)

Thieliche, Helmut, The Waiting Father, trans John Doberstein (San Francisco: Harper and Row Publishers, 1958)

Throckmorton, Burton, The Gospel Parallels (Nashville: Thomas Nelson, 1992)

Weatherhead, Leslie, The Will of God (Nashville: Abingdon Press, 1944)

Young, Robert, Analytical Concordance to the Bible (Maclean, VA: MacDonald Publishing Company)